WAR STORIES

From a New York City Cop
in the Seventies and Eighties

JACK FITZGERALD

I dedicate this book to my wife Susan.

She accepted my career choice and stayed by my side through the good times as well as the all-too-frequent tumultuous times. She lived the life of a cop's wife and "rarely" complained. I love you, babe!

I thank my son-in-law Rob. Without his tutorial skills this book would never have been written.

I want to identify several members of the NYPD who were a big part of my 26 year career... Tommy Deger: My first partner in the 75 Precinct. We were the classic example of "the blind leading the blind" in a very hazardous area in Brooklyn. Somehow we survived while getting the job done... Bob McClellan: Without a doubt the bravest man I ever worked with. Bobby was absolutely fearless. I worked with many very good police officers, Bob McClellan was the best... Lieutenant Elwood Selover: My mentor for most of my career. A wonderful boss... Jeff Musheno: The toughest man I ever worked with. One of my boxing trainers and a very strong man... Sergeant and eventually Captain Timmy Snyder. Timmy just may be the classiest man I ever met and a great boss. As a sergeant he led from the front.

Thank you all.

1

INTRODUCTION

I was born in Brooklyn, New York, into a family of public servants, as in Police Officers.

My father was a police officer, as were three of his four brothers. When our family got together for parties, dinners, et cetera, the primary topic of conversation was usually "The Job."

I grew up listening to police-related issues and tales of occurrences they all told. When our family got together, the brothers would occupy the living room, my mom and aunts would be in the dining room or kitchen and I would be in the street playing ball with my cousins. After dinner, my cousins and I would usually join our fathers in the dining room and we all listened to their "war stories."

My cousin Larry Muchow was the first of the cousins to join the force, followed by his brother Raymond.

There came a time in 1967 when I took the test for NYC Police Officer. I got a very good mark and was appointed on April 3, 1968. My cousin John eventually took the test for the New York Port Authority Police and was appointed to that department.

A BRIEF BIOGRAPHY

I grew up in Brooklyn playing stickball, punch ball, football and just about any other kind of ball you can imagine . . . in the street. The closest park we had was Putnam Park, behind Bushwick HS, where the Halsey Bops (our local gang) hung out. We rarely went to that park, so the street was our playground/park. Grass, the only grass we had in our neighborhood, was the grass the Bops smoked in Putnam Park.

The ethnic breakdown of the kids I went to school with and played with was Irish American, Italian American, German American and a mix of all the above. I went to Catholic school, St. Brigid's, and in the late '40s and early '50s we had a lot of German and some Italian kids in our school whose families immigrated to America and New York City. They were fleeing the devastation inflicted on those countries by the Allies during World War II.

Our neighborhood was typical to New York City and part of the large melting pot. All new arrivals were treated just like any other kid. We weren't taught hate in my home. My parents as well as the nuns and Brothers in St. Brigid's taught us to treat everyone as we wanted to be treated. I retained that lesson through my life and still do to this day.

On April 3, 1968, I found it necessary to adjust my ideology. I found myself hated, for the first time, by people who didn't have a clue about who I was. All they knew was I wore the uniform of a New York City police officer. That's all it took to generate extreme hatred.

As a member of the Tactical Patrol Force, I would be part of a response team. When there was a riot we responded. Most of the riots we responded to were generated by African Americans. That first summer the assassination of Martin Luther King Jr. was the cause of many riots in NYC. Ninety-nine percent of the rioters were black. I and every member of my squad were assaulted. We were called PIGS simply because we were trying to keep the peace.

I grew to hate those black rioters.

Then, during that same summer, we had riots at Columbia University. Most of those rioters were white ultra-left-wing Liberal students. We were called PIGS and assaulted for doing what we were ordered to do: Keep the peace.

I grew to hate those white rioters.

That's the way it went that first summer. It didn't take me long to realize I wasn't being assaulted and called PIG because they didn't like Jack Fitzgerald; they didn't like what I represented. I was standing in their way. They were anarchists. They wanted to bring down the fascist police and wreak havoc on our civilized society.

I want you, the reader, to understand that during my twenty-six-year career in the NYPD I learned to hate. I learned to hate the criminal who killed the store owner because he/she didn't give up their hard-earned money fast enough. I learned to hate the guy who came home from work drunk and beat the ever-loving shit out of his wife and kids because he had a bad day. I learned to hate the low-life piece of crap who snatched an old lady's purse after she cashed her social security check. I hated the drug dealer who sold poison to kids and others, who then had to rob innocent people of their rent money for their fix. I learned to hate and you will feel my hate as you read my book.

You will also feel the love I have for those people I was able to help, especially when they said, "Thank you, Officer Fitzgerald." A thank-you wasn't required, but it didn't hurt.

I want you, the reader, to understand I never was and never will be accused of being a racist by anyone who knows me. As a police officer I worked with and had many friends of color: That's white, black, Hispanic and I even had a couple of friends of Chinese descent.

I want you, the reader, to understand the words I used to identify the ethnic background of some of the people I interacted with on a daily basis are words and terms used by neighborhood people. The people of that culture. I grew up in that culture and we all used those words to identify each other. No one took offense because none was intended.

About this book, why I wrote it and the title.

On any given hot summer night and after eight hours of almost nonstop police work, it wasn't unusual for one of the men to say, "Anyone up for a couple of cold brews?" The answer was always yes. At least a few, sometimes more than a few of our third platoon would be looking forward to spending an hour or so "unwinding from the stress" with brother officers while enjoying a cold beer.

Every precinct had a "cops" bar where we could gather without concern about running into the guy we locked up last week. The bad guys knew that bar was off-limits and they were not welcome. They stayed away.

After that first cold beer the conversation would usually begin with, "Let me tell you what happened to me and my partner tonight. You won't believe what happened." The storyteller would embellish his most recent policing experience and a good storyteller would always add just enough drama to keep everyone interested. Of course there was always a follow-up by someone with another story and that's the way it would go until it was time to leave. Those stories became known as "War Stories," as in, "Do I have a war story for you guys tonight."

From time to time and while enjoying the company of my wife, family and close friends, I would tell one of my war stories. They would always be on the light side as I tried to entertain my audience with some of the strange but true incidents that happen during a tour of duty. Never anything dark.

There came a time when my wife Susan was joined by a very close friend (like family) Roberta Rissmeyer in saying: "Jack, you really should write a book." Due to their encouragement I decided to give it a go. I wrote a total of thirty-two chapters. "This isn't so difficult. I'm almost finished."

I was almost finished just before Christmas about four years ago. During Christmas Eve I told one of my family members about the book I was writing. I was happy when he offered his help with my venture. I sent him several chapters and he returned them with his edits. Not exactly what I had in mind. How could I expect someone who had zero experience in the policing business to tell my stories? I decided that wasn't going to work so it's time to go to plan B. Thank goodness he was patient. He came to my home and spent a good two hours giving me a crash course in writing 101.

This book is written to the best of my recollection and each chapter is its own story. I will begin where all books written about the life and times of a New York City police officer should begin— from day one and going forward in chronological order.

One last detail I want to address before asking you to turn to page one:

I want you to understand there is a lot of emotion in police work. I mean a L.O.T.

Sooner or later every police officer will have experienced just about every emotion humanly possible. I addressed the hate part, but there were also many times when I loved being a cop. I loved being able to respond to a violent family dispute and leave with both combatants laughing . . . It happened. There was fear: Man on the roof with a gun and you're the first man through the door.

From a report of a man shot and you roll up to the scene and find a dead man with four bullet holes in his body and the next job you get is an aided case where a woman is about to give birth. And sometimes the last job you receive and the one you will take home with you is: Eight One Charlie Investigate a three-year old baby girl out a fourth-floor apartment window. (One of my chapters and definitely the saddest day of my career.)

There was much more, but the bottom line is that a police officer is expected to go from one emotional extreme to another without skipping a beat. Without catching his/her breath. I am going to write one sentence on behalf of every police officer:

It ain't easy being us!

3

MY VERY, VERY SHORT-LIVED CORRUPTION-FREE CAREER

P rior to my appointment, my wife Susan and I were invited for coffee and cake with my cousin Ray Muchow and his wife. We lived in the same area in Queens, about a mile away from one another. As the evening progressed, Sue and Donna got into their own conversation in the living room while Ray and I did the same in the kitchen. I must mention we were having a few beers while I tutored Ray.

Now remember, Ray was on the job about two years already and I was waiting to be called. I was an idealistic civilian and Ray had a problem listening to me go on about how police officers should never expose themselves to any form of corruption, not even a free cup of coffee.

I was clearly making a fool of myself and Ray was growing impatient with my end of the conversation. Finally, Susan decided it was time to leave. It was getting late, so we thanked our hosts for an enjoyable evening and as we walked to our car Susan told me she was driving. I had no problem with that. There was total silence for the first thirty seconds and then she let me know what a fool I had made of myself.

She went on and on about how stupid I sounded, yada, yada, yada until we came to a red signal light. When she stopped the car

I got out and told her I didn't have to take her criticisms, but didn't use that word. I slammed the door and she peeled out down Sixty-Ninth Street, leaving me standing in the middle of the road. I looked at the car as she drove away and said to myself, "I showed her."

I walked the mile to our apartment just hoping someone would try to rob me so I could vent some of the rage I felt due to my stupidity. When I finally arrived home Susan was in our bedroom, possibly asleep, but I wouldn't give her the satisfaction of sleeping with her, so again, I showed her who the boss in our family was. I slept on the couch. The good news is I got wiser as I got older.

(The following series of events took place on April 7, my first tour on the street and I was assigned to the Eighteenth Precinct.) I have it out of sequence because it directly relates to the above short story.

We were ordered to report to the Eighteenth Precinct in Midtown Manhattan where we would work from eight p.m. to eight a.m. until further notice. My partner that first tour was John Miller, another member of company 6824. Our post was Forty-Ninth Street between Fifth and Sixth avenues. That block is well known as the home of Radio City Music Hall.

After roll call, we left the station house and proceeded to our post and neither of us knew what we were doing. Think about it. Four days ago we were civilians and now we're police officers wearing a six-gun with almost no knowledge as to what we were expected to do.

The last order our sergeant gave us before sending us out into the cruel world was, "Unless you are being assaulted or you see someone else being assaulted, don't do anything. Be alert and be visible."

John and I were born and raised in New York City, I spent my first twenty-one years in Brooklyn and John was raised in the Bronx. Neither of us was new to "The Street" so we figured we could always wing it.

The first thing we did was to scope out our post. We had no clue as to what we were looking for but we knew, if we found it, we would know what to do. ABSOLUTELY NOTHING.

As we walked back and forth from Fifth to Sixth avenues, there came a time when we met several police officers at the corner of Fifth and Forty-Ninth. Lo and behold, one of the boys in blue was my wife's cousin John Sekorski. He had been sworn in about a year prior, but we hadn't seen each other in that time.

He didn't know I had been appointed, so we chatted for several minutes and finally he asked me where my partner and I were going for dinner. I hadn't given any thought to food, but I did ask him for our available options.

He directed my attention to a restaurant about one hundred yards away, the Cattleman. He suggested we go there and see the doorman, Bill. Bill would take care of us. He added that there weren't many reasonably priced restaurants in that area and the Cattleman was good to the boys in blue.

I knew exactly what he meant, so when ten p.m. rolled around, we took our assigned meal break and went to see Bill. I was very familiar with that restaurant because my wife and I dined there often. They had good food at reasonable prices. As we approached the restaurant I made eye contact with Bill.

"Will you be dining with us tonight, Officers?"

"Yes, please."

"Follow me."

Bill took us through a side room to the kitchen and then down a flight of stairs to a small room on the lower level. It was a nice room set up with a large table and chairs. We discovered that was the room used by their employees on their breaks and for their meals.

Bill told us we could leave our hats and coats as they would be safe and asked us to follow him back to the kitchen. We returned with salad and soda and met our server, Mario.

"Good evening, Officers. My name is Mario and I will take

care of you this evening. You have several choices, but I recommend the brisket."

"Brisket sounds good to us."

"Enjoy your salad and I'll be back shortly."

It took Mario about ten minutes to arrive with our food. We enjoyed our first meal and spent time making our memo book entries. We were ready to return to our post with fifteen minutes to spare. We were both anxious to get back to being police officers.

We left something for our waiter and as we exited the restaurant I asked Bill how much we owed him and he said, "Have a nice night, Officers." We tried to give him something in appreciation, but he wouldn't accept it.

As I walked back to our post I remembered that evening at Ray's house. I looked at my wristwatch and realized it took me exactly two hours and forty-five minutes to become a corrupt cop.

Okay, maybe the word corrupt is a tad harsh, but I had to admit that my foolish idealism went out the window when introduced to the way it was done in the street . . . at that time. I came to the conclusion there was a lot more to being a street cop than I anticipated, a lot more.

Looking back over my twenty-six years on the job, I freely admit I accepted many free or discounted meals, but I never took a bribe or allowed my integrity to be compromised for profit or consideration.

4

BACK TO THE BEGINNING

I was appointed to the NYPD on Wednesday, April 3, 1968. After the swearing-in ceremony, we went to the auditorium where we received a lesson in the proud history of the New York City Police Department. The captain then went on to identify what we had accomplished and what would be expected of us after raising our right hands and taking the oath required of every recruit.

We received the ultra-abbreviated version of our benefits as well as a printed version of our schedule for the next two weeks. After his one-hour talk we were given a twenty-minute break, followed by two additional hours of informative talks.

We listened to representatives from the many fraternal organizations as they invited all eligible officers to join their ranks. Eventually the captain returned and told us we would be given an early dismissal so we could spend time with our families on that special day.

The next day was pretty much the same with a four p.m. dismissal. That evening, April 4, Martin Luther King Jr. was murdered as he stood on the second-floor balcony of the Lorraine Motel in Memphis, Tennessee. His assassination ignited riots in every major city in America, including New York City.

On April 5, I reported to the Police Academy at eight a.m. as scheduled. We assembled outdoors, on the fourth-floor muster deck. A roll call was taken, followed by an order to proceed to the auditorium on the second floor to await further orders.

Okay, now what? I took my schedule out of my pocket and confirmed what I already knew; we were supposed to be in room 435 for a class on the penal law. As the auditorium began filling up I heard someone instruct the overflow to proceed to the gym.

So we waited and waited and while waiting for several hours we got to know our classmates in company 6824

Finally a sergeant took the stage:

It is now eleven thirty. You will break for a meal. You will return to the muster deck no later than twelve thirty and await further orders."

At twelve thirty we were ordered to report to room 321, where we met Sergeant Cassidy.

"Due to the assassination of Martin Luther King, the two-week schedule you received is no longer in effect. The revised schedule is as follows: I will give you a lesson on the penal law until it is your turn to report to the equipment section at Four Hundred Broome Street. Upon arrival you will receive a duffle bag, a box containing your service revolver, which you will not open, your handcuffs, all leather goods as well as your probationary police officer's uniform. You will place all that equipment in your duffle bag and return to this classroom, where I will be awaiting your arrival. Is there anyone here who doesn't understand what I just said?"

About twenty minutes after our first lesson began, we were ordered to report to 400 Broome Street. After receiving our uniforms and equipment we returned to the Academy and room 321.

The new schedule was to have all 691 recruits visit one of the two shooting ranges to qualify with the .38 caliber revolver. Most companies did qualify, but our company and one other didn't, as it just got too late.

Our revolvers were collected by Sergeant Cassidy and we were ordered to return to the Academy the following night, Saturday, at eight p.m. in civilian clothes. We were dismissed at about seven p.m.

We returned as ordered and reported to the indoor range.

We spent about four hours in the classroom with our range officer. We learned just about all there was to learn about the revolver and "round ball" ammunition. During those first four hours we had several fifteen-minute breaks but that didn't give us time to leave the building for coffee or other refreshments.

"It is twelve fifteen. You will break for meal and be back at your desks no later than one thirty. You will leave your revolvers, in the box, on your desks. Are there any questions? Good. Dismissed."

The Academy was located on Twentieth Street between Second and Third Avenues. At midnight there weren't many unlicensed (No alcohol served) restaurants to choose from. (It is a violation in the Patrol Guide for police officers to dine in a restaurant that serves alcohol.) We all went to the Blimpie on the corner of Twentieth and Third.

Being a Brooklyn guy I knew what a "hero" sandwich was supposed to taste like. It had to be made using real Italian bread and always with Boar's Head cold cuts unless you were ordering a hot hero. You could get just about any kind of hero you wanted, but it absolutely, positively had to be made on Italian bread.

I don't know where the people who opened the first Blimpie came from, but it definitely was not New York City. Their version of a hero began with something that resembled Italian bread but the East Cupcake version, which tasted like cardboard. "Yuck." Then they sliced their no-name cold cuts wafer thin, so thin the meat almost dissolved as it hit the crummy bread. Finally they topped it all with shredded lettuce, tomato, and then some kind of oil and vinegar to mask the taste of all other ingredients. I took a couple of bites before throwing it in the trash. I got a container of coffee.

We returned to the classroom, stood roll call, followed by the range officer leading us to the actual shooting range where we met two more range officers. We were assigned firing positions and given a box containing fifty rounds of .38 caliber ammunition. For the first time we were ordered to remove our revolvers from "the box."

The NYPD range officers are recognized as some of the best in the world. I won't go into the lesson plan, but when they completed their instructions, all thirty-two members of my company were reasonably proficient with our revolvers. We all qualified.

The shooting and qualifying part of our tour went from one thirty to six with several fifteen-minute breaks. At six we were given a half-hour break allowing us time to leave the Academy to buy a cup of coffee. We returned and waited. Finally our class was called to order.

"I'm happy to inform you everyone has qualified. You will join the rest of your class already assigned to patrol. You will work twelve hours on and twelve hours off until ordered to return to the Academy. You will report to your assigned precinct tomorrow at seven thirty p.m. in full uniform."

Our instructor began calling our names and when he got to John Fitzgerald he said, "You are assigned to the Eighteenth Precinct located on West Fifty-Fourth Street."

When he had completed that task, all thirty-two of us had been assigned to either the Fourteenth or the Eighteenth precincts. Both were in the high-profile midtown area, the Times Square area.

Seven out of every ten people we would come in contact with would be either tourists or theatergoers and the mayor wanted a strong police presence in that area during that tumultuous period.

(I have written a separate chapter about my first tour, so I will pick up after that eventful night.)

After that first tour on the street I realized I could get by using common sense and my wit. There were several minor issues with the never-ending prostitution condition in the Times Square area, but during the twelve days we spent on patrol I don't recall any memorable policing incidents.

We continued with our twelve-hour tours for the twelve days and in the NYPD there was no such thing as overtime. As far as I was concerned, that wasn't an issue. We were well aware of the benefits before joining the force and I would have worked twenty-six hours a day. I was doing what I was born to do and I was enjoying every minute of my time on the street.

After that first night I teamed up with a member of my company, Harry Peters, who lived near me in Maspeth, Queens. We arrived at the precinct early and found the sergeant who would be giving us our assignments. There was no prepared roll call, so we asked if we could work together and he had no problem with our request.

During our first evening, as we patrolled Broadway near Forty-Second Street, two couples from California stopped us and asked why some of the police officers wore blue uniforms and some, including us, wore grays. I couldn't pass up the opportunity, so before Harry had a chance to respond I said we were assigned to the NYPD Special Forces and usually worked in high-crime areas in the city.

Our intense training was the reason we were the first responders whenever there was a riot. Now we were assigned to the midtown area to assure that the people visiting our city during these trying times were safe.

They were impressed and I felt a little guilty for my "untruth," but there came a time on June 2 when that's exactly what happened. I was assigned to the Tactical Patrol Force (TPF) and that is what the officers in that special detail did.

On the humorous side: I do remember another happening that first night, when I tried to get my revolver out of my holster. You can imagine our leather goods were new and stiff, but the holster we were issued was far beyond stiff and bordered on wooden.

The holster had a piece of leather near the top that acted as a locking device for the revolver. It's a little hard to describe, but if you needed to remove the gun from the holster you used your thumb to slide that piece away from the cylinder, allowing the removal of the weapon.

At about two a.m., while we were patrolling a quiet street, I decided to test my skills at revolver removal. I followed the range officer's instructions, but I wasn't very successful, as in—I couldn't get my gun out of the holster.

It was locked in there. I did my absolute best, but I just couldn't get it out. Harry tried to help. I used both thumbs and pressed as hard as I could while Harry pulled the gun up by the stock. No dice, we just couldn't get it out. This is not funny!

We found a very secluded place where I took my gun belt off, I held the holster while Harry pulled the stock and finally my gun came out. Now it was his turn and we went through the same exercise. As we stood in the dark with our revolvers in our hands, we knew we needed to make an adjustment.

As we reviewed our options we came upon two members of our company patrolling an adjoining post. We asked them if they had tried to get their guns out of their holsters and they both said yes. Obviously they were a tad more advanced than we were.

I asked how they solved the problem. Peter Boyle said he placed one of his son's marbles in the holster so the gun never went in far enough to lock. His partner did the same. That solved one problem, but created another. The revolver now sat rather high and it was not secure in the holster, so anyone could come up from behind them and just pull the gun out. Or, if they needed to chase someone the gun was loose in the holster and could come out.

Now we had our first dilemma: Do we patrol unable to remove our revolvers or do we go with plan B and have the gun loose in the holster. I decided to force a dime into the bottom of my holster. The gun didn't lock, but it was pretty deep. Yes, someone could pull it out if I let them get that close, but at least I could get it out if needed. Harry followed my lead and at least we had a temporary solution to that problem. (I worked on my revolver removal technique and eventually solved that problem)

After twelve days of twelve on and twelve off, we were given two days off and ordered to return to the Academy to resume training.

We reported to the gym, where we received our schedule for the week. Now it was time to begin our first official classroom experience. The instructor began by informing company 68-24 that our instructor was on extended sick report. There was no projected date for his return, so our class would be joining his and others as our lesson plan progressed.

As I looked around the room I realized we had about sixty-five recruits in our classroom and it went that way for the entire five weeks we spent in the Academy. I'm talking about an extremely poor learning environment. In fact I clearly recall that first class: The sergeant began with the penal law and as he identified what illegal activity was required to charge the perpetrator with a crime, someone raised his hand and began asking a question. The sergeant stopped him by saying, "Don't ask me any questions, you don't know enough to ask questions."

A few minutes later another hand went up and someone asked what if . . . The sergeant responded with a stern, "What part of don't ask any questions didn't you understand, probationary police officer?" With that, we all got the message and there were no more questions, at least on that day with that sergeant.

Eventually we discovered the instructors were told they had to use an abbreviated lesson plan. Our class would soon be sent out on patrol for the summer and possibly longer.

Every lesson was street oriented and narrowly related to the law and the use of force with little time spent on NYPD procedures and the Patrol Guide was given almost no time.

We did spend an ample amount of time in the gym learning how to defend ourselves as well as how to frisk (search) a suspect or prisoner. We were introduced to very basic boxing and we even received some karate from our own, in-house, black belt karate master, Al Griffin, who was one of our gym instructors.

The mayor's office knew it was going to be a very busy summer for the police department. Police Commissioner Leary was told to get as many bodies on the street as soon as possible.

May 29, we receive our assignments. We were ordered to report to our commands or details on June 2 in full blue summer uniform. No more rookie grays.

During my five weeks in the Academy, a sergeant asked every member of our company what assignment he looked forward to after graduation. I had heard about the Tactical Patrol Force and that sounded pretty good to me. TPF was every active cop's dream assignment and I was going to be an active cop. It was the "special forces" in the NYPD at that time. Working high-crime areas, the first responders to all riots, I definitely wanted to work in TPF.

June 2 I got my wish. I reported to Sergeant Brennan's fourth squad in the Tactical Patrol Force. That night we were assigned to the Sixth Precinct in Greenwich Village. Our hours were always six p.m. to two a.m. Greenwich Village was a break from the high-crime areas TPF usually worked. "The Village" was a low-crime tourist attraction unto itself. I write more about that area in another chapter, "My first riot," but I must admit I enjoyed that first night.

My second tour was very different from the first. Our squad was assigned to one of the worst precincts in the city, the Seven Nine, in the Bedford- Stuyvesant section of Brooklyn. I was assigned with PO Delaney to patrol Myrtle Avenue. There were two additional two-man teams assigned to adjoining posts. One new kid with one veteran. (In TPF a veteran had about three years on the job.)

Before separating to patrol our posts, one veteran suggested we check out the projects a block away where we might make collars. The way this went down was four of us climbed the ten flights of stairs to the roof in building number one while two men remained on the ground floor of building number two. Once on the roof we had access to the next building, where we could surprise anyone doing drugs at the top landing.

I later found out that on any given evening you could find junkies shooting up on the top landing. Now we're on the roof and Jimmy Ortiz opens the door and sure enough there were three guys smoking dope on the top landing. Before we could grab them they booked down the stairs and out of sight. They never hit the ground floor, so they must have had an opened door ready just in case. The stupid druggies were in jail, the rest knew the routine.

Okay, that didn't work. Mike Puglissi said maybe it was time to patrol our assigned posts. We all walked down Myrtle Avenue and as we were about to split up and go to our assigned posts we saw a car pull up in front of a bar in the middle of the block. Six guys got out and ran into the bar. About twenty seconds later, those six came running out being chased by about ten more from the bar and when they hit the middle of the street all hell broke loose.

They began fighting with their fists and a few had knives and that's when one of the senior men called a Ten Thirteen assist patrolman. We went after the large group and caught them by surprise. As we laid into them with guns drawn and nightsticks at the ready, one man came at me as he tried to get away.

I saw he had a knife in his hand. I was between him and freedom and as he tried to get past me he came down with the weapon in a slashing motion. I blocked his arm with my stick and hit him on the head with the corner of my revolver, that right angle piece below the barrel. He fell to the ground. I could see he was bleeding . . . bad, I'm talking "head wound gushing blood" bad. He was definitely out of this fight.

I left the thug bleeding on the sidewalk and got back into the melee. The entire mob was now fighting us.. We were outnumbered and it wasn't looking good for us. That is, until we all heard that sweet sound of sirens. Very few people will ever know how great it is to hear the cavalry coming, especially when you are in a life-and-death fight.

As the sectors arrived and screeched to a stop, the rioters began their attempt to get into the wind. Some ran back into the bar while a few just booked down Myrtle Avenue.

The cops in the Seven Nine precinct were pros. They were used to responding to Ten Thirteens and when they saw someone doing a "felony run" away from the scene, they grabbed them. That evening two sectors grabbed five fleeing felons.

The rest of us went into the bar and collared everyone we suspected of being involved in the fight. That left the bartender, an old rummy and a woman who was obviously a working girl (prostitute).

With the five fleeing felons caught by the responding sectors and the nine prisoners from the bar in cuffs, I returned to the corner where I left my wounded combatant. Lo and behold he was gone. As I approached that corner I heard a voice from above: "The guy you hit was put in a car by another guy and they drove away."

I looked up and there was a woman in the window of the second-floor apartment. "The guy was out of it and the other guy had trouble getting him in the car. I think he be dead."

I went to where he fell and by using my flashlight I could see there was a lot of coagulated blood, no doubt that perp was seriously injured. I also found his knife. A knife used to cut linoleum. It had a hook blade and was very sharp. If he had caught me with his slashing blade I would have been the one bleeding on the sidewalk.

It wasn't even seven thirty yet and all six of us had prisoners, as did three of the sector car teams.

As soon as we arrived at the Seven Nine precinct with our prisoners, I called Cumberland Hospital. I identified myself and asked if they had anyone there being treated for a head wound and was told no. I had no idea what could have happened to that guy because Cumberland was the closest hospital and considering the amount of blood he lost he was definitely in need of medical attention.

We processed our prisoners by midnight and were given an early dismissal because we had to return at seven a.m. to transport our prisoners to Brooklyn Criminal Court.

We charged everyone with riot, but that was plea-bargained down to disorderly conduct at arraignment. We didn't object to that deal because none of the combatants were seriously hurt during the melee and we couldn't charge anyone with assault on a police officer because we weren't assaulted. I should mention when it came to the plea deal no one asked my opinion nor did anyone care. I was a new kid on the block and did as I was told.

My time assigned to TPF, from June 2 to the middle of December, was a learning experience. I enjoyed every minute in that assignment.

In mid-December, most of us on temporary assignment from the Academy were transferred to either Safety Unit A (lower Manhattan) or Safety Unit B (midtown Manhattan); I was assigned to midtown and Unit B. Our job description was simple. We worked one of two tours, from seven a.m. to three p,m, or three p.m. to eleven p.m., and during rush hour we directed traffic at major intersections. Off hours we issued summonses. That was it.

I want to remind you that our lessons in the Academy were extremely abbreviated. We received absolutely no training in the art of directing the gazillion vehicles moving through the streets of Manhattan while interacting with another gazillion pedestrians trying to get from point A to point B without getting run over.

I wasn't crazy about directing traffic because after six months in the Special Forces I felt I could be of greater value in some other crime-fighting capacity. I made the best of it, as I knew it was another temporary assignment.

Now about my five weeks in Safety Unit B:

I will use my very limited traffic duty experience and say, in my opinion, there is no secret to directing traffic. It doesn't require much training or experience (I am the best example for proof positive in that regard). Simply put: You must be alert at all times and use common sense.

Most of the time I would let the signal light do all the work, but from time to time a smart ass would try to make a turn from the wrong lane, which would obstruct the traffic flow. Very often that move resulted in a moving violation.

Then came the night I will never forget, which is why it is my primary story in my traffic directing diary. It was a very cold, snowy Saturday afternoon and I was working the three p.m. to eleven p.m. tour.

There is one thing I forgot to mention that comes into play in this chapter; our authorized department tailors were overwhelmed with the number of recruits appointed in 1968. Every probationary police officer had to have his uniform made by one of about ten authorized tailors. There was the February class, our April class, a June class and an October class. Our class had 691 men, so if we were the average that meant the tailors needed to make uniforms for about twenty-five hundred men.

They made two pair of winter pants, two pair of summer pants, a summer/dress blouse and a winter blouse that was not at all warm and designed for sector car duty. Finally there was the winter overcoat, aka the blanket.

My tailor didn't get to my overcoat, so during the winter of 1968 my warmest garment was the winter blouse. The good news was while wearing that jacket we didn't need to wear a uniform shirt, so I wore a warm sweater and a sweatshirt under it all winter.

Getting back to that Saturday evening: After changing into my uniform I reported to the muster room and read the assignments for that tour. I found my name and saw I was assigned to work the intersection in front of Lincoln Center (Broadway and Sixty-Fifth Street). I had never been to Lincoln Center nor had I ever come within ten blocks of Lincoln Center and I most certainly didn't know anything about the traffic conditions at that location.

I had worked Forty-Second Street and all the avenues intersecting Forty-Second and they were very busy posts so I really wasn't too concerned; an intersection is an intersection, right?

WRONG! I'm sure there are other very busy intersections . . . IN THE WORLD . . . but to my knowledge that intersection was the absolute busiest in the northern hemisphere.

(To get a better understanding of what I am writing about, I suggest you Google Lincoln Center in Manhattan and work your way to where Broadway, West Sixty-Fifth Street and Columbus Avenue intersect.)

At 2:55 p.m. our platoon stood roll call, followed by the sergeant's order, "Officers, take your posts." As I approached the door, the sergeant called my name and asked to speak to me. I knew him from his prior visits to my post over the past two weeks and found him to be a good boss. He was about thirty-five years old so he wasn't one of the "Old School, don't even think about talking to me" bosses.

He asked me if I had ever worked that post before and I said, "No, Sergeant." He knew I had little experience in S.U.B (Safety Unit B), so he asked if I thought I was up for a busy evening and I said yes without thinking. I would never in a million years say no, I can't handle it, Coach, put me on the bench. Never ever ever gonna happen.

He gave me the prime-time hours for that post, which were six p.m. to eight p.m. with an eight meal; I had to be back at nine p.m. He added that I had to be out there (at the intersection) during those hours. He noticed I was carrying my raincoat and he gave me a thumbs-up for that move. I knew it was supposed to snow, it was very cold and the rubber raincoat would act as a windbreaker for my not very warm winter blouse. Finally, it had illuminating tape reflectors that would make me more visible in the dark.

He told me he would see me on post and his parting words were, "So you think you can direct traffic? Well, Officer Fitzgerald,

I guarantee if you survive this night you will be an expert before you sign the return roll call." As I walked to the bus that would take me uptown I figured, how bad could it be? I arrived on post by 3:45 and found a coffee shop on Columbus Avenue. I had a cup of coffee and made my entries in my memo book. I didn't need to be at the intersection until six so I issued summonses to illegally parked cars on Broadway as well as Columbus Avenue.

By five p.m. it was getting pretty dark, so I walked to Sixty-Fifth Street on Broadway to check out my intersection. I had made a brief pass earlier, but it took on a different dimension in the dim lighting conditions that were common in NYC in the sixties and seventies. I checked the signal lights to make sure they were working properly and they were, thank goodness.

(At this time I need to help you to visualize so you have a mental image of what I am writing about. That intersection is a little hard to describe, but I'll try: There are three lanes of traffic moving east on Sixty-Fifth. There are six lanes of traffic traveling on a slight angle from NE to SW on Columbus Avenue and then I had Broadway. Broadway has three lanes traveling north and then after a twenty-foot divider I had three lanes traveling south. The bottom line was I had fifteen lanes of traffic crisscrossing at one intersection. I repeat: To get the full picture, do Google searches.)

I looked at my watch, it was five twenty, so I decided to have another cup of coffee and use the restroom before returning to my post. As I left the coffee shop it began to snow. I have never shied away from a challenge, so the snow was only going to add to my challenging experience.

I donned my raincoat, removed my official white NYPD-issued whistle and my flashlight from my gun belt and put them in my raincoat pocket. I put my gloves on as I returned to my intersection.

I stood on the sidewalk between the north and south lanes on Broadway and absorbed the scene. It was snowing pretty hard and very dark, but the streetlights were working and the headlights from the cars illuminated the street, so I really wasn't concerned about not being seen.

It was now five fifty and time to get started. I waited for a lull in traffic before entering the intersection and once there it didn't take long to get acclimated. As I look back it was like standing on the edge of a pool getting ready to dive into the water; after the initial shock of the cold water it's not so bad and after a little while you begin to enjoy. It didn't take long before I actually began to enjoy what I was doing, I enjoyed the challenge and I think a big part of it was the conversation I had with the sergeant.

He was an expert; no, make that, the supervisor of experts. He let me know, up front, my post was going to be very difficult. He was a good boss and wasn't going to put me in a no-win situation if he thought I wasn't up to the assignment. I was in the ring and the bell was about to toll, let's get it on.

There was a lot of traffic, more than I had ever seen in one place before. I let the signal lights do most of the work as I maintained order by working on the gridlock. Gridlock/spillback is the primary cause of traffic jams and I wasn't going to allow that condition to hinder my job performance.

The later it got, the harder my job got, trying to move back and forth between Broadway north and south and Columbus Avenue. I didn't feel the temperature; I knew it was cold, but my body was as warm as could be and my adrenaline was pumping.

I blew my whistle almost nonstop and my flashlight was on for the entire two hours as I used it to stop and move the cars.

Just before eight I noticed the sergeant's RMP (Radio motor patrol car) parked just off Sixty-Fifth Street on Broadway, making his observations of my performance. He pulled up to where I was standing and said, "Get in, kid."

The word "kid" was used by anyone with more than five years on the job when speaking to anyone with less than five years on the job. It's still used today in that regard.

He asked me how I was doing.

"Officer Fitzgerald, I've been watching you for the past five minutes and it seems as though you have everything under control. You are doing a fine job."

"Thank you, Sergeant."

"I know you're new to this area and you have an eight o'clock meal. You're doing such a good job we will drive you to one of our favorite Italian restaurants in this precinct."

A sergeant driving a nobody rookie probationary police officer to a restaurant... unheard of.

As I exited the RMP, the sergeant said, "Officer, tell Angelo, Billy B. and Sergeant Rocco said hello."

As I entered the restaurant I was greeted by an elderly Italian man who said,

"Welcome to my restaurant, my name is Angelo. Please take any table you want."

Good evening, Angelo, I will sit in the back in the corner. Sergeant Rocco and Officer Billy B. said to say hello."

"You know Sergeant Rock and Billy?"

"Well, Sergeant Rocco and his chauffeur are watching my back tonight. I'm new to traffic duty and I have Lincoln Center this evening. I'm on my meal hour and Sergeant Rocco told me you served very good food. I guess that's why he drove me here."

"If they brought you here they must like you. I will take very good care of you tonight."

There was a woman waiting tables, but Angelo came over and gave me a menu.

"Officer, can I offer you a hot cup of expresso?"

"Yes, Angelo, that sounds good."

"Can I sweeten it with Sambuca?"

"Thank you, but no thanks, expresso will be fine."

"What would you like for dinner?"

"How's the baked ziti with eggplant?"

"Delicious and I just took it out of the oven not ten minutes ago."

"Sounds good to me, thank you."

As I began making my memo book entries, Angelo returned

with bread and asked if I would like a glass of his special home-made wine. I said no thanks, but I would like a Coke.

Ten minutes later my food arrived. A large portion of one of my favorite meals: baked ziti with eggplant. Hot and delicious, perfect for a cold snowy night.

Before I had a chance to butter my bread he returned with another large plate containing a huge piece of veal cutlet parmigiana

"Angelo, I didn't order the veal."

"Officer, tonight I have a special; when you order baked ziti with eggplant you get a side order of my special veal cutlet parmigiana

I finally got the message. The offer of Sambuca, the home made wine. Now I happened to come in on the special day when you get a huge side order of veal cutlet parmigiana with my ziti. Either I'm the luckiest cop in the neighborhood or it's good to know Sergeant Rocco and Officer Billy B.

Angelo must have returned at least five times during the next thirty minutes to see if I needed anything. I finished most of my meal, had another cup of expresso and asked Angelo for my check.

As I was putting my blouse and raincoat on he returned with my bill: Three dollars. My meal should have come to about fifteen bucks with the gigantic portions including the delicious veal. Then I had two expressos and the soda, so I gave him a ten-dollar bill and began to leave when he stopped me and said, "Officer, your change." He gave me a five-dollar bill and five singles and said, "Please come back and see us again. Any friend of Sergeant Rock and Billy is my friend."

I was still having difficulty accepting free meals, so I returned to my booth and left a five-dollar tip. What an enjoyable meal and Angelo took very good care of me.

It was almost nine, so I took a brisk walk back to my post.

As I approached my intersection I was surprised to see the traffic had slowed to a trickle. It was still snowing, but just enough to add to the holiday season. I didn't feel like writing any more summonses, so I entered the arena once again. I went through the motions of directing traffic, but I definitely wasn't needed, at least for the next thirty minutes.

By nine thirty Lincoln Center was letting out and the cars were returning. It got busy, but now I was a more seasoned veteran. As far as I was concerned, after that first round of intense traffic, I was ready for anything.

I was a little disappointed because I wanted that challenge again. I wanted that adrenaline rush one more time tonight, but it never came. The final traffic rush was over in about thirty minutes. I took on the best the City could send my way and I was successful. No gridlock, no accidents, nothing to report.

I returned to the coffee shop, had another cup of Joe and made my final memo book entries. It was now ten fifteen, time to call it a day, or evening.

I caught the bus downtown to the old Sixteenth Precinct Station House, which was now the home of Safety Unit B. I arrived with time to spare before my "end of tour" at eleven p.m.

As I was in line to sign the return roll call Sergeant Rocco came over to me and said, "So, Officer Fitzgerald, you survived."

"Yes, Sergeant, I did. Sergeant, I want to thank you and Officer Boyle for driving me to Angelo's. His food was great and he took very good care of me. He told me to say hi to you and Officer Boyle."

"Jack that was your reward for the fine job you did this evening. I visited your post several times during your tour and I do believe you would do well in Traffic Duty. Would you like me to submit your name for consideration for Safety Unit B?"

"Thank you, Sergeant, but I would like to try precinct patrol duty for a while."

"Well, if you change your mind you know my name and you know where you can find me."

As I drove home that night I likened my evening to that of a matador in a bull ring, only I was better. All he needed to contend with was one bull and I had roughly fifteen cars coming at me from different directions in the snow and in the dark, so I figured if I ever decided to move to Mexico I could get a job.

The only other memorable experience I recall during my five weeks in SUB was another evening I worked that three to eleven p.m. tour. My post was Madison Avenue and Fiftieth Street, the intersection at the rear of Saint Patrick's Cathedral.

I was directing traffic in the middle of that intersection when I noticed cars double-parked halfway down Madison. Those cars were creating a traffic jam as far as I could see. I walked to the cause of the problem, which was two double-parked cars in front of a large office building on the west side of Madison.

As I approached the vehicles I realized they both had diplomat plates, which meant they were unsummonsable. As I continued to investigate my dilemma, I noticed the parking signs. That entire block was restricted parking for DPL plates only. The first three cars parked at the curb were DPLs, then there was a limousine with a driver behind the wheel and finally another two unoccupied limos. I ordered the driver of the first limo to move his car and as he began to object to my order I told him to move or I would give him two summonses.

He moved. I then proceeded to issue summonses to the other two limos. That didn't solve the bottleneck problem, but at least I did something about the cause. I returned to my intersection and continued directing traffic for another twenty minutes until it was time for my meal. I walked to the sidewalk and began making a memo book entry when a limo pulled up and stopped in the traffic lane just in front of where I was standing. I looked up as the passenger, a man about fifty-five years old and neatly dressed, exited the rear seat on the traffic side and yelled, "Hey you." As I looked in his direction he crooked his finger, directing me to walk to him.

I ignored him. He saw me look up and he saw me ignore him,

which, I'm sure, really pissed him off. I pretended to continue writing in my memo book as he stormed over to where I was standing and shouted, "What is your name?"

I responded: "Police Officer Fitzgerald." He said, "It figures," then he asked me for my badge number and I pointed to my shield. He took out a piece of paper and began to write while saying, "Do you know who I am?" I said, "Yes, you're the guy who just got out of the car that I'm about to issue a summons to for double-parking if the driver doesn't move NOW." He had this shocked look on his face as in—I do not believe this lowly cop just raised his voice as he threatened to summons my chauffeur.

As I walked into the street I opened my summons book. He followed me and as I approached his car he said, "I own that building where my driver was waiting for me." I said, "You mean the car parked in the parking spaces designated for DPL plates?" He ignored my words.

He then told me he was friends with the captain of the Seventeenth Precinct, which is the precinct his building was located in. He was going to have me transferred and I would never give another ticket in Manhattan. I responded, "So I guess the one I'm about to give your chauffeur will be my last." His face got beet red, he got in the backseat and sped off.

The reason I have total recall of that incident is because it was at that time I realized the power and authority I had as a police officer. That authority came with the sometimes extreme responsibility we accepted when taking our oath of office.

Here I was, a twenty-four-year-old nobody, enforcing the laws that required me, in some instances, to tell people what to do. The best part was if those people failed to comply, there were penalties to pay.

In that most recent interaction I was going toe-to-toe with a billionaire who, I could see by his condescending attitude, was used to talking down to just about everyone he came in contact with.

I really ruined that guy's night because a lowly cop ordered his driver to move his car from in front of his building. Then, to make the entire situation ten times worse, when he attempted to intimidate me by using his relationship with the captain by threatening to have me transferred out of SUB, I didn't cave. I responded by ordering him to move his car.

I could read his mind: What the F*** just happened? The audacity of that nothing of a public servant. How dare he be so contentious? I would bet a lot of money that jerk hadn't had anyone stand up to him in many years, not even the captain, but I did and the best part was there wasn't a thing he could do about it. I was right because I was doing my job. I truly enjoyed that evening.

P. S. With regard to the captain in that precinct: He had absolutely no control over my assignment. . He was a precinct commander and I worked in a totally different branch in the department. Again I must clearly state I was doing my job and did nothing wrong.

Time to Finish What We Started Back on April 3.1968

5

BACK TO THE ACADEMY

I guess it was during the first week of January 1969 when our entire class was ordered back to the Academy to complete our training. By now we were all hairbags (a term used to describe a cop who had time on and knew the ropes). Of course we weren't and we didn't, but we thought we did and the best part was as of January 3 we were off probation and the department couldn't dismiss us without a trial. No more "Probationary Police Officer Fitzgerald."

We spent the next five weeks in a classroom, in the gym or at the indoor range in the basement of the Academy. We never did have our own instructor, so we always doubled up with another company. I have no doubt company 68-24 was the worst-trained company in the history of the NYC Police Department. Every other company came in a close second. Our classroom training was very poor at best.

On Friday, February 8, we were given the weekend off and ordered to report on Monday, February 11, to the armory in the Nineteenth Precinct to practice for our graduation ceremony. Before being dismissed for the last time we received two green admission cards to be used by our guests to gain entry to our graduation ceremony.

It began snowing early Saturday morning and continued until late Sunday night and when I awoke Monday morning we had about fifteen inches of snow on the ground. I made my way, on foot, to the subway on Queens Boulevard, which was about a mile away, and took the train to the armory.

I found the main hall and joined my classmates. We gathered in small groups talking among ourselves and spent most of the morning waiting for someone to begin the graduation practice.

At about noon, a sergeant called for order and took a roll call. Upon completion he ordered us to report to the United Nations Building on the East River where, upon arrival, we would receive further instructions. Finally he told us that due to the snowstorm that crippled the city there would be no graduation exercise for the April 3 class.

We were ordered to return to the armory the next morning, in uniform, at which time we would receive our permanent assignments.

No graduation. Nice, now we were complete. The April 3, 1968, class would eventually become known as "the infamous April Third class." We had set three new records in the NYPD record book before completing one full year that, to this day, have never been broken and never will be.

First: Our class spent less time in the Academy, by far less time, than any preceding class prior to being sent out on patrol.

Second: A member of our class, not my company, was shot in the line of duty in the Fourteenth Precinct with less than one week on the job. The two probationary officers were on foot patrol into their third tour. A car, occupied by several black men, pulled up and opened fire, striking one of the officers.

Third: We never experienced the time-honored graduation ceremony. I still have the two green admission cards in one of my scrapbooks,

Over the years we broke many records, but the two I find most interesting are: 1—we received the most department-generated complaints for alleged violations of the Patrol Guide. 2— we received the most medals for valor, awarded by the mayor, for acts of bravery performed in the line of duty at imminent risk of death. I received both.

On the morning of February 12, I rose early because I knew I had another long walk to Queens Boulevard and I didn't want to be late. As I walked down Grand Street, in full uniform, a patrol car pulled up and asked me if I needed a ride. It was an RMP from the One Twelve Precinct and they knew I was walking to the subway because they didn't know me as a member of their command.

I said yes and got in. They drove me to the subway and wished me luck in my new assignment. I took the train to the armory and arrived early, so I got on a short line to get the news.

(I should now mention that my father still had influential friends in the NYPD. Inspector Green was assigned to police headquarters and he asked my father where I would like to be assigned after graduation. He asked me to give him three precincts and hopefully I would be assigned to one of them. I enjoyed the Sixth Precinct, the West Village; I also liked the midtown area, to wit, the Fourteenth and Eighteenth Precincts. Those were my three precincts / choices.)

As I waited on line I decided the Sixth would be my first choice. Finally: "Name and tax registry number?" Police Officer John Fitzgerald, tax number 858***, Officer Fitzgerald, you are assigned to the Seven Five Precinct in Brooklyn. Next!"

Okay, I knew the Seven Five after working there many times in TPF and it was the direct opposite of the tourist area I requested. I knew I would be exposed to the "Real Deal" police work and I figured if I had to be assigned to an area other than my three choices I might just as well work in a very busy precinct where I could learn the job through exposure. The Seven Five would most certainly give me that opportunity.

(During my two years in the Seven Five, we were ranked the busiest precinct in the entire city. The most UF 61s, the most radio runs. I must be fair and identify several other extremely busy precincts: the Four One, aka Fort Apache, the Two Eight and the Three Two in the heart of the Harlem crime zone. The midtown Fourteenth and Eighteenth precincts were very busy and generated many crime reports, but their criminal activity was usually nonviolent.

Then we had Brooklyn's Seven Three, Seven Seven, Seven Nine, Eight One and the Eight Three. Queens had one really bad precinct, the One O Three. All very busy and dangerous places to work, but the Seven Five was #1 . . . Considering the Seven Five covered a larger area, that did account for our numbers.)

My father asked me to call him as soon as possible after I got the news, so I found a pay phone and made the call. He answered and I said, Dad, I got the Seven Five. There was dead silence on his end of the phone. Finally he told me he would try to find out what happened, but the good news was he knew the captain's clerical man, aka captain #2, who he worked with while assigned to the Sixth Precinct.

It took me over two hours to get to the East New York section and then another ten minutes to walk to the station house (SH) at Liberty and Miller avenues. I entered the building and walked over to the desk. "Police Officer Fitzgerald reporting for duty, Lieutenant."

The desk officer (DO) responded by telling me he was waiting for my arrival, then he made a phone call and I heard him tell the person on the other end, "Fitzgerald just walked in." As I stood waiting for the second shoe to drop, the door to the office behind me opened and a police officer (PO) came out and said, "Jack, my name is Walter Pierce. Your father called and told me you were assigned to our command, welcome. Let's go upstairs and find you a locker."

He asked me to follow him, at which time he took me to the second-floor locker room.

"Jack, find an empty locker and you will need to share it with another member of your class when he arrives."

I didn't have anything to put in the locker, which was a good thing because I didn't have a lock. There was a blank tag attached to the locker door and Walter told me to put my name on the tag. We returned to the first floor and another office, where he introduced me to the roll call man, another good person to know.

The roll call man gave me a post description and told me I was assigned to the fourth squad. Finally I returned to the desk.

The DO said, "Officer Fitzgerald, where were you assigned while on probation?"

"I was assigned to TPF for most of that time and worked SUB for five weeks during the month of December and into January before returning to the Academy."

"Did you ever work this precinct?"

"Yes sir. Many times and I'm happy to be here."

By now it was about one p.m., so he gave me a foot post on Blake Avenue with a one thirty meal. I knew where to get a decent lunch, so off I went to the coffee shop at Liberty and Pennsylvania avenues.

By 1:45 I was walking to my post, which was five blocks away. As I walked I couldn't help but think that six months ago I was patrolling these same streets, but with another police officer. Now I was alone and I would need that old common sense I grew dependent on from the beginning.

That first tour was uneventful and I returned to the SH by 3:55. We all waited outside the landmark building until the third platoon (four to midnight tour) came out, at which time we entered to sign out.

Officer Pierce was already watching out for me by having the roll call man assigning me to the fourth squad. My sergeant was Sergeant Henry and I would have the next two days off. I was scheduled to work my first late tour, to wit, midnight to eight on February 15. I left the SH in full uniform and got the train to Fresh Pond Road and Palmetto Street in Queens. That was as close as I was going to get, using public transportation, so now I needed to walk the remaining mile and a half to my apartment in Maspeth.

As I began my walk a Lindy's car service cab pulled up and asked me if I needed a lift. I said yes, but I didn't want to take him out of his way and I definitely didn't want to pay the five-dollar-plus fare it was going to cost me for the ride. I was young and walking wasn't going to kill me even though I was a little tired.

The driver said get in, which I did. He then asked me where I wanted to go. I told him and off we went. The streets were still covered with snow, but vehicles were moving and it took about ten minutes for him to get me close to home.

He told me he had to pick up a fare not far from where we were. I was now a few short blocks from home. I thanked him, exited the car and gave him a two-dollar tip. He didn't want to accept it, but I insisted. In five minutes I was home with my wonderful wife Susan and I spent the rest of the evening staying warm after a shower and an enjoyable dinner.

On Friday, February 14, I left early for my first late tour. Upon arrival the first thing I did as I entered the building was salute the desk officer. That was an absolute must, followed by a climb to the second-floor locker room and my locker.

It was empty, so I put in my uniforms, service revolver, gun belt, et cetera, and affixed my new lock to the hasp. I changed into uniform and returned to the ground floor and the muster room. I now had my overcoat. (That tour was the one and only time I wore that overcoat, which I still have, in new condition.)

I checked the roll call and discovered I would be working with Chester Genaro at a fixer (fixed post) on New Lots and Livonia avenues. Our sergeant called the roll and off I went with Chester, a seasoned veteran who also happened to be a great guy.

As we walked to our post I asked him why there was a fixer at that corner and he told me during the summer there was a riot in front of the candy store at that location and it was a fixed post ever since. It was also the end of the line for the elevated/el train, which meant they had a depot at the end of the "Last Stop" platform.

I still recall a good part of that first night and I recall Chester asking me what I looked forward to as a police officer. I responded by telling him I wanted to make a lot of arrests and be the best cop I could be. He said, "Jack, I can assure you that if you stay in the Seven Five for a couple of years you will make arrests for just about every crime in the penal law." I remember that so clearly because over the two years I spent in the Seven Five I did make many arrests. I may not have covered the entire penal law, but I got close.

As time went on I continued making many arrests. Every time I collared someone for something new I added that crime to my list of accomplishments and while doing so I thought about that late tour with Chester.

We spent about an hour standing in front of the candy store and finally the sergeant on patrol pulled up to give us a scratch. Chester had about eight years on the job, so he had "Time on," which meant as long as I was with him I wouldn't receive additional attention from the sergeant. A two-man post was very unusual, but that fixer called for two men.

About ten minutes after the "Boss" drove away, Chester told me to follow him as he climbed the stairs to the el platform. We walked to the depot at the end of the platform and that's when he told me he was going to rest for a while and if I needed him I knew where to find him. I returned to the front of the candy store where I spent the next three hours.

It was February and it was very cold, so I spent as much time inside the store as out and the store owner was happy to have me there. Every once in a while a car would pull up and the driver would come in for a container of coffee or a pack of cigarettes, but for most of the next few hours it was me and Meyer.

Every time I came in out of the cold he would greet me with, "Would you like a hot cup of coffee, Officer?" After the third container I declined his offers. Meyer had owned the candy store for many years. After the initial small talk there came a time when I asked him if he knew why there were two police officers assigned to the corner in front of his store twenty-four hours a day.

His answer was pretty much like Chester's:

"Officer, last summer there was a riot in front of my store. A gang of punks came off the el station and they began fighting with another gang from the neighborhood. They had guns and knives. Five kids were shot and two died. It was terrible. From that day until now I have had two officers, from your precinct, in front of my store twenty-four hours a day."

"Meyer, do you know what started it?"

"No, but in this neighborhood it doesn't take much to start a riot. I can see by your new uniform you are new to the police department, right?"

"I have a little less than one year on the job, but I have worked in this area before. I know what you say is true."

In the late sixties and early seventies there were many riots in our city and Brooklyn had more than their share.

Chester came down the stairs at about four and asked me if I wanted to rest my eyes for a while, but I declined. Our meal was at five. At 4:45 the sector car pulled up and both officers got out and gave Chester the keys. To the best of my almost total recall this was my first time ever ride in a bona fide, official, real deal NYC police car.

Chester drove us to the Galaxy Diner located on Pennsylvania Avenue and Linden Boulevard, which was located in his sector. (On the night we worked together he was working overtime.) We entered the diner, took a booth, had breakfast and when the check came Chester took it to the cashier who he knew. He gave her a five-dollar bill and received several bills as change.

He returned to the booth and left a two-dollar tip. When I asked him how much I owed him he said, "It's on me, kid." Chester drove us back to our fixer and returned the keys to our relief. At about seven forty we began walking back to the SH to sign out.

I decided to use one of my four vacation weeks from 1968, so as soon as I signed out I went to our roll call man.

"Good morning, Officer Cline, my name is Fitzgerald and you may recall Officer Pierce introduced me to you a few days ago. I would like to take one of my vacation weeks from last year. I would also like to use my lost time to take the next three days off."(In 1969, when members of the department worked overtime we were compensated with time back, also known as lost time. While in TPF I amassed about 100 hours of lost time on the books.)

He went into a drawer, took out a UF Twenty-Eight (request for time off form) and told me to fill it out. He said he would ask the desk officer to sign it.

(Thank you again, Walter. If any other "new kid on the block" would have made that request without the required one-week notice, the roll call man would have laughed him out of the office. Being the son of a very well-liked and respected retired police officer had advantages.)

He told me to see him before I went home. I did and he told me to have a good vacation. This was going to be the first vacation I had in a long time because probationary police officers were not permitted to use vacation time until off probation. While assigned to TPF, I made over fifty arrests in six months, so I was able to build a sizeable "lost time" account, ergo, I did have several mini vacations with my wife while on probation.

Working in a precinct was very different from the TPF detail and very different from SUB., I learned every precinct had its own structure and steadfast rules as well as customs that were handed down from generation to generation.

In 1969, I was taught the same unwritten rules my father learned when he joined the NYPD in 1946. There were many, but to mention a few: You never called for the Sergeant on Patrol unless you absolutely positively had to. You always remained visible on post until the sergeant came by to give you a "Scratch" (sign your memo book).

On cold nights you took your private vehicle to your post, which would give you somewhere to warm up, but you always let the sector covering your post know where you could be found if needed.

(That was a violation of the Patrol Guide, but everyone did it and it was overlooked unless you were on the sergeant's shit list.)

On a late tour you always checked your post for any signs of criminal activity (breaks) before returning to the SH at the end of your tour. There are many more that I will get to as I write.

Getting back to the structure in the Seven Five Precinct. The commanding officer in the Seven Five was a deputy inspector, one rank above captain, which was common in very busy precinct. The desk officer, usually a lieutenant, was the highest ranking member of the command we interacted with on a daily basis and the sergeants were there to supervise the PO s on patrol and they didn't want to do the police officer's job.

One of the first unofficial rules I learned occurred when our squad sergeant, Sergeant Henry, called the roll on a four to twelve. There was an unusually large number of young police officers present. He said, "Men, you're all over twenty-one. You must think on your feet and make your own decisions. Call me when you need me, but only at that time."

I still remember Sergeant Henry and his Irish brogue. He was different from most of the other old-time sergeants primarily because he wasn't that old. I think he was one of the youngest sergeants we had and he was always on patrol, which was a bit unusual back in '69, '70, and '71. He really didn't mind a call unless it was for something dumb, but I don't recall any of my brother officers ever making that mistake.

We may have been rookies, but we all had almost a year's worth of experience during a very trying period in New York City's history. When we arrived for that first tour we came knowing the score.

I worked in Sergeant Henry's fourth squad the two years I spent in the Seven Five and enjoyed working for him. Sergeant Henry continued moving up in the ranks and retired as an assistant chief inspector, a three-star chief.

During my two years minus one day spent in the Seven Five Precinct, I learned much about police work. Most of what I learned was due to exposure while working with some of the best police officers in the world.

I also learned that most of what was taught us in the Academy "From the Book" was written by people with little or no street experience. On February 11, 1971, I cleaned out my locker and said good-bye to some of the best cops I would ever work with. I received a long-sought-after transfer to an undercover unit called Taxi Truck Surveillance Unit.

Postscript

I don't think Sergeant Healy would mind me using his name in my book so I will. He was one of my favorite supervisors. A great boss who worked a full eight-hour tour.

6

MY FIRST RIOT

June 20, 1968, I parked my car about a block away from the Charles Street Station House (the Sixth Precinct) located in Manhattan's West Village. I was assigned to the fourth squad in the Tactical Patrol Force. TPF was formed to deal with the riots that began in the mid '60s. Watts had their riots; Detroit had their riots, Washington, DC, had their riots and New York City most certainly had our riots. East New York/Brownsville, Bed-Sty, Harlem and the South Bronx were battle zones and entire neighborhoods were set ablaze.

The police officers assigned to those high-crime/hazardous commands were not equipped to deal with the onslaught of organized mayhem. The assassination of Martin Luther King Jr. on April 4, 1968, caused the "Summer of '68" riots.

King was a man of peace, which was made clear by his "peaceful protests." Unfortunately, after his assassination, the radical activists took a different approach when demonstrating. That approach was called "RIOT." I could never understand the thought process that motivated black ghettoites to burn and plunder their own neighborhoods.

Think about it; before the riots, the people living in the poorer, primarily black and Hispanic areas of many cities had decent, subsidized housing. They had public assistance in the form of welfare and food stamps and if they chose not to work or couldn't find work they were supported by the various federally funded programs. What caused them to be in that economic dilemma is and has been a debatable subject, but that's where they were in life.

Then, something would spark a riot and entire blocks would be burned to the ground. Good people were killed and local businesses were burned out of existence. I have witnessed this destruction many times and it's still a mystery to me, but the NYPD didn't rationalize the cause. We simply responded and did our best to protect life and property.

There came a time when the hierarchy in the NYPD came up with a brilliant idea: Let's form a group of volunteer police officers and train them in riot control. They will work the high-crime areas in the city and they will work peak crime time: six p.m. to two a.m.

The police commissioner gave the thumbs-up and the Tactical Patrol Force became an integral part of the NYPD.

To be accepted into that special assignment you had to be physically fit and have a neat appearance and in all modesty, I must admit I qualified. We received advanced training in crowd control, but the forte of TPF was the more hazardous riot control. We always patrolled on foot with another member of our squad. The bottom line is TPF was the Special Forces in the NYPD at that time.

When not working in the high-crime areas in Brooklyn North, our squad was assigned to Manhattan South, which was far less stressful. Or so it was supposed to be. We had completed our third week in Brooklyn before catching a break in the Sixth Precinct, which encompassed Greenwich Village.

The residents of the Sixth Precinct were diversified. There were students attending New York University, one of the best schools in the country. There were hippies and beatniks who came to the village because it was cool and they opened coffee shops, jazz joints and a few nightclubs. There were the longtime, born and raised, residents, living in the many tenements that can still be found on the lower west side of Manhattan.

"The Village" was home to many ultra-wealthy New Yorkers as well as celebrities from stage, screen and the world of sports. The West Village was and still is the heart of the Gay community in NYC . . . Very diversified.

The night I am writing about wasn't my first night assigned to the Sixth Precinct, but it was most certainly my most memorable tour in that command. I was assigned with five other police officers to Washington Square Park, which is one of the best-known parks in the city. Very popular with the locals, tourists and especially the resident students at NYU.

As my partner Ralph C. and I walked our post, we came upon an elderly couple sitting on a park bench. The woman called us over and handed me a flyer, which read, in big bold letters at the top: "Up against the wall Mother F***er." It went on to inform the reader that there was going to be a demonstration that evening at the fountain and the purpose of that gathering was to protest the excessive use of force by a member of the fascist NYC Police Tactical Patrol Force.

Ralph used his portable radio to request a meeting with our sergeant just outside the park. As we walked toward that meeting, a student from NYU stopped us.

"Officers, are you aware of the demonstration scheduled to take place in the park tonight?"

"Yes, we just heard about it. Do you know what caused the demonstration?"

"Yes, I do. Two nights ago I was here, hanging out with my friends when we saw one of the local druggies climbing a tree, trying to catch a squirrel. They think it's cool to have a pet squirrel on a string/leash. One of your TPF officers went to stop him. The jerk fell out of the tree and broke his arm. The officer arrested him, but then he took him to St. Vincent's Hospital for treatment. His doper friends contacted the local Black radical agitators who hang out in this park just looking to start trouble."

When Sergeant Brennan arrived we gave him the copy of the flyer and introduced him to the student, who repeated what he told us. The sergeant walked with us as we reentered the park and I could see him scoping out the scene. It was nearly eight and he said there were a lot more people gathering around the fountain than we would have on a normal summer evening. It was also obvious there were no tourists or students in that mob.

Sergeant Brennan got on his radio and ordered all members of our squad to respond to the park. Eventually our six-man detail grew to twenty-five, but the crowd was also growing by the minute. I heard him request backup from another squad assigned to the nearby Ninth Precinct. As the sun went down the crowd grew larger and more animated. Even I, with very limited experience in such matters, could see there was going to be trouble that night.

During my first three weeks in TPF, I had been assigned to the worst areas in the city, but that was reasonably tame compared to what was happening this night. I don't mind admitting I was feeling the adrenaline rush.

Sergeant Brennan gathered our squad in an out-of-the-way corner and told us we were going to monitor the demonstration without getting too close. He also told us that the squad he requested from the Ninth Precinct was delayed due to an issue in that precinct. (Looking back on that night I can understand why our sergeant was well liked by our chief, Chief McCarthy, and why we received so many difficult assignments.)

With no prior warning, Brennan needed to address a crowd control condition at best and possibly a full-blown riot with one squad. He also had to consider that about one third of his squad had very little patrol experience and had never been in a riot.

Under his direction we kept our distance and finally a speaker/agitator got up on the elevated lip running around the large fountain in the center of the park. The guy was a black man, as was 90 percent of the mob.

I was standing near a senior member of our squad very familiar with the park and heard him say the demonstrators were not regulars. The bigmouth ranted and did his best to fire up the crowd with anti-police/anti-TPF rhetoric. I don't recall exactly what he was saying because I really wasn't paying much attention, we were all too busy watching the people in the crowd.

Finally, after about twenty minutes of his tirade, he began leading the mob out of the park through the Washington Square Arch and onto Fifth Avenue. Sergeant Brennan led our detail as we followed them toward Eighth Street. The demonstrators were kicking the parked cars as we walked. I saw another black man pick up a garbage can and throw it through the windshield of another parked car. As we turned off Fifth Avenue and began walking east on Eighth Street, they began throwing anything they could get their hands on at the store windows that lined the sidewalk, breaking many of them.

I could not believe all we were doing was following and watching. The leader of the crowd did an about-face and began walking west on Eighth toward Sixth Avenue. The now totally out-of-control crowd followed him as he returned to the park, but they did a lot of damage along the way. They had been emboldened by our "do-nothing" response to their riot.

By now there had to be at least two hundred demonstrators and still only twenty-five of us. We continued in a follow mode, returning to the park several minutes after the "Leader of the Pack."

As we approached the entrance at the Arch, we could see most of the trash receptacles had been set on fire. The large dumpsters near the park house were ablaze and the rioters were now breaking the antique lights that illuminated the park. Most of the park was dark.

A bottle came flying out of the crowd aimed at us. Then another and another, but fortunately we were able to dodge them and thank goodness no one was injured, because we were not prepared for this riot. We did not have our helmets.

The leader returned to the fountain where he resumed his rant, bringing the rioters to a fever pitch. We were now standing directly under the Arch about one hundred feet from the fountain. As I looked around I was able to gather my thoughts: What the F*** was happening?

I could not believe what was taking place. I can clearly recall thinking that if this is what being a police officer in NYC was going to be like I would need to reconsider my career choice. I was thoroughly disgusted with the way we policed/controlled this incident/riot. We were the police, we were supposed to protect life and property, but we were allowing the mob to wreak havoc on that neighborhood.

I overheard a message Sergeant Brennan received on his portable radio. The Ninth Precinct squad had arrived and was on their way to the park. Chief McCarthy was also responding.

As we continued to "monitor" the rioters, our reinforcements arrived. Leading them up the path from MacDougal and West Fourth Street was none other than our chief.

I was standing about thirty feet from that entrance when they arrived and I saw a bottle flying through the air, just missing the chief's head. It was very close and clearly got his attention. He continued toward the fountain and finally gave the order on his handheld megaphone: "Officers, clear the park." Those words were music to my ears. Clear the park.

With the additional squad our manpower grew to about fifty men and I was happy the odds were getting better. Using wedge formations, learned in riot control training, we divided the crowd into smaller groups, which were then forced out of the park and onto the side streets. There wasn't as much resistance as I hoped for.

I wanted to kick some ass, but the cretins got the message. The party's over, it's time to leave. There were a few skirmishes here and there, but none close to me. Finally the only people left in the park were wearing blue.

By midnight the fires had burned themselves out without leaving much damage. A few trees showed some burns and there was quite a bit of damage to the very old, circa 1860s, light posts. I have no idea how many reports were prepared for the hundreds of thousands of dollars of damage to the cars and the store windows.

By one fifteen, the only police presence was our original six men. It was totally dark. Ralph and I were standing in a small fenced-off area by the park house. It was near the end of our six to two tour and we were getting ready to begin our fifteen-minute walk back to the Sixth Precinct SH for return roll call.

As unbelievable as the following paragraph is, it is true.

As we stood there in total darkness, just the two of us, with no light source save that provided by the moon and the couple of streetlights from the surrounding area, we couldn't believe our eyes. Guess who came walking along the narrow path between the park house and a wall of shrubs?

If you guessed the leader/organizer of the riot, mister bigmouth agitator, you are correct. We were shocked and couldn't believe our good fortune. I now must ask you, the reader, to put yourself in our shoes for a moment. You have just spent the last six hours watching and following a large mob as they rioted through the city streets. Intentionally causing untold damage to private property as well as city property. Setting fires as they went and no one was arrested. No one would be punished for their criminal actions. But here comes the person who organized the entire evening's entertainment. I ask you to use your imagination. Put yourself in our uniforms at that moment. What would you have done? Now try to understand why I will not write another word about our last few minutes spent in the park.

I will admit that after that brief encounter I decided to remain a member of the NYPD, which I did for twenty-six years.

7

MOLLY'S

In the summer of 1968, I was assigned to the Tactical Patrol Force. One sweltering summer evening, my partner Ralph Riccio and I were assigned a foot post in the Seventh Precinct, which encompassed the Lower East Side of Manhattan. If you are unfamiliar with that part of the city, it would be fair to say: What once was is no more.

During the latter part of the nineteenth century and into the mid twentieth century, that entire area was occupied by Jewish immigrants and, to a lesser degree, still retains some of that old Jewish neighborhood charm.

My favorite kosher style deli anywhere in the world, Katz's, is still going strong on Houston Street. In 1888, while Jack the Ripper was making headlines for his murder spree in London's East End, the Iceland brothers opened a deli on the lower east side. In 1903 Jerome Katz joined them and in 1910 that deli became known as Katz's.

Then there is Orchard Street, aka "Jew Town" to old-time New Yorkers. Third- and fourth-generation Jewish merchants still own and operate a few clothing, luggage and other shops in that area.

On that sweltering evening we found one of those holdouts while looking for a cold drink of water.

Ralph and I were assigned to patrol Rivington Street. After about an hour and a half of constant foot patrol we came to the conclusion a cool drink of water was needed. As we patrolled we saw store after store locking their doors. No restaurants, no bodegas. Nowhere to get a drink of water. It's time to make a decision, so I broke one of the many rules in the Patrol Guide by walking off post, one block, to Delancey Street, looking for water.

I found a Cohen Optical store, but it was closed. I could see a security guard inside, so I knocked on the window and he opened the door. He opened it just enough to allow me to ask if my partner and I could get a drink of water.

"What do you want?"

"Sorry to bother you, but would it be possible to get a couple of cups of water?"

"No. I'm not allowed to let anyone in after closing."

"I can see your water cooler; can you just fill two cups with water for me?"

"No!"

With that "No" he closed the door. Come on, give me a ****** break. I'm in full uniform wearing a shiny NYPD badge already. I realized that black security guard did not like cops. I returned to my post and gave Ralph the bad news. We continued walking toward Essex Street dying from thirst, but we were young, we were tough, we would suck it up.

As we patrolled Rivington Street, we came upon a restaurant we hadn't noticed before. It was several steps below street level. We must have walked past it five times, but never realized it was a restaurant until they turned their lights on.

We went down the steps, opened the door and walked into a beautiful classic old-time New York City restaurant. It was a good-size dining room with about twenty tables, all covered with white linen tablecloths. There was a piano player and a man playing the violin. Real Class.

At eight p.m. they were not busy, maybe five occupied tables. As we walked into the dining room, a waiter came over and asked if we would be joining them for dinner. Ralph said no, but asked if we could have some cold water. As we were speaking to the waiter a well-dressed, very attractive lady wearing a beautiful blue dress walked over. She was about fifty years old and added charm to this fine restaurant. She belonged!

"Good evening, Officers, my name is Molly, thank you for coming to my restaurant this evening. Please follow me."

The waiter told her all we wanted was a glass of water. Molly stopped, turned and asked why we weren't staying for dinner. Then she added, "None of the boys from the precinct come in anymore." We explained that we didn't have our meal hour until ten, but we were thirsty and we would really appreciate a cool glass of water. She smiled and told the waiter to get us a bottle of seltzer. She said seltzer is better when you're thirsty. She asked us to sit as the waiter returned with the seltzer, which came in the old-fashioned blue bottle with the little lever on the side.

We sat at a nearby table as the waiter brought two glasses with ice cubes. We made memo book entries stating that we were taking a "Personal," so we were covered for twenty minutes. Molly began chatting about the heat, the neighborhood and finally she reminded us that we had our meal at ten and invited us back for dinner. Ralph and I finished our seltzer, thanked the waiter and told Molly we would see her at ten. She responded "Don't forget" just the way my mother would have said those words.

We left the restaurant and returned to our post. As we walked, I asked Ralph how much money he had with him; nine bucks. I had about the same and we both knew between us we didn't have enough for one meal at that fine restaurant. We had planned on going to Katz's, which not only was the best restaurant in that area that we could afford, but just about the only one open and then there was the fifty-percent discount for the "boys in blue."

In 1968, you could get a gigantic corned beef or pastrami or brisket sandwich, all top-shelf quality kosher meat with pickles, for about seven dollars. For us . . . four with a soda, and that sandwich back then, as it is today, weighed about one pound. Today it costs about twenty bucks and is still a good deal.

We discussed our dilemma as we walked our post. Our problem was, we'd told Molly we would return for dinner, but we knew we didn't have nearly enough money to pay for our meal. We felt confident that Molly's invitation to have dinner with her meant we would not be given a check, but we couldn't be sure. That's when Ralph said, "Sometimes it's not easy being a cop." We both laughed and decided we could not break our promise to Molly as she was very sincere with her invitation.

We passed Molly's several times and watched as the fine expensive automobiles pulled up and parked nearby. Everyone going in was wearing either a suit or a nice dress, Molly's was definitely a high-class restaurant.

At exactly ten we walked down the few steps, opened the door and were again greeted by that same waiter. He said, "Welcome back, Officers, please follow me." He showed us to a table in a corner as far away from "center stage" as possible. Molly was singing a song while the piano player and the guy with the violin played. I told Ralph that I couldn't recall ever having dinner in a restaurant as upscale as this. He said he didn't know of any restaurants like Molly's.

Our waiter brought us a couple of menus and as we went down the list I found many items that I had never heard of before. This was clearly a gourmet menu in a fine Jewish restaurant, but the one section we had no problem understanding was the price.

We knew going in the door we wouldn't have enough to pay for our food, but by now it really didn't make much difference how much our selection would cost, it would be too much. If only that security guard had given us some water.

When our waiter returned to take our order, I asked if it would be possible for us to get a couple of sandwiches. He hesitated and said he would need to ask the chef because they didn't have sandwiches on the menu. As he was about to walk away, Molly came over to our table and thanked us for returning as promised.

She asked what we would like for dinner and before we could answer our waiter said, "They want sandwiches." Molly must have known our dilemma and asked if we liked brisket. Brisket? We loved brisket. She said, "If you like brisket you'll love my brisket," and told our waiter to bring us two brisket dinners. End of that problem, at least for a while.

As our waiter walked away, Molly asked us what we would like to drink. We both responded, "The seltzer was very good," so she called another waiter over and told him to get us a bottle of seltzer. As we waited for our food, Molly sat with us engaging in small talk.

"I don't know why the boys from the precinct don't come in anymore."

"I'm sorry I can't answer that question; we're assigned to the Tactical Patrol Force."

"So that's what TPF on your collar stands for."

"Yes."

That's when she told us the only one who did come in was Inspector Rubin and then we knew why "the boys didn't come in anymore." The inspector, a high-ranking member of the department, enjoyed dining at Molly's and wanted to keep this fine restaurant to himself and his high-ranking associates. He put the word out to the precinct CO.to instruct the members of his command Molly's was off-limits. TPF was off the radar so we didn't get the word; ergo, here we were enjoying a dinner at Molly's.

There came a time when Molly excused herself and told us our food would be out in a few minutes. She returned to the two musicians and as she began another song our waiter arrived with our brisket. Two large plates loaded with brisket, potatoes, vegetables and gravy. We enjoyed every last morsel and it was delicious. Molly returned and asked if everything was okay and we said it was great and we thanked her very much.

She was really a nice lady and she made us feel welcome. As

our waiter returned to clear the table she said, "Bring the boys some nice warm apple strudel with cream."

Ralph and I said, "Molly, thank you but we couldn't eat another bite. The brisket was delicious and we are full. Can we have our check?"

"No check for you boys, it's a pleasure having you join us tonight. Promise me when you're in the area you'll come in again."

"Molly, thank you very much for your generosity. We really appreciate it. It has been a pleasure meeting you. We promise we'll be back."

We got up from the table, shook her hand and thanked her again. Then I said, "Molly what time do you think you'll close tonight?"

"About one."

"We'll be waiting outside when you leave to make sure you're okay."

"That will be nice and when you get thirsty or would like a cup of coffee, please come in."

Ralph and I each gave the waiter a five-dollar tip. We climbed the stairs and resumed patrol. Molly got a lot of attention from us that evening.

At about twelve thirty we realized our post was as quiet as could be. The only place open was Molly's, so we returned to the restaurant staying close, but not too close.

When her lights went out we walked to the front door. When Molly and her staff came up the steps we escorted them around the corner to the parking lot where we waited for them as they got into their cars. Before Molly got in her car she said, "I hope you both come back soon." We stayed with them until they drove away.

We promised Molly we would stop by and we did. Ralph and I carpooled to work as we lived about a mile apart in Maspeth, Queens. On many occasions we would make early arrests, go to Night Court and get an early dismissal, usually before midnight.

Whenever we worked Manhattan and had that early dismissal we would stop at Molly's. She would always join us as we had a cup of coffee or shared a bottle of seltzer. We wouldn't leave until she turned off the lights, then we walked her and her staff to their cars.

We traveled to work in uniform, always wearing a light jacket over our uniform shirts, but the patrons could see who we were and Molly liked that. She definitely liked a cop and we liked Molly.

Over the next several months we got to know her a little better and she invited us to come in with our wives, but that never happened. I knew her generosity would never allow a bill and I could never take advantage of such a nice lady. That one time was just something that happened, but neither Ralph nor I ever accepted more than coffee or seltzer after that and I think Molly understood.

Postscript

During the summer of 1968, Governor George Wallace from Alabama was running for president. He held a rally at Madison Square Garden. (I will return to that event in another chapter.) There came a time, after the rally, when Wallace supporters were handing out "Support Wallace" items including Wallace for President bumper stickers.

For those readers who may not be familiar with George Wallace, that man was a true southern bigot, ergo the need for the Tactical Patrol Force at his rally.

He was anti-black and probably anti everything else good in our country, but most definitely anti-black. Maybe the word racist might be more descriptive, but who am I to judge. As we watched those in attendance exit the Garden, a campaign worker came over and gave us all a few "Wallace for President" bumper stickers. I folded them and put them in my pocket as there was no place to trash them.

When Ralph and I returned to my car I tossed them in the backseat and forgot about them . . . until the night of the "Big Thirst."

As we walked our post, dying for a cool drink due to the black, cop-hating racist, security guard denying us a friggin' cup of water, I remembered the bumper stickers. When the sun went down I returned to my car and found one of the Wallace for President stickers. With Ralph as my lookout I attached a sticker to the rear bumper of the guard's car, which was parked in front of the store. I do believe that "out of character" deed was caused by the lack of salt in my body and the severe thirst I was experiencing.

I know when my time comes to join St. Michael the Archangel in Heaven, I will have time added to my purgatory sentence for that dastardly deed, but on that very hot evening in the summer of '68, revenge was sweet.

8

THE WALLACE RALLY AT MADISON SQUARE

In 1968, and while assigned to the Tactical Patrol Force (TPF), our fourth squad would frequently be assigned to very sensitive areas during demonstrations, as in this instance I am writing about: Ground zero at the Governor Ralph Wallace Presidential Rally held at Madison Square Garden. Our squad was the only unit assigned to the front of the Garden, where the radical demonstrators were gathered. Their only purpose for being there was to disrupt that event.

I should begin by mentioning that Ralph Wallace, the governor of Alabama, was considered by many to be the classic example of a southern "redneck" politician. He was a Democrat but in 1968 he ran as the American Independent party candidate for president.

He came to NYC to campaign and held a huge rally at the Garden. On this rare occasion eight squads from TPF had a tour change from our usual six p.m. to two a.m. to a ten a.m. to six p.m. tour.

Our squad had worked the previous evening and I recall our sergeant telling us to make sure we had our hats and bats (helmets and nightsticks) as well as our raincoats when we reported for duty. He added we wouldn't need our uniform hats. We always had our helmets and nightsticks in our cars, but I wondered how the sergeant knew it was going to rain the next day.

By nine forty-five the officers in our squad began to gather just off the northwest corner of Seventh Avenue on Thirty-First Street. By ten we were all present and awaiting the arrival of Sergeant Brennan.

He exited the Garden at about ten fifteen and had a brief roll call before taking a few steps back. He looked us over; every permanent member of the squad had a raincoat while every probationary member had none. It was warm and sunny and there wasn't a cloud in the sky. We didn't need a raincoat, right? Wrong. On that day I learned two things: Always listen to your sergeant and sometimes a raincoat can do more than keep you dry.

Sergeant Brennan was a very patient man. I never saw him get flustered and I'm sure he wasn't surprised finding us "raincoat-less." He told us we had a ten thirty meal with a return to post at eleven thirty with raincoats. My carpool partner and I walked to my car, retrieved our raincoats and got a cup of coffee before returning to our corner.

Okay, everyone had their helmet, raincoat and a nightstick. As we awaited further orders we could see large groups of demonstrators gathering across the street from the Garden on the northeast corner of Seventh Avenue at Thirty-Third Street. There had to be at least two hundred demonstrators and many were wearing motorcycle helmets with face shields. We all knew there was going to be trouble today.

Several agitators, standing on wooden boxes, were working the crowd into a frenzied mob. There came a time when Sergeant Brennan ordered us to move the demonstrators. They were blocking pedestrian traffic while using loud and abusive language. Both violations of the penal law.

We approached them in a wedge formation and moved them north on Seventh Avenue. As we moved, the mob resisted; they were experienced demonstrators. They locked arms, so now we needed to use our batons. Every move we made was in the Tactical Patrol Force handbook. .

We held our batons horizontally while pushing the demonstrator's north on Seventh Avenue toward Thirty-Fourth Street. There came a time when they began grabbing our sticks, trying to take them away from us. Not a good idea.

We were definitely outnumbered, but riots and demonstrations were our forte. I must say that at no time did we lose control. We used that necessary force required to get the job done and no more. Yes I'm sure there were some minor injuries on both sides, but I don't recall anyone needing medical attention and the "mob" was dispersed.

Finally we come to the raincoats: The standard operating procedure for most demonstrators was to create public disorder and while doing so try to agitate the police to a point of overreaction. With luck, those incidents would be recorded by the news media covering the demonstration. If they got very lucky someone might even get a "front page shot" of a cop hitting some poor defenseless demonstrator over the head with a nightstick. (Not much has changed over the past forty-nine years since that rally, except now everyone has a movie camera in their pocket.)

It was also common practice for those protesters to record every cop's shield number, which would be used when making false civilian complaints. Our helmets did not have shield numbers and while wearing the raincoat as an outer garment our shields were not visible because they were affixed to our shirts. Ergo, no shield numbers and no civilian complaints.

Our fourth squad was the only squad assigned to crowd control outside the Garden, but if we needed backup it was available from the seven squads inside the Garden. Sergeant Brennan was a very wise man.

9

MY FIRST DOA

There are two assignments in the NYPD most police officers dread.

#1—Guarding a dead human body.

#2—Being assigned to a fixed post.

Both are always given to officers on foot patrol.

With regard to the second, many precincts, especially those in midtown Manhattan, have numerous fixed posts. Every embassy required at least one assigned officer and sometimes more than one. My first command in the Tactical Patrol Force eliminated any chance of me getting either of those two assignments because we were not part of the precinct patrol force.

As a police officer in the Seven Five Precinct I was fair game for both. We had one fixed post, a synagogue, where I stood guard . . . once. Those were seven of the longest hours of my career. It was in February on a four to midnight tour and I still feel the cold. To this day, in August when the temperature hits one hundred ten degrees, I still get a chill just thinking about that night.

When you got a fixer you never even thought about leaving until relieved. Imagine standing in front of a building for seven hours with the thermometer reading twenty degrees. Nowhere to sit or get out of the wind. You had to be visible and alert. You could expect a visit from every Sergeant on Patrol at least once during your tour. You were relieved for meal and two twenty-minute breaks for personal necessity during your eight-hour tour.

There were no ultra-warm thermal long johns or ski skins, no electric hand warmers, no superduper warm socks to keep your feet from coming close to losing all your toes due to frostbite. You get the picture. On that night in February it was friggin' C. O. L. D.!!!

I sucked it up and survived to tell the story.

P. S. There came a time in the eighties when the PBA negotiated a change to the fixer assignment. A fixed post was limited to four hours per officer.

One evening as I walked my post on Blake Avenue, a sector car pulled up and the driver said, "Get in, kid, we have a job for you." I knew it, just by the way he said those words, it was a DOA . . . He told me that I had a DOA in the projects on Linden Boulevard, but I was lucky because it was a homicide and the body was fresh.

That made all the difference in the world. I won't go into detail, but having to sit with a "ripe" dead human body was the worst jobs you could get. The law required a police officer to be present to safeguard the property of the deceased until he/she was removed to either the morgue or a funeral parlor. All valuables such as cash and jewelry had to be vouchered awaiting disposition by the Chief Clerk's office.

When I arrived at the apartment I was met by the Sergeant on Patrol and he introduced me to the crime scene. He asked if this was my first homicide/DOA assignment and I said yes. He went on to review what I needed to do as well as the entries I was required to make in my memo book. He told me this was going to be a busy evening for several reasons.

This DOA was a homicide crime scene. It occurred in a City Housing project located in our precinct, so the Seven Five detectives would be handling the case. No doubt the NYC Housing detectives would make an appearance. Crime Scene investigators would arrive to do what they do best and finally the medical examiner would be paying me a visit.

I need to take a moment to comment on the Housing Police from its inception and up to the great changes that were made in the early 1980s.

As far as I am concerned, and I know most of the NYPD patrol force from the 1960s and '70s will agree with my following evaluation: The Housing PD was a farce. I should begin by referring to that city agency as they were referred to by 99.99 percent of the real deal NYPD, to wit, "Housing Guards." They were as useless as useless could be. In fact using the word guard is a put-down to all the security guards working and doing a good job in the city.

They were assigned to patrol the housing projects, but I don't recall ever seeing a member of the HPD on patrol, ever. Their base of operation (station house) was an apartment in one of the buildings in the project and that's where you could find them sleeping or watching TV most of the time.

What really created a major issue with the NYPD officers on patrol was that we were required to respond to every job in a housing project and the guards rarely responded. It was common for a sector, after receiving a job in a project, to ask central to have the Housing Guards respond, knowing they would never arrive.

In the early eighties, that agency was assigned a new Chief of Patrol and he made a lot of changes, all good for the city and the NYPD. There came a time when the Civil Service Department made a change to the hiring practice for all policing agencies, resulting in one exam for NYC police officer.

When a list of applicants was published, the recruit could be assigned to any one of the three city police departments, the NYPD, the NYC Transit PD or the Housing PD. With the changes in their top bosses as well as hiring quality police officers, the Housing PD was looked upon more favorably by all. The Transit PD always did a great job and quite frankly I wouldn't want to trade jobs with them. They earned their money.

Returning to my crime scene: Our detectives responded within a short time and they called for the Crime Scene Unit. The sergeant had the T.S. (telephone switchboard) operator notify the medical examiner's office and he was on the way. The last thing the sergeant said to me before leaving was, "Officer Fitzgerald, do not allow any unauthorized sightseers to enter this apartment. Have I made myself clear?"

"Yes Sergeant, crystal clear."

The crime scene was a small apartment with one bedroom, a small kitchen, living room and bathroom. The victim, an elderly Jewish woman, was in the bedroom. She had been beaten to death and her apartment had been ransacked.

I watched every move our detectives made and when they realized I was interested they took time to explain what they were doing and why they were doing it. I was totally engrossed in that scene and our detectives were some of the best in the city.

By the time they completed their part of this investigation I had learned a lot. They concluded that due to the fact that there was no sign of forced entry the victim most likely knew the person, or expected someone and allowed that person entry into her apartment.

The detectives interviewed people living in adjacent apartments on her floor and they all said the victim was a nice lady who lived alone. She was known to give money to needy neighbors on occasion. She usually kept several hundred dollars in her apartment to avoid traveling to her bank more than once a month. No one could recall seeing her for a couple of days, but that wasn't unusual.

They inquired about her daily habits and asked where she shopped. There was a supermarket within a short walk from her building and that's where she did most of her shopping. She usually used a small cart to carry her packages home, but on occasion she would have her groceries delivered.

Upon completion of the interviews, the detectives returned to the apartment. As they were bringing me up to speed the doorbell rang. The medical examiner had arrived. He spent several minutes viewing the body, and finally he ruled this death a homicide. The detectives and the medical examiner left, leaving me alone . . . but not for long.

Soon the Housing Guard detectives arrived. They viewed the body, looked around and then one of them asked me if the Seven Five squad had been there . . . Yes.

Those Housing Guard detectives were at the crime scene for about five minutes, five friggin' minutes and this was a homicide within their zone of influence. No canvassing, no interviewing neighbors, no interest regarding means of entry. Those two bozos couldn't have cared less about the victim.

When the CSU detectives arrived, things got interesting again. One man began dusting for fingerprints while his partner took photos of the scene from every angle He measured the rooms, recording the numbers in his log as he went.

They searched the chest of drawers, the closet and the refrigerator. They actually searched every inch of that apartment, but found nothing incriminating. I obeyed the sergeant's orders and made entries in my memo book. If and when I needed a reference log I would have it.

While CSU was doing what they do, the doorbell rang. I opened the door and came face-to-face with two Housing Guards. I asked what they wanted, one said they heard there was a homicide committed in the apartment and they wanted to take a look at the crime scene. Before I had a chance to respond they both tried to push past me. I stood in front of them and told them unless they had reason to be there I would not allow them entry.

"Yo, this is our project and you can't tell us we can't come in. We got every right to be here."

"Can I have your names for my report?"

"Why you want our names?"

"Because I'm going to call my sergeant and tell him two officers from the HPD have arrived and want to take control of this homicide crime scene. I know he will want your names. I'm sure he will also want to speak to your sergeant as well as the two detectives who just left. If you will give me your names and the name of your sergeant as well as the phone number where he can be reached, I will make my call and leave. Then you can take control of this crime scene and I can resume my patrol duties."

If looks could kill I would be a dead man. They knew I was right. The Crime Scene detectives took about an hour and a half to complete their job. As they were leaving they said they were going to stop at the Seven Five SH to speak to our detectives. About twenty minutes later, the sector arrived to relieve me for meal. It was late, so I told them that I would remain on the scene until relieved by the late tour. They left and I watched the TV until my end of tour relief arrived at twelve thirty.

My first DOA and my first homicide scene under my belt on the same tour.

I didn't give much thought to that murder victim after that night, but about one weeks later one of the detectives assigned to that case called me to the squad room and told me that they had finally solved that case. He said the CSU lifted many fingerprints, but only one set appeared over and over on drawers, a jewelry box and other areas in the apartment.

They ran the prints and they came back to a nineteen-year-old man who had been arrested for burglary several times. That person had been released from prison two months before the murder. They checked with his probation officer and he lived in the Seven Five Precinct. He also worked as a delivery boy for the same market where the victim did her shopping.

He was interviewed and admitted that he delivered groceries to her that evening. He'd heard she had a lot of money in her apartment, so when the woman opened the door he demanded money. She told him she only had a few dollars and he could have it. He wasn't happy with that, so he pushed her onto the floor and that's when she began to scream. He began hitting her until she stopped. She stopped because she had a heart attack and died. Due to his prior criminal record he received twenty-five years in Attica.

10

THE BURGLARY AT FORTUNOFF'S ON LIVONIA AVENUE

After about four months in the Seven Five Precinct, I received a change of assignment from foot patrol to sector car duty. My father, retired Patrolman Fitzgerald, had many friends in the department, so he called in a favor from the inspector's clerical man, aka Captain #2 and I "got a seat." I wanted the busiest sector and I got what I wanted. Sector C as in Charlie was the busiest sector in one of the top three busiest precincts in the City of New York.

The man I was scheduled to work with was transferred to a plainclothes detail two days prior to my reassignment, so I worked with different men every day. There came a time, about one month later, when Tommy Degar was assigned as my "Steady Partner."

Sector Charlie was in the heart of a NYC ghetto. Most of the residents were low income or no income on welfare, 75 percent black and 25percent Hispanic. If you could afford to leave that section of Brooklyn you were off like a prom dress.

In 1922, Max and Clara Fortunoff opened a store on Livonia Avenue. At that time East New York Brooklyn was 100 percent Jewish. There came a time when they opened a second store on Livonia Avenue, one block away. Both stores were upscale and profitable and grew into rather large department stores selling fine china, jewelry, clothing, furniture, et cetera.

In the early sixties, that neighborhood began to go downhill. By 1969 to 1971, there were entire blocks leveled to the ground from Pennsylvania Avenue to Hinsdale Street.

There came a time when the owners of Fortunoff closed their doors for the last time and relocated to Westbury in Nassau County on Long Island.

One December night while working a late tour (twelve to eight) we received a 10-52 dispute in our sector. While we were on that job sector Queen was assigned to investigate a burglary in progress at Fortunoff, also in our sector. We handled the dispute and got back on the air in time to hear that sector requesting backup to assist in the search at Fortunoff, which was a large two-story building.

As we pulled up in front of the well-lit store we saw Joe Russo covering two men in handcuffs. We also saw that one of the large windows had a huge hole in it and there were boxes of merchandise all over the sidewalk.

Within a minute we were joined by two additional sectors. Joe told us his partner was in the store and needed help with the search. We all went in via the broken window and found Pete Adams. With seven of us searching it didn't take long to come to the conclusion the building was empty. Before resuming patrol I had a brief conversation with Joe Russo:

"Joe, would you like us to transport your prisoners to the house for you?"

"No thanks, Jack, we haven't decided if they're under arrest yet. If we need transportation we'll call you. Would you go to the SH and pull the card on Fortunoff and notify the owner they need to respond to safeguard this break?"

"Consider it done. If you need anything, just call."

Tommy made the call while I brought the desk officer up to speed. We returned to Fortunoff with two containers of coffee and told Joe and Pete the manager was on the way.

They had released their suspects and told us they never saw them in the store or in possession of property, so they cut them loose. They thanked us for the coffee and said they would remain at the scene to safeguard the premises until the manager arrived.

Sector Charlie went 10-98 (resuming patrol).

At eight a.m. it was end of tour and time to go home. Late tours were difficult for me. The most I could expect was about five hours of broken sleep, so by the time I returned to work I was still tired. It went that way for the entire week.

On that day in December I didn't try to sleep. I planned on attending our precinct family Christmas party at the local chapter of the Knights of Columbus. The party began at two p.m. My wife and I took our daughter to see Santa. They served lunch for everyone with ice cream and cake for the children. Santa would give the gifts we brought and I wanted to be home by four. If all went as planned I could get my five hours' sleep before returning for another late tour.

As we entered the hall one of my friends asked me if I had responded to Fortunoff that morning. I said yes and he told me to join him in the kitchen. I found a table for my family with a friend and his family and proceeded to the kitchen.

As I walked in I could see several of the men who worked the previous late tour in conversation and they were not having a good time. Jimmy Doyle, one of our PBA delegates, was doing most of the talking. He told us there were several representatives from the Fortunoff Corporation at the station house meeting with our commanding officer and a one-star chief, the second-in-command of our Brooklyn South borough.

Jimmy added, to make things worse Fortunoff security director brought two eyewitnesses to the station house. They were willing to swear, under oath, that the cops who responded to the burglary at Fortunoff stole a lot of property from the store. They said they watched as the cops filled their police cars with the boxes and drove away.

I knew that wasn't true because every responding officer was busy searching for the burglars in the store. I saw that two sectors resumed patrol while Tommy and I stayed on the scene helping the assigned sector move the numerous boxes found on the sidewalk back into the store via the broken window.

The assigned sector remained on the scene safeguarding the premises. Tommy made the call to the manager and then we resumed patrol. About an hour later we drove past the store and saw the Fortunoff maintenance crew boarding up the broken window and securing the building. The assigned sector had already resumed patrol.

Getting back to the party—I asked the delegate what we could expect from what was happening at the SH. He said we had to wait to see.

Now try to understand; I was twenty-six years old and had never been accused of a crime before. I was not a thief and didn't appreciate being accused of stealing from that store. This was definitely a first for me and I wasn't enjoying the experience.

I returned to my family and suffered through the two hours it took before Santa gave the present to my daughter. As I drove home my stomach was in a knot. When we arrived my wife took care of our daughter while I took a shower and went to bed, trying to get some much-needed sleep.

Of course that wasn't going to happen. I tossed and turned for about an hour and finally gave up. I returned to the living room and watched TV until it was time to go to work.

I lived about five miles from the SH, so when working late tours I left home at about 11 p.m. That night I left at 10:30 and by the time I arrived I was totally exhausted both mentally and physically.

I gave up caring about what I was walking into. All the stress and anticipation had been drained out of me, so when I entered the SH and the desk officer asked if I had responded to Fortunoff the night before I just said, "Yes sir."

He told me to stand by after roll call; our commanding officer was going to speak to all responders. I was already in the last stage of numbness, so I was prepared for anything. I climbed the one flight of stairs to the locker room and as I began changing into my uniform, Jimmy Doyle entered the room.

After he spoke to us at the Christmas party, Jimmy returned to the Seven Five SH and continued representing us in the ongoing investigation.

As he approached I said, "Jimmy, what's going on?"

"Jack, don't worry, everything is under control. It's been a very long day and I'll explain after roll call."

I changed into uniform and returned to the Muster Room, where I met my fellow falsely accused members from the previous late tour

At 11:55, our sergeant entered the room and began calling the roll. When that task was complete he told everyone who had responded to Fortunoff the night before to stand by. He added that our PBA Delegate wanted to speak to us as he closed the two large doors, giving us privacy.

The delegate began by telling us that he and our commanding officer were looking forward to concluding a long, stressful day.

"You all responded to the burglary run at Fortunoff last night and most of you are aware there was an allegation made by Fortunoff management this morning. I will now give you the details of what took place today.

"At approximately ten thirty, a vice president and two senior managers arrived wanting to speak to the commanding officer about police misconduct during the burglary at their store earlier this morning. They told our CO that they received a phone call from two eyewitnesses who claimed they saw police officers stealing boxes of goods from their store. They also said they watched as the cops loaded those boxes into their police cars. The inspector requested the property voucher log and discovered no property was vouchered on that tour."

They provided the names of the witnesses as well as a call-back number. Our CO asked them to call the witnesses and have them come to the SH to be interviewed. The call was made and the two men came in. Jimmy figured with the two witnesses coming in, this was not looking good.

Our commanding officer interviewed the two men and they repeated their story. They didn't see who broke the window, but they did see the cops go in and come out with a lot of stuff that they put in their police cars.

After that interview our CO called the Borough Office to report this very serious criminal allegation.

The deputy chief responded to the Seven Five SH to meet with the very irate people from Fortunoff in person. Jimmy Doyle was present during the entire session and there came a time when he felt certain that members of our command would be placed under arrest before the end of the day.

He told us that while the chief and our CO were at their meeting, a woman called the telephone switchboard and asked to speak to the desk officer. That woman was a member of our local community board and wanted to commend the officers who had responded to the burglary at Fortunoff the night before. The desk officer asked her if she would like to speak to our commanding officer and she said yes.

Our CO listened as the woman told him she lived directly across the street from the Fortunoff store and happened to be awake when she heard the window break. She went to her window and saw two men go into the store and begin throwing large boxes out onto the sidewalk. She saw them leave the store and that's when a police car pulled up and the cops put handcuffs on the two men.

As she watched she saw more cops arrive. They all went into the store and after a while they came out and began putting all the boxes the two crooks tried to steal back into the store. Our CO asked her if she would have time to come in to the SH if he sent a car for her. She said she would be happy to come in and speak with him.

As they awaited her arrival, the CO asked the two "eyewitnesses" if they would mind meeting with the detectives, who would take their statements. Our commanding officer was a very smart man. I have no doubt he smelled a rat with the two guys who claimed what they were claiming.

When the woman arrived he asked her to repeat what she told him on the phone. Without missing a beat she gave the same blow-by-blow description of what she saw.

"Mrs. Jones, can you describe the two men you saw coming out of the store?"

"Yes, I can."

As she described the burglars, our CO realized there was a very good chance his assumption was right. This lady was describing the two guys now with the detectives and they hadn't even changed clothes.

He called the detective doing the interview and told him he had a witness to the burglary and he was bringing her up to view the two "witnesses." He wanted the two guys in the side room visible via the one-way glass used in lineups.

The woman took one look at the crooks and said, "That's them." Our CO said, "That's who?" She responded, "Those are the two men I saw coming out of the broken window at Fortunoff."

"Are you sure, Mrs. Jones?"

"I'm positive."

The detectives arrested the two burglars and notified Fortunoff's management that they needed to have someone meet them in court the following day to sign a complaint.

As Jimmy ended his report our Commanding Officer came into the muster room.

"Men, I'm sure your delegate has explained the series of events that took place here today. There was an allegation of police corruption made, based on so-called, eyewitness reports. My faith in the integrity of every member of our command was proven justified. Another witness came forward to commend your good work. Now I want to add my appreciation for a job well done by the men of the Seven Five Precinct.

"The two Fortunoff witnesses have been arrested for the

burglary and Chief Sullivan will contact the Brooklyn District Attorney's office to make certain those two felons receive the full effect of the criminal justice system. Thank you again for a job well done. You are dismissed, take your posts."

As I exited the old building I felt great. Like a huge weight was removed from my body. I understood that if it were not for that lady coming forward to tell her story, there was a very good chance eight police officers, including me, would have been arrested that day.

At that time I realized not everyone in prison was guilty and that is a fact that I always remembered when I had doubt with an arrest

Postscript

There came a time when the arresting detective asked the two former witnesses why they went as far as they did with their allegations. They told him that wasn't their plan. They were pissed that they were handcuffed and because of that they called the store.

After they told their bogus story to a Fortunoff manager, he asked them to come in. He added that if they cooperated with him they would be rewarded for their time. They asked what kind of a reward and he promised they would be happy.

They weren't happy. They were charged with burglary, obstructing governmental administration and falsely reporting an incident. They pleaded guilty to attempted burglary and due to their extensive criminal history received two years in the Iron House.

11

MY 3:00 AM MEETING WITH THE RIFLEMAN

O ne of the most interesting and exciting parts about working in the Seven Five precinct was I never knew what to expect. The "Seven Five" was one of the top three worst precincts in the city and the worst in Brooklyn. (There were several also very bad but we were larger and had more crime.)

It was 3 AM on an unusually quite Sunday morning. I was behind the wheel cruising our sector as my partner Hank S. tried to enjoy the few rare moments of tranquility. I turned off Pennsylvania Ave onto Glenmore and right there, not twenty feet in front of our RMP was a guy standing in the middle of the street holding a rifle. He was pointing it at a group of about 15 people as they stood motionless on the sidewalk in front of him.

I slammed on the brakes and we bailed out, guns drawn using the doors for cover. I yelled "Drop the rifle." He took off with the gun and ran around the corner and into a six story walk-up. I pulled the RMP to the front of the building while Hank pursued on foot. As I got out of the car I could see the mob from the sidewalk running toward me. I got back into our vehicle, got on the radio and called for backup. I then ran into the building to join Hank with the pursuit.

Before I took my third step I noticed a rifle lying on the ground to the left of the stairs. I retrieved the weapon before resuming my climb. As I reached the top floor Hank was banging on an apartment door. A woman opened the door dressed in a nightgown and in a heavy Puerto Rican accent asked what we wanted.

We didn't answer as we pushed past her and ran into the apartment. Hank went into the kitchen as I entered the bedroom where low and behold I found "The rifleman" hiding in a closet. As I opened that door he came lunging out trying to get past me. I tackled him as Hank entered the room.

After a brief struggle we were able to cuff him with his hands behind his back. He was still very combative and continued to resist as we lead him out of the apartment.

As we began walking him down the stairs he broke away from us and jumped down the eight steps to the next half landing. Every half landing had a very large window and he hit that waist high sill with such force his momentum was carrying him out the window. With his hands cuffed behind his back Poncho was three quarters out.

Hank and I jumped the same eight steps and pull him back from the brink. If we hadn't moved as fast as we did he would have dropped five and a half stories. Not good. I couldn't imagine trying to explain how our handcuffed prisoner ended up dead after falling out of a window.

We were struggling with our prisoner going down the stairs when off in the distance we heard the sirens. The cavalry was on the way.

As we walking the prisoner out of the building we we're rushed by the drunken crowd. I knew that was inevitable because Poncho disrespected them. He threatened them with his rifle and they wanted revenge. They were going to take him away from us and beat the crap out of him.

Our back up arrived and took control of the mob. Hank got in the back seat with the prisoner and I asked one of the responding officers to canvas the crowd for reliable witnesses. Everyone he considered worthy of an interview should be brought to the S.H.

The desk officer was waiting for us and asked what we had and who was taking the collar. We gave him the facts and I was up so I was the arresting officer. After the search I took my prisoner into the muster room. There was no arrest processing room so our muster room was used as an all-purpose room where just about every procedure requiring space within the S.H., away from the front desk, took place.

I advised Poncho of his constitutional rights. He spoke broken English but we were able to communicate.

"What is your name?"

"Poncho Gonzalez."

"What happened tonight?"

"Man, I went to the club and was having a good time with my friends. A guy wanted to fight with me because I danced with his wife. I didn't want to fight so I went home."

"When we first saw you, you were in the street but you just said you went home. What happened? If you went home why did we find you in the middle of the street with this rifle?"

He didn't answer. It was at that time when I picked up the gun and said:

"Poncho, where did you get this rifle?"

"I got it from my friend."

I made a memo book entry regarding that Q. and A. By strict interpretation of the law I could not prove the rifle I had recovered from the floor was, in fact, the same weapon I observed him use to menace the mob in the street. His response sealed the deal.

Sector Queen arrived with four complainants/witnesses. They also had the names and contact info for three more. I asked Hank to take the prisoner to the detective squad room for fingerprinting while I interviewed my complainants.

When I completed those interviews I had four solid complainants who agreed to sign affidavits and proceed to trial if necessary. I had answers to the: Who, what, when, where and why questions I would most certainly be asked by the ADA when preparing the affidavit (Accusatory instrument) needed at arraignment.

This story is almost identical to so many I've heard over the years while working in precincts with a sizeable Puerto Rican population. It always begins in a social club. I have learned that in Puerto Rico the social club is where most of the locals went to hang out and party.

On that evening, the owner of the social club was hosting a birthday party for one of his regulars which was the norm on Saturday evenings. For some reason they thought a private party allowed them special dispensations from the Liquor laws but it didn't and we didn't care anyway. Poncho, decided he would go to the party without his common law wife who was home taking care of their 4 children.

As reported by all four witnesses: Poncho did a lot of drinking and dancing at the party. There came a time when he fell in love with Carmen, a foxy lady who was also drinking and dancing but Carmen had a boyfriend. The boyfriend, we'll call him Jose, was very jealous and he didn't like anyone dancing with his girlfriend (Wife) and he definitely didn't like anyone making lewd remarks about her.

Poncho was doing both so Jose told him to stop. Poncho was just drunk enough to disregard the fact that Jose was bigger and stronger than he was. He told Jose to kiss off, but he didn't use the word kiss.

Jose took out his knife (No macho man ever went to a social club on a Saturday evening without his knife) and threatened to cut Poncho into little pieces. Poncho was drunk, not stupid so he left the club but before he did he threatened Jose.

"Jose, don't go anywhere. I'm coming back to take care of you."

"Poncho I'll be waiting for you."

Jose figured Poncho was trying to save face with his threat and wouldn't be back. After about 20 minutes he decided he had enough partying for one night. He took his lovely foxy lady home and as he left he said in a loud voice: "If Poncho comes back tell him I said he is a madacone" (Homosexual in English)

That's the worse insult you can use when disrespecting a Puerto Rican. The second is to say something bad about his mother. Either of those two will very often result in bloodshed. Fathers, wives, children are way down the list of deadly insults.

About 10 minutes later Poncho returned looking for Jose and sure enough he was packing some heat. He had a rifle. Someone told him what Jose called him and now Poncho had to save face. He went looking for Jose in the street followed by 15 partiers including my witnesses.

They probably wanted to see someone get shot or stabbed because come on, it was Saturday night/Sunday morning and no one got assaulted yet.

Poncho walked about 4 blocks before giving up. When he stopped searching, someone in the group said maybe Jose was right and that he was a madacone..... I personally believe that's when Poncho decided he had two choices; he could move out of the neighborhood because he really was a punk madacone or do something to save face. He couldn't find Jose but he had to shoot somebody so he turned the rifle on the crowd and it was at that exact moment when we turned the corner.

My interviews were complete. I thanked my witnesses/complainants and escorted them out of the S.H. By the time Poncho was fingerprinted and I completed the arrest forms and voucher for the rifle it was almost eight AM.

I got transportation to Brooklyn Criminal Court where I lodged him with the department of corrections.

The ADA working the arraignment part requested high bail due to Poncho's extensive criminal record. He had numerous arrests and convictions for assaults, weapon possessions, burglary and sales of drugs. He was held in $50,000 bail. Due to my two day swing (Regular days off) the return date was three days away.

The ADA told me to be sure to have a ballistics report at the hearing because the defendant's attorney would try to have the weapon I recovered "Thrown out". (Stricken as evidence.) When I returned to the S.H. I informed the desk officer I needed to have the rifle taken to ballistics ASAP due to my imminent court date. At the hearing I had the ballistics report in hand.

When my case was called I was ready. The ADA also had my four witnesses prepped and ready. I wasn't at all concerned with the prosecution part but the Judge was another story.

I had several hearings before him in the past. He was liberal and very often the defendant's attorney was given more latitude then what was considered the norm. I've seen times when the defendant was treated more like a victim then the victim but this was Brooklyn and that's just the way it was.

There came a time, during my testimony, when the ADA wanted to have the rifle admitted into evidence.

I produced the weapon and the judge asked me to describe it: "Your honor, this is a Marlin single shot 22 caliber rifle."(The gun looked like a repeating rifle because it had a fake lever action and a false feeding tube under the barrel but it was, in fact, a single shot rifle.

Now the Judge caught an attitude with me. I really think he didn't like cops so he said in a loud authoritative voice, "Officer Fitzgerald I can see that weapon is a multi shot rifle. Do you have a ballistics report?"

"Yes sir I do."

"May I have the rifle and will you please read the report."

I handed him the gun and began reading the report. Before I got past the make, model and serial number he stopped me. He returned the weapon and said no need to read on, you're right it is a single shot rifle.

I completed my testimony without being questioned about where I found the rifle. I'm sure Poncho's lawyer considered my testimony as well as the four witnesses who were ready to testify and was sure this case would go to trial.

He wanted to hold off exploring the possession of the rifle for the main event. The ADA didn't have the witnesses testify. No need, the judge held this docket for trial with no further testimony.

Poncho's lawyer, who was also his uncle, posted his bail and he was released. The return date was 3 weeks away.

On the day of the trial I met with the ADA and our four witnesses. I reviewed my testimony given at the hearing. We were all ready to proceed. The good news was the trial Judge was great. He was fair and that's all I asked for. The defense chose to have a Bench Trial so the judge would be the sole decision maker. Guilty-Not guilty it was all up to Judge Kennedy.

I was the first to be called. I won't review my entire testimony but I had to explain exactly what took place resulting in my arrest. As I completed my testimony the ADA said I have no further questions. Now it was "Uncle Lawyer" turn.

I know most of us have had the experience where you walk into a room, lets say at a party or gathering and after a few moments you take a dislike to another guest. That's what happened to me with this lawyer at the hearing. I usually interact with defense attorneys in a professional manner. They have their job to do as I do mine but this guy made it personal. Now, here we are at trial. The gloves are off and I'm ready.

Mr. Ortiz thought he was the reincarnation of F. Lee Bailey as he strutted in front of the judge during questioning. I had been cross examined by very competent lawyers many times so this bozo was not about to rattle my cage with his posturing.

I was expecting him to use every trick in the book and I wasn't disappointed. I was ready. He began his first question while standing directly in front of me and continued as he walked away lowering his voice as he walked. I strained to hear the entire question but couldn't hear the last part. (I had seen this trick used before and the purpose of that maneuver was to force me to ask him to repeat himself over and over making me look foolish.) I did ask him to repeat his question.

The second time he tried that stunt I said:

"Your honor, would you please ask Mr. Ortiz to raise his voice, I'm having difficulty hearing his questions."

"Yes Mr. Ortiz, I'm also having difficulty hearing your questions. Please raise your voice so we can all hear you."

He went on with his questions until he decided it was time to begin his second shot at our Q. and A session. A review of my answers: Officer Fitzgerald, what time did you first receive the call for service at the location of occurrence?"

Only 10 minutes before, I testified we came upon the scene while on routine patrol.

"Councilor, as you may recall I testified I came upon the defendant while on routine patrol. I observed him standing in the middle of the street menacing a group of people with a rifle. There was no call for service."

He immediately objected to my use of the word "Menacing" which the judge overruled and he added "Councilor, when someone points a firearm at another that's menacing".

From that point I guess he realized I was onto his game so he kept it reasonably proper.

He asked questions about lighting conditions on the street where we made our first observations. He ask how many lights were in operation at that location and I told him again that he would need to request that information from the proper authority, to wit, the people in charge of maintaining the street lights.

I reiterated that I had a clear and unobstructed view of the defendant standing in the middle of Glenmore Ave. pointing a rifle at a group of people who were standing in front of him on the sidewalk. He didn't want to hear that again so he tried to interrupt me but I continued to completion.

Then he began questioning me about the foot pursuit into the building; He asked me to describe the lobby. What were the lighting conditions, how far from the entrance were the stairs. He wanted to know where I was in relation to my partner and the defendant. He asked me if I ever lost sight of the defendant, was I yada, yada, yada? This cross examination was defense attorney's "Routine personified".

Then he explored the actual apprehension of his client. I explained how we gained access to his apartment and where we found him hiding. I also went into his struggle as he resisted being handcuffed and that covered the resisting arrest charge.

He continued doing his best to cloud the issue but he had already made a big mistake. If he would have gone with a jury trial he had a shot but this judge wasn't buying into his shenanigans.

Mr. Ortiz went on about the distance between me and the defendant when I saw him enter the building and where my partner was in relation to us both. He really didn't have much to go on but he did his best to confuse me. In all modesty, I was always good on the stand. I focused, I concentrated. I don't recall ever losing a case due to poor testimony at a hearing or trial.

There came a time when Ortiz arrived at his final destination: The rifle or I should say the possession of the rifle.

This was his moment to shine. He knew the possession of evidence laws and he was sure he had me. I found the rifle in the lobby. I never saw him drop it. I never saw the defendant in possession of the weapon I submitted into evidence!!! Mr. Ortiz was going to win this trial with one question.

"Officer Fitzgerald, was my client in possession of this rifle when you apprehended him in the apartment?"

With that question the ADA stood up and objected to his line of questioning. (Come on already you should have objected 15 minutes ago).

"Your honor, Officer Fitzgerald had already testified with regard to the rifle. If Mr. Ortiz would like the stenographer to review his testimony he should ask for that reread. If not can we move on? The judge agreed and asked Ortiz if he had any unasked questions for me."

I could see Ortiz doing his posturing act again. He walked

over to the table and picked up the rifle. I knew what was coming. With a smirk on his mug he said:

"Yes, just one more question Judge: Officer Fitzgerald, if you didn't see my client drop the rifle you recovered from the floor in the lobby how can you be so sure this rifle you have entered as evidence is the rifle you saw my client with in the street?"

I had been waiting so long for that question.

"Mr. Ortiz there came a time, after advising your client of his constitutional rights, when I held that rifle in my hands and said: Poncho where did you get this rifle"? He said "I got if from my friend."

Ortiz immediately asked the judge to strike his question and my response but the judge said: "Councilor, you asked the question you bought and own the answer". The defense rested his case. The Judge deliberated for about 3 seconds and said: "Mr. Gonzalez I find you guilty as charged." The complaining witnesses were never called to testify. Bench trials are usually less dramatic and in this case the main point of contention was the weapon possession.

He remanded the defendant for a return date at which time he would be sentenced. With that remand I knew he was going to put Poncho away for several years. Considering his past criminal record and with this judge, I figured 5 years, maybe more.

The judge told me to take my prisoner to the department of corrections for fingerprinting and lodging. Now Ortiz had to try one more cheap shot: He said " Judge I would like it noted for the record that my client is unmarked and in good physical condition" The judge asked him why he made his request and he replied that he did not trust the arresting officer, to wit, me and he wanted to make sure I didn't harm his client.

Before the judge could respond I said: "Your honor maybe Mr. Ortiz would like to accompany me and his client to the department of corrections to assure his clients safe arrival. He can watch as Mr. Gonzalez is printed and lodged. The judge said good idea officer and he ordered the idiot to do just that. I knew he didn't like the lawyer any more than I did so I thought he would accommodate my request. I took my time and enjoyed every second of the next 45 minutes I spent with the gruesome twosome.

Epilogue

My partner, Hank Stewart, took the test for and was eventually sworn in as a Suffolk County Police Officer on the east end of Long Island.

He was a great man to work with and a proactive cop in the Seven Five precinct, one of the busiest most dangerous places to work as a police officer. He bought a house in Suffolk County and his wife was happy that she didn't need to worry about him every time he left home to report for duty in Brooklyn.

Hank was killed in the line of duty in Suffolk County.

12

THE BURGLARY AT THE BOTANICA

It was four AM, Tommy Degar and I were about to resume patrol in the Seven Five Precinct. As I drove north on Pennsylvania Avenue we came upon another sector traveling South. We couldn't help noticing they had a very large piece of furniture sticking out of their trunk. I stopped and said:

"Lenny, what's in the trunk?"

"We found this stereo in the street on Blake Ave. and I'm taking it down to the wastelands off Penn. I'll come back after work and take it home."

We didn't give it much thought until about twenty minutes later, when we received a call of a past burglary at a Botanica on Blake Avenue. When we arrived the owner of the store was waiting for us. He had responded to his silent alarm and found the large front window broken.

After entering he took a quick look around and discovered it wasn't just a simple broken window, this was a burglary. Someone broke in and the first thing he found missing was a large stereo he had on display in the front of his store.

As Tommy began taking the report, a woman, who lived across the street, entered the store wearing a housecoat over her pajamas. She went to the owner, who she knew, and began speaking to him in Spanish. I don't speak Spanish, but Tommy did and as she began talking Tommy stopped writing and began listening. Finally, when she ended her conversation we could see the owner was very upset and told us he wanted to go to the precinct to talk to the person in charge.

Tommy told him we would meet him at the SH. As we left the store, he said, "Jack we gotta get a hold of Lenny and Pete . . . NOW."

In Spanish, the woman told the owner that she saw exactly what happened regarding the break-in. She woke up when she heard someone break the front window. She saw two men go into the store through the broken window. They were in the store a couple of minutes and she watched them carry the stereo out of the window and down Blake Avenue. She saw a police car driving down Blake Avenue and when the two men saw the police car they tried to hide the stereo between two parked cars and then they ran away.

When the cops saw the stereo they stopped, picked it up and put it in their trunk. Then they drove down Blake right past the broken window. Now I knew why the owner was so pissed off. Who could blame him?

We requested the location of their sector. We met and Tommy said, "Lenny, you have a problem."

"Why?"

"About ten minutes ago we got a past burglary job on Blake. It was in a Botanica and you won't believe what was stolen."

"A stereo."

"Right. While we were taking the report an eyewitness showed up and told the owner what she saw, including you and Pete putting the stereo in your trunk. They're on the way to the precinct to make a complaint. We'll cover for you and stall, but you better get that stereo into the house ASAP. You also better come up with a reason why you're so late."

We drove to the SH and as we entered, the owner and his witness were giving the desk officer a lot of grief. They were both very loud and very accusatory, telling the lieutenant "his" police stole the stereo.

Now I must explain; the DO on duty that night was a good boss who was fair and would go out of his way to make life easy for a cop if possible. There is no way he would condone what "his" police were accused of doing. I could see he was upset with the allegation being made, because it happened on his watch and he knew just how much trouble the sector team could be in.

The owner and witness seemed to be decent, respectable people. The woman was very sure of what she saw and the store owner wasn't about to let this go away regardless of how diplomatic the DO could be.

Tommy and I were standing behind the two complainants so I was able to catch the attention of the DO without them seeing me. I winked and gave him a thumbs-up and at that moment we could see a slight smile on his face. He knew the thumbs-up meant everything was under control.

A few minutes later the front door swung open. Lo and behold who came walking in carrying a stereo but Lenny and Pete.

"Lieutenant, while driving down Blake Avenue, Pete and I found this stereo in the street, so we put it in our trunk. We were on our way in to voucher it as found property when our car died. We had no power so we couldn't call for a tow. I kept trying to start the car and finally it started and here we are. Pete will prepare the voucher and I'll call department tow to have the RMP towed to the shop."

I wish I had a camera to take a picture of the faces of the two, now very shocked, complainants, as well as the look on the DO's face as he said, "Now aren't you ashamed of yourselves. You came into my station house accusing my officers of a crime. Did you ever consider the possibility of a motor vehicle breakdown? Well, now you know what happened. The officers will complete the crime report, and then you can take your stereo with you."

The owner looked at his witness like she was the one who caused his now-embarrassing dilemma. Tommy told the store owner to join him in a side office where he continued with the UF 61 for the burglary and I told the witness she could leave.

She walked out the door into the cold winter night wearing her nightgown and slippers. As I watched her walk out the door I stopped her and told her to come back. I couldn't allow her to walk home in the cold. We would drive her home. She did nothing wrong; in fact, she tried to do the right thing.

(Lenny and his partner were definitely wrong. I won't even try to justify their actions that morning except that I knew they were good cops and there is no way they had any reason to believe the stereo was the proceeds of a burglary. They should have brought the stereo in to be vouchered as found property.)

The desk officer was happy because Tommy and I helped Lenny and Pete dodge a serious allegation as well as an Internal Affairs investigation. After that night he always treated us with a little more respect.

Lenny invited me and Tommy to the Galaxy Diner as his guest for breakfast. I told him I didn't make a habit of eating with criminals, but in this case I would make an exception. The desk officer ordered Lenny to buy breakfast for him and the two men assigned to the 124 room (clerical office) as well as the telephone switchboard operator, for the stress he generated.

13

ROUTINE TWELVE AT FAMILY DISPUTES

Family disputes were usually dangerous assignments for police officers. The typical scenario: The man comes home drunk and when the woman asks what he did with the paycheck or the welfare check money he gives her a smack. Now I admit this is not an everyday occurrence, but I have had many similar calls for service during my career.

That job will most often end in one of two ways: The dispute is temporarily resolved when the man leaves for the night or we arrest the man and remove him from the home. In my twenty-six-year career I have made my share of arrests while trying to bring peace to a warring couple.

Every time the woman, it was always the woman who had the man arrested, would drop the assault charges the next day. Whenever possible we would try to avoid an arrest by negotiating a peaceful solution. When there was no injury requiring medical attention we could give the victim the option of having "him" arrested or, if he left for the night, just refer it to court. Usually removing the assailant from the home would solve the problem, at least temporarily.

On those occasions I would go to what I called routine twelve. I came up with that ruse early in my career in the Seven Five

Precinct (seven plus five equals routine twelve) after responding to a family dispute where there was no injury. The woman just wanted her husband out of the apartment and he refused. "Lock me up, I don't care." I heard those words a gazillion times. Lock me up, I don't care.

Our "husband" was gainfully employed as a truck driver and didn't believe we had the right to evict him from his apartment. We didn't want to get tied up with a bullshit arrest and it was at that moment I had a brainstorm: I told my partner to keep both people busy in the kitchen and I went into the living room. I took my off-duty revolver—most of us carried two guns on patrol—emptied it and placed it between two cushions in the sofa with the tip of the handle sticking up just enough to be visible.

I returned to the kitchen and told the husband to follow me into the living room. It was SOP to separate the combatants . . . As I walked into that room I said, "Listen, I don't want to arrest you, but if you don't leave I have no choice."

"I don't care. Lock me up. I didn't do anything wrong. I'm a hardworking man and I'm not leaving."

I made my way to the sofa, maintaining a distance between the husband and my secreted gun. With great drama I discovered the revolver hidden between the cushions. Now try to visualize the scene: This guy had a job and neither of the two participants were skells (lowlifes) . . . He went into shock and immediately sobered up.

"What the **** is this?"

"That ain't mine, Officer. I never saw that gun before."

"Well, if it's not yours it must belong to your wife."

"No, no, no. It ain't hers either. I swear I never saw that gun before."

"Well, it's in your apartment, so I gotta arrest somebody."

I could see this black man going pale. He was defeated. I had him. He was mine.

I took my handcuffs out and as I walked toward him, I said, "Okay, who's it going to be? You or your wife?"

"Officer, I swear I never had no gun in this house and my wife never had no gun either."

"Who else lives here?"

"No one, just me and my wife."

"Oh, so maybe I put the gun in your sofa?"

"No, I didn't say that, but I know we didn't have no gun."

Now it's time to bring this show to a close.

"You look like a decent guy. Your wife seems like a nice lady. I really should arrest someone, but I can't prove who owns the gun, so this is what I'm gonna do. If you leave the apartment for the night and promise you won't come back until tomorrow, I'll make the gun go away. But if we need to return you are going to jail for possession of a loaded firearm, a felony."

"Officer, I'll leave and I promise I won't come home tonight."

I escorted my new friend back to the kitchen where my partner was still talking to the wife.

I explained that her husband had decided to leave for the night. I added that if he returned she should call, at which time he would be arrested. He packed a small bag and we escorted him from the building. He kept his word, he did not return that night.

I used routine twelve under similar circumstances and as a last resort. It always worked.

14

MRS. B'S POOLROOM

While on patrol in the Seven Five Precinct my partner Tommy Degar and I came upon two of our local teenage criminals fighting in front of Mrs. B's poolroom. As I pulled the car to the curb they saw us and ran into Mrs. B's. We followed them in and as we entered, the door slammed shut behind us. At that moment I knew: This is a setup.

Tommy and I were very active police officers. We made a lot of arrests, many drug-related arrests, which made the criminals residing in our sector very unhappy. This was a message. This was payback as well as a warning: Lay off. We received that information from the girlfriend of one of the men we arrested.

I could see Tommy to my right swinging his nightstick at anyone trying to get close to him. Then I felt a sharp pain to the back of my head. I was dazed and as I turned to see who hit me the punk came at me again swinging his pool cue. I ducked and threw a strong right hand catching him in the chest. We were definitely in a life-and-death fight and when the adrenaline kicked in, it amplified the force in my punch. He went down to the floor and just lay there.

I knew he was out of the fight, so I redirected my attention to the crowd in the room. By now Tommy had used his stick on several assailants and they were on the floor, but others kept trying to move closer. They were throwing pool balls and swinging pool cues. Time to increase the volume.

I took my gun out and pointed it in the general direction of the mob. Tommy did the same. They froze. They knew we were both ready to shoot. They were right.

In 1969, only foot patrolmen had portable radios, so I ran out to our RMP and used the handset to call for assistance. I returned to the poolroom, where Tommy was still holding the group of about twenty at bay. Most had given up, which left a few hard-core kamikaze dope dealers looking to take us out. (Thank God guns were not as available then as they are today.)

I could see a few thugs moving into position to Tommy's left, so I hit the guy closest to me with my nightstick and I ordered the rest to get down on the ground. This riot was over and they came in second. As we were catching our breath we heard the sweet sound of sirens. The cavalry had arrived. First sector John, then sector David, finally three more sectors.

As our backup entered the poolroom we identified everyone under arrest. They began placing handcuffs on our prisoners.

We probably could have taken more, but we stopped at eleven including the owner, Mrs. B. I arrested her because at one point, after we drew our weapons and before I went out to the sector car, I saw her standing, watching the melee. I knew who she was and ordered her to call nine one one; she refused. That was a misdemeanor as in failing to come to aid of a police officer when ordered to do so.

The guy I hit was still down and unconscious, so I called for an ambulance. The prisoners were transported to the Seven Five Precinct and the injured prisoner went to Brookdale Hospital with an assigned "foot man." Tommy and I went to Kings County Hospital, where we were treated for bruises and I was x-rayed and treated for the egg size lump on the back of my head.

We returned to the Seven Five, where we spent the rest of that tour processing our prisoners. By four a.m. we had completed our paperwork. I said, "Tommy, how you feelin'?"

"I'm beginning to get a little tired."

"Good thing you're only a little tired because we still have another twelve hours to go."

I went to the desk and said:

"Lieutenant Gallagher, Tommy and I would like to take a break. If possible we would like to take part of the meal hour we didn't get on our four to twelve."

"I think I can make that happen. Have sector Adam respond to the station house. When they get here I'll have them guard your prisoners."

The sector arrived and took charge of our prisoners. Tommy and I went to the locker room for a shower and a change into a clean uniform. Twenty minutes later I was at the desk again.

"Lieutenant, we're off to get a couple of containers of coffee, can I bring you something from the diner?"

"Jack, now you can do me a favor. The lads in sector Frank are stuck on a DOA, so they won't be available to meet the bakers at Maxwell's Bakery. Would you and Tommy take care of that for us?"

"Consider it done, Lou," (Maxwell's was a large bakery on Atlantic Avenue and every morning, when available, the sector covering that bakery would be waiting when the bakers arrived for work. The bakers were happy to have a police presence and they always gave the "lads" a cake and anything else they wanted from what was left over from the previous day.)

We did the pickup at Maxwell's, drove to the Galaxy Diner and bought six containers of coffee. We returned to the station house to share our coffee and cake with Lieutenant Gallagher and the Palace Guard (the two police officers working the 124 room and the telephone switchboard operator). That was our breakfast.

At seven thirty, the Paddy Wagon arrived to transport our prisoners to 120 Schermerhorn Street, also known as Brooklyn Criminal Court.

With our prisoners safely lodged with the department of correction we proceeded to the second floor, where we met with an assistant district attorney to "draw up" our complaints. The ten assailants were charged with assault second degree on two police officers and riot, both felonies. Mrs. B was charged with failing to comply with a lawful order of a police officer and failing to come to the aid of a police officer, both misdemeanors. The prisoner in the hospital was identified as Calvin Williams and I had no further information regarding his condition.

Our next stop was to the arraignment part, room 101 where our prisoners were officially charged with their crimes. As we entered we were met by relatives of our prisoners and a lawyer who was representing Mrs. B.

Now about Mrs. B: She was an elderly Jewish lady, a holdover from the late '50s and early '60s, when East New York was primarily a Jewish neighborhood. They still had a large synagogue at the corner of Pennsylvania Avenue and New Lots Avenue. Her husband had passed away, but she kept the poolroom as a source of income. With this one exception we never had a call to that location. She had a good rapport with her customers.

As we left the courtroom for a short recess her lawyer approached me. He began telling me about his client and how hung she was politically. She knew congressmen and councilmen, et cetera, et cetera. Finally he asked if I would be opposed to a plea bargain. I said, "Why are you talking to me? Go talk to the DA."

As we returned to the courtroom a man approached me and identified himself as Robert Williams. He told me I was going to pay for killing his nephew.

"What nephew, what killing? What the hell are you talking about?"

I hadn't given much thought to the prisoner in Brookdale Hospital. Now I had time!!!

"Mr. Williams, what are you talking about?"

"I'm talking about my nephew who you killed last night in the poolroom. He's dead and you are going to pay."

"What makes you think I had anything to do with his death?"

"I have two witnesses who saw you punch my nephew in the chest. Now he's dead and you are going to pay."

"Did your two witnesses see him try to take my head off with a pool cue?"

No response. There was nothing more to be said. I give him one of my stone-cold glaring looks as I walked into the court-room. What I felt like saying was: Your nephew assaulted me with a weapon and I defended myself. Too Fu***n bad and I'm not the least bit sorry he's dead . . . I wasn't sorry, but I didn't say another word.

At one o'clock the judge broke for lunch, giving me time to call the Seven Five desk officer. I knew he would know the condition of my prisoner and he did. He told me Calvin Williams was pronounced dead at twelve forty-five that morning and the cause of his death would be determined by an autopsy.

I went to see the DA assigned to the arraignment part and informed him of Calvin's demise as well as Uncle Robert's threat. The DA said, "We'll deal with that issue later, now I want to have my lunch and I advise you to do the same and don't worry about the uncle."

We returned to the courtroom early to confer with our ADA. Tommy and I spent a lot of time in court and knew most of the ADAs, but the guy working that part was new and neither of us knew him. He was a recent addition to the Brooklyn DA's office, but he definitely had experience. He asked for a blow-by-blow description of what took place the night before and then he asked us what we wanted as far as punishment for the now ten defendants.

Tommy and I agreed that we weren't seriously hurt, some bumps and bruises, but they had to be punished for what they did. Then I had the dead Calvin Williams to contend with. He asked if a guilty plea for assault three with a considerable fine would be acceptable and we had no problem with that.

We both had experience in "the system" and we knew the liberal judges in Brooklyn weren't going to actually punish the thugs with jail time, so any penalty was okay. A police officer seriously injured in the line of duty was handled seriously, but bumps and bruises were an everyday occurrence and part of being a cop in New York City.

As far as Mrs. B was concerned, we requested that her license to operate a poolroom be suspended for one week. When court resumed our dockets were called and the DA met with the two attorneys. The Legal Aid lawyer agreed to the guilty plea with a five-hundred-dollar fine for each of his defendants, but Mrs. B's attorney balked at forcing her to close for a week. She persisted with her "I did nothing wrong" position.

He argued that the melee was something she had no control over and she believed if Tommy and I hadn't chased the two combatants into her establishment we wouldn't be in court. I said if we hadn't been assaulted in her poolroom and if she would have made the call to nine one one as I ordered her to do she wouldn't be in court, but she didn't and now she had to answer for her indiscretion.

The DA understood how we felt and it was our good fortune that we both weren't hospitalized that night. He told her attorney to pick an adjourn date and then he told the Legal Aid lawyer that if Mrs. B didn't accept his plea offer the entire deal was off. We would go to trial. The defense requested a second call (request to have this docket called again in a short time giving him time to speak to his client, Mrs. B.)

When our dockets were recalled both attorneys agreed to the plea deal, which brought an end to most of this issue. The only remaining concern was the dead Calvin Williams. The DA told us to wait until the judge took an afternoon break. At that time we all went to his office. He called the medical examiner's office and requested the results of the autopsy, which was performed earlier that afternoon.

The result was Calvin died of internal injuries to his chest and heart. The sternum was broken, piercing the heart, which caused his death. He said, "Rest easy Officer Fitzgerald. I have no intention of presenting this to a grand jury. You and Officer Degar were assaulted and injured during a riot. There were several people injured, including Calvin Williams."

The bottom line is there was no civilian complaint or allegation of excessive use of force made against us.

I felt relieved and returned to the Seven Five Precinct with a load off my mind. I had absolutely no remorse for what happened to Calvin. I was fighting for my life and if those criminals had gotten the best of us, who knows what they would have done. They would have had our revolvers and we would have been at their mercy and in the ghetto, at that time, the word mercy was rarely used. I never heard another word about that incident, but I did get a chance to read about it in the *Daily News* as it made page three in the Brooklyn section.

15

NEVER TAKE THE WORD OF YOUR WIFE'S BOYFRIEND WHEN HE HAS A KNIFE IN HIS HAND

Policing the streets of New York City was a high-risk occupation. Policing as well as living and working in high-crime Precincts in NYC was downright dangerous. It was dangerous for the police officers, it was dangerous for the business owners and it was extremely dangerous for the residents who had no escape from the everyday violence.

Black on black crime, especially murder, was out of control. It was out of control when I worked the ghetto in the late '60s and into the '70s and our Seven Five Precinct homicide numbers were usually into the seventy-eighty-plus a year. That's one precinct in Brooklyn

One summer evening in August of 1970, Tommy Degar and I received a call to investigate a past assault at 834 Glenmore Avenue. As I pulled our RMP to the curb we came upon several people, including a woman who told us her husband had been stabbed and was bleeding to death in their cellar.

We entered the home and found a blood trail. We followed the blood down the stairs and into the cellar. I knew the husband was in bad shape because every time he stopped on his journey he left a baseball-size pool of coagulated blood on the floor. Finally we found him in the back room lying in a child's plastic swimming pool.

He was lying face up and the bottom of the pool was about one third covered in blood. Now I know the volume of blood in a human body is about seven percent of the body weight. Considering the amount of blood in that pool I figured that guy must have weighed about 175 pounds. That's a lot of blood and he was definitely dead. In fact if there were degrees of dead he would have been a ten, but he hadn't been stabbed; his throat was cut. There was so much blood I couldn't actually see the gash, but it was definitely enough to end his life.

I called Central and requested an ambulance and a sergeant. I also informed Central we had a possible homicide. (No member of the NYPD can pronounce a person dead, ergo the need for the ambulance and an EMT.) I began questioning possible witnesses as Tommy gathered information needed for our reports. I had no idea so many people in that neighborhood were blind and deaf. Absolutely amazing. Nobody saw anything and nobody heard anything. Then I met a friend of the victim who was not afraid to talk to me.

"Good evening, Officer, my name is James Walker and I saw what happened to my friend Thomas."

"Mr. Walker, would you mind joining me in your friend's apartment where we can have some privacy?"

"No, we can talk in your police car."

James joined me in the RMP and began by telling me his good friend, Thomas Wright, was married to a tramp named Clara and she was no good. Thomas loved Clara, but Clara didn't love Thomas as much as she loved Leroy, Rodney, Jerome, et cetera, et cetera. She was a wicked woman. On that afternoon he was hanging out on the stoop with Thomas and a few friends having some wine when this guy named Robert came looking for Clara.

Robert had been seeing Clara for quite a while and wanted to take her to a party at a local bar that night. Thomas had other plans. He went into his house and in a few minutes came out looking for Robert. He was looking for him with a large kitchen knife in his hand. When Robert saw Thomas with the knife he took a straight edge barbers razors out of his pocket.

My witness told me that the two men circled each other for a short time until Robert finally said:"I don't need a knife to kick your ass, let's drop our knives and fight like men." Thomas said okay and tossed his knife toward the house. Robert moved in and slashed Thomas's throat. Robert ran and Thomas went into his house.

Now mortally wounded, Thomas made his way to the cellar where he collapsed into the pool and died. The Seven Five Precinct detectives arrested Robert three days later and charged him with murder in the second degree.

James Walker joined me at the grand jury where Robert Brown was indicted as charged. He pleaded guilty to a lesser charge in Brooklyn Supreme Court.

16

VIOLENT FEUDS IN EAST NEW YORK'S SEVEN FIVE PRECINCT

Disputes were very different from feuds in the ghetto. Disputes usually involved two, sometimes three, at the most four people. Feuds were always like the Hatfield's and McCoy's. During my two years in the Seven Five precinct I responded to many of both, but the feuds were always bloody brawls.

"Seven Five Charlie, respond to a large family dispute, front of One Thirty-Five Williams Street."

We arrived at the early stage of the melee and we could see about thirteen people, men and women, fighting, without weapons, which was very unusual. This was not a family dispute, this was a feud. Tommy called for backup as we attempted to bring order to this mini riot.

As we tried to separate the combatants I saw this three-hundred-plus-pound, six-foot-three monster of a guy pick up a garbage can. I then saw him bring it down across Tommy's back. Tommy went down. He was hurt and dazed, but the good news was there was no blood. I helped him up, then I drew my revolver and that's when everyone ran into the first-floor apartment.

Ghettoites weren't stupid. They were very street smart and they knew when the police are outnumbered seven to one and they take their guns out, the party is going to get rough and possibly deadly. Okay, so now we have the mob in the front room and they're still fighting.

I could see Tommy was coming back to reality. He was hurt, but not out of the fight. Adrenaline is an amazing hormone. When it kicks in, well, you all know what happens when the adrenaline kicks in. We both entered the house. I ran down the hall and I could see Mr. Grizzly Bear in the kitchen, but now he had a carving knife in his hand. This guy didn't need the knife, but the weapon made my job easier. I pointed my gun at him and yelled, "Drop the knife or I WILL shoot you."

This was one of those moments every street cop experiences from time to time. There was no way on earth I could allow him to get away with assaulting my partner; no friggin' way was that going to happen. He knew I was serious. He also knew, at that moment, I actually wanted to shoot him for what he did to Tommy and what he was about to do to me.

No, don't drop the knife; bring it on so I can shoot your big grizzly ass . . . Wow, this guy read my mind. He threw the knife down. I told him to get on the floor, which he did, and I cuffed him to a pipe going to the stove. He wasn't going anywhere.

I saw Tommy in the front living room doing his best to stop the fight. As I went to help him I ran past a bed in a middle room. That's when a large German shepherd came from under a bed and bit me behind my right knee. Her canine tooth went deep and she held on until I smacked her on the head several times with my slapper (a blackjack type weapon, but much more effective). She finally fled back under the bed.

As the dog went whimpering away, sectors Boy and John arrived and the six of us "used necessary force" to bring an end to the melee. Eventually another three cars, including a sergeant, responded.

The thirteen prisoners were transported to Brookdale Hospital while Tommy and I went to Kings County Hospital for treatment. Tommy went for X-rays while a doctor treated my dog bite. My bite was actually a severe puncture wound with a minor tear. The doctor told me he couldn't stitch it due to the strong possibility of infection, so he applied ointment before doing a bandage job on me.

Then he gave me the bad news. The good doctor told me I absolutely, positively needed to get the dog to the ASPCA so they could check it for rabies. If that test wasn't done I would need to undergo rabies shots, which I knew were painful.

After Tommy was x-rayed we both received prescriptions for pain and we returned to the Seven Five. The first thing I did was inform the desk officer that I needed to go back to the scene of the crime to get the dog.

"Lieutenant, the doctor told me I need to get the dog that bit me to the ASPCA and have it tested for rabies. I have to go back to the apartment and get the dog. I'll take the dog noose with me and I'll need help."

"Is your partner able to go with you?"

"Yes."

"Be careful. Don't get bitten. . . again."

I got our dog noose and we returned to the apartment. I knocked on the door and a girl about sixteen years old answered. I told her why we were there; she had to be the only resident that wasn't arrested.

"What is your name?"

"Wendy."

"Okay, Wendy, where is your dog?"

"What dog, we don't have a dog"

I was in no mood to play games; I pushed my way in, went to the bedroom and lifted the bed, exposing the dog and her pups in a large box. The shepherd began growling and snarling, so I used the noose to gain control. As Tommy and I took the dog out of the apartment the girl began screaming, "You can't take my dog, the puppies will die." I didn't respond. I had no choice. The dog had to be tested, End of story.

I walked the dog the five blocks to the SH and put her in the cage we had in the basement. I called the ASPCA and explained what happened. The ASPCA is a great agency and they knew the importance of that test. I was told they would have someone respond within four hours, maybe less at which time they would take the dog for the required test

I asked Tommy how he was feeling. I saw how hard he was hit with the garbage can and knew he had to be hurting. "Jack, I'll let you know when the pain pill wears off."

My dog bite was a tad painful, but the pill was working. We didn't want to leave the mountain of paperwork for the two men who would be assigned to complete the arrest processing after we went on sick report, so I went to the desk.

"Lieutenant, before Tommy and I go sick we want to do as much of the arrest processing as possible. How about if I call Brookdale and ascertain how our prisoners are doing?"

"If you feel up to it, I'm okay with that."

I called the hospital and spoke to Jimmy Dykman from sector John.

"Jimmy, what's happening with our prisoners?"

"We have seven treated and released, just waiting to get transportation back to the house."

"Tommy and I should be there in about ten minutes and Jimmy; sorry you and Frank got stuck with this mess. Tommy and I will complete as much of the arrest processing as possible, but when the pain pills wear off, we're gone."

"Jack, do us all a favor; you and Tommy need to call the Sick-Desk and go sick. Me and Frank will take care of your prisoners."

"Jimmy, we don't want to leave you with this mess."

"Jack, you're not listening to me. Tomorrow is our RDO and we can use the overtime. You and Tommy are hurt and need time to recuperate. What part of go sick don't you understand?"

Tommy and I were team players. We didn't want to leave the mountain of paperwork for another sector, but if they didn't mind, we were happy to call it a day.

"Lieutenant, we're going sick. The pills wore off and it's time to leave."

"Call the Sick Desk, make out your aided cards and I'll do the rest." Tommy and I went sick, changed into our civilian clothes and went home.

The end result was twelve of the thirteen prisoners were charged with disorderly conduct, to wit, acting in a violent and tumultuous manner. The guy that hit Tommy with the garbage can was charged with felonious assault on a police officer.

We couldn't charge them with riot because they were simply fighting among themselves. We couldn't charge anyone else with assault because they all refused to press cross complaints. All thirteen prisoners were treated for injuries, minor cuts and bruises, sustained in the melee. The only two people with reported injuries were me and Tommy.

Everyone charged with dis con pleaded guilty to that violation and received a conditional discharge. The guy who hit Tommy pleaded guilty to assault third degree. He had an extensive prior arrest record with numerous violent crime convictions, so he spent three months in jail and was placed on probation for another year.

The dog that assaulted/bit me was not rabid, which was good news, but the ASPCA classified her a stray simply because no one in the home claimed ownership. Considering the fact that she was now a "known biter," she was put down. Tommy and I returned to work after a week of recuperation.

17

THE NEW YEAR'S EVE HOT PURSUIT

December 31, 1970. New Year's Eve assigned to sector Frank in the Seven Five Precinct with my partner Hank Steward. It was a relatively normal day tour until Central advised us that Nassau County PD units were in pursuit of four men wanted for robbing a Locust Valley bank. During the robbery they kidnapped a teller and threatened to kill her if they were stopped.

Our Twelfth Division operator told us they were at Kennedy Airport. The NCPD didn't want to stop the vehicle, so they were in a "follow" mode. They kept us informed as the airport wasn't far from the Seven Five Precinct.

We didn't give it much thought and figured the pursuit would never come into Brooklyn. Wrong! Within fifteen minutes we received a call.

"Seven Five Frank, Nassau County has informed us they left the airport and are traveling west on Conduit Boulevard. Respond to Atlantic and Pennsylvania and await further orders." They had three other sectors respond to major intersections as well.

By this time a NYPD helicopter had joined in the pursuit and was giving the NCPD vehicles the route being taken by the robbers. The Nassau officers were out of their element and had no idea where the streets were, ergo—as long as they had eye contact with the vehicle they were okay.

We didn't need to wait long. Within a few minutes we could see the vehicle coming our way on Atlantic Avenue followed by at least ten NCPD RMPs with their emergency roof-rack lights flashing. They all made a right onto Pennsylvania Avenue, which became Bushwick Avenue as they drove north.

Hank was driving.

"Jack, I'm going down Broadway, maybe they'll come our way." (Broadway ran parallel to Bushwick and one block south.)

"Good idea."

With our lights flashing and sirens blaring it didn't take long to catch up with the parade but one block away. The bird kept us informed. As we approached Hancock Street, we heard that the crime car made a left onto Hancock. Hank made a right. Now they were coming our way and Hancock is a narrow street with room for one car.

Yes, there was a risk to the hostage, but there was a greater risk to every pedestrian in the path of the pursuit. Someone had to make the tough call and Hank did it. When he made that right turn the criminals had nowhere to go, we were blocking their escape route and do or die, this chase was over.

As we ran the fifty feet to the crime car, two Nassau police officers beat us to it. They were dragging the driver and the passenger out of the front seat. The hostage and the other two perps were still in the rear seat.

I opened the rear door and was just about to pull the guy sitting there, motionless, out of the car when a gigantic Nassau County Highway Patrol officer came over me like a tsunami wave, knocking me to the ground. He yanked . . . no make that he plucked the criminal out of the car and began using him for a heavy bag.

That cop had to be nine feet tall or at least that's how he appeared to me, looking up at him from the blacktop. There was no way I or anyone else was going to take that fleeing felon from him and quite frankly I could understand his mindset. I've been there.

In any pursuit the body's adrenaline begins pumping through your veins. Most of us have felt that rush. At the time of apprehension, when necessary force is needed to make an arrest you feel that rush kick in. This was about ten times worse than a routine pursuit.

Another Nassau Highway PO dragged the last criminal out from the other side. Hank and I helped the female passenger/hostage to our car and as we drove to the Eight One Precinct, which was the precinct of apprehension, I said, "My name is Police Officer Fitzgerald and my partner is Officer Steward. Are you hurt in any way?"

"No, thank God."

"I know you're still in shock and I'm sure you will need to be checked out by a doctor, but do you feel any pain? Did they assault you in any way?"

"No."

"Can I have your name, please?"

"Edith Reagan."

"I can't imagine what you just went through."

"No you can't, Officer Fitzgerald. I thought they were going to kill me. I have never been so frightened in my life, but I'm happy it's over. When can I go home?"

"We're taking you to a police station where you will be interviewed by detectives. They will want to know what happened today. Then I'm sure Nassau officers will take you to a hospital in Nassau County to be checked out. Before we drive to the police station, can we stop and get you a cup of coffee, tea or anything?"

"A cup of coffee would be nice and I'm dying for a cigarette. Those bank robbers weren't very considerate; they didn't let me take my purse. Yes, a container of coffee and a pack of Newport's would be very nice. Thank you."

This lady wasn't as fragile as I thought. She was about thirty-five years old and had just gone through a two-hour life-threatening ordeal. She was kidnapped, held hostage by four armed low-life criminal bank robbers and all she wanted was coffee and a pack of Newport cigarettes.

I got the coffee and Newports before we escorted Edith into the Eight One station house. That building was over one hundred years old and small. The rooms were small and by the time we arrived there had to be at least thirty members of the Nassau County PD as well as about twenty-five members of our department. It was a beehive of police activity.

Chiefs, deputy chiefs, detectives, you get the picture. Then the Port Authority Police arrived (they got involved in the pursuit at the airport, which is their zone of influence).

As we were waiting to speak to the desk officer, a Nassau PO was showing him the two loaded handguns, a bag of money, as well as several bags of heroin and marijuana they recovered from under the front seat.

Eventually Hank and I were able to introduce the hostage to the Lieutenant.

"Lieutenant, this is Mrs. Edith Reagan, the lady who was held hostage by the criminals."

"Mrs. Reagan, are you okay?"

"Yes. I just want to go home."

"Please give me a minute to locate the inspector from Nassau County; he will want to speak to you."

With those words I asked the DO if we could leave.

"Lieutenant, if it's all right with you, my partner and I would like to return to the Seven Five."

"Not yet, Officer, you will need to speak to Detective Johnson."

We gave the detective a full description of our involvement in this caper. Blow by blow, which took about a minute and a half. When that was completed we found Mrs. Reagan, who was still waiting to speak to the Nassau County boss.

"Mrs. Reagan, my partner and I are leaving now. We have to get back to our precinct. Is there anything we can do before we leave? How about another container of coffee. You still have your Newports, right?"

"Yes, Officers Fitzgerald and Steward, there is one thing you can do, get me the hell out of here. Please. Let me go with you. I'll call my husband from your precinct and he'll come and pick me up. I just want to go home, NOW. I'm ready to just walk out that door, but I don't know where I am."

"Let me see what I can do."

I went back to the desk officer and told him about the conversation I just had with the victim. He went and found the inspector from Nassau County and told him his complainant/hostage/victim was about to leave if he didn't speak to her now.

That inspector finally came over and introduced himself to Mrs. Reagan.

We knew there was nothing more we could do. We said goodbye to a very nice, strong lady. As we walked away, she came over and shook our hands and said, "Thank you both very much."

When we got back to the Seven Five, our desk officer, Lieutenant Wallace, wanted to know where we were and what we did for more than an hour. (He needed to prepare a UF 49—official report —identifying what we did during this major, newsworthy event.)

"Lieutenant, you may not believe this, but Hank and I almost single-handedly brought this catastrophic incident to a successful conclusion."

"You're right, Jack, I don't. Now tell me exactly what happened."

The 49 was brief. We really didn't do too much. We were NYPD cops and we did what NYPD cops do.

That evening my wife and I had several couples over to our home to celebrate New Year's Eve. When the eleven o'clock news came on, the number one story was about the chase from Nassau County to Bed-Sty's Eight One Precinct. They had video of the chase from their news helicopter as well as the apprehension including a great overhead shot of me being knocked to the ground by Goliath. Its incidents like that which caused me to become addicted to the adrenaline rush.

Before you read the next two sub-chapters chapters I want to make it clear I have no animosity toward firemen. My very close friend, Richie Sullivan, was a fireman. One of my most memorable times spent with him was one day after attending a half day at the NYPD outdoor range on City Island in the Bronx.

His firehouse was nearby, so he invited me to spend time with him. It was great. I slid down the pole and even got to ride in the cab of a fire engine on a run. I felt like a kid again. Firemen have a tough dangerous job and I respect almost all firemen. Save the two I am about to reveal to you, the reader.

The Lying Fireman Part I

One evening while on routine patrol in the Seven Five Precinct, we came upon a building in flames. It was a two-story, two-family residence and after notifying central to have NYFD respond we asked the many people on the street if they knew of anyone still inside. An elderly resident told us everyone was accounted for. We then made sure the adjacent buildings had also been evacuated. As we awaited the arrival of the FD, a young boy ran up to me and yelled that his puppy was in the cellar.

I went to the cellar door, kicked it open and could see the flames hadn't reached that lower level and the smoke wasn't very thick. I went in. Looking back I probably shouldn't have entered a building that was in flames, but I am an animal lover and I felt bad for the kid, so I did what needed to be done.

I used my flashlight and made my way through the smoke while searching for the dog. I reached the rear wall; enough already. It was getting very hot, the smoke was now thick and I was having difficulty breathing.

As I began to leave I could no longer see the front door. That's when I heard the dog whimpering. I entered a small storage room and found her cowering in a corner. I reached down to pick her up and she jumped into my arms. That shepherd pup knew I was there to help.

I could no longer see the door and my eyes were burning from the smoke. How do the firemen do this every day?

I made my way to the front wall and found the door. As I climbed the few steps and hit the fresh air I thought, thank God, I can breathe again, that was a tough one.

As I was enjoying the sweet fresh air the crowd saw I had the puppy and yelled their approval. One of the rare times I received that type of response for my work in the ghetto. The boy came over, took his dog and thanked me while my partner, Tommy Degar, told me I was crazy and he added that I looked like hell.

The Fire Department arrived and took control of the fire scene. The sector concerned arrived for the crowd control and I drove to the SH. I went to the restroom and took one look at myself in the mirror; my face was covered in black soot and sweat. Tommy was right, I did look like hell. I knew I needed to change uniforms because I smelled like smoke.

I showered and changed into a clean uniform and we completed our tour without further incident. The next day when I arrived for work my sergeant, who knew what took place the evening before, greeted me with, "Jack, you are not going to believe this."

He showed me the front page of the *New York Daily News*. Yes folks, right there on the front page was a fireman holding the same puppy I pulled out of the burning building the night before and the caption read, "Fireman saves puppy."

That wasn't the last time a fireman took credit for work a police officer did.

The Lying Fireman Part II

Nine Four Precinct Youth Car; investigate a man stabbed front of 76 Eagle Street. Upon arrival we found the victim lying on the sidewalk bleeding out. He had been stabbed several times and was losing a lot of blood. That guy was in very bad shape and waiting for a bus wasn't an option. We helped him to our RMP and raced to Greenpoint Hospital with lights on and siren blaring.

Bobby Mack called ahead, so they had a gurney waiting. As we waited to gather the information needed to prepare the required paperwork, we met two members of our command who were there with a "possible psycho." Their guy was in the quiet room waiting to be evaluated by a psychiatrist.

The ER was very busy and shortly after our arrival three firemen walked in to be treated for smoke inhalation. As we all waited in the rather narrow hallway, the psychiatrist came out of the quiet room to inform Gerry Beady that the man he brought in needed to be transported to Kings County Hospital's G building (their psych ward) for further evaluation.

The doctor was careless; he had not secured the door to the quiet room. Gerry and his partner were talking to the doctor. Bob and I were waiting to get into the ER to speak to our stabbing victim when this guy walked past us and went right over to Gerry and ripped his revolver out of his holster.

He grabbed the stock and yanked it so hard that the stitching gave way. As he pulled the gun upward it struck one of the firemen just above the left eye, causing a deep gash.

The psycho now had the revolver in his hand. I was standing a few feet away, so I grabbed the gun and tried to wrestle it away from him. Gerry immediately jumped in and stuck one finger behind the trigger so the gun couldn't be fired, then he pushed the cylinder release button. The cylinder opened and the six bullets fell to the floor. Brilliant moves by Gerry.

Now the weapon was empty. We were able to pry the gun out of his hands and put him in handcuffs. He was now under arrest for robbery and possession of a loaded weapon, so KCH was no longer an option. Gerry and his partner transported the prisoner to the SH for processing while Bobby and I returned to our stabbing victim.

That should be the end of this story, but not so. The next morning when I arrived for my eight to four tour I began reading the *Daily News* and I couldn't believe my eyes. I came upon a story about a fireman, being treated in Greenpoint Hospital, who saved the lives of four police officers as well as his two firemen coworkers. The hero fireman single-handedly wrestled a loaded gun away from a crazed man who took it from one of the police officers.

WHAT?????? WHAT?????? . . . My blood pressure went so high I'm surprised I didn't begin bleeding from my ears. I showed the article to the desk officer and told him exactly what occurred in the hospital. Then I went to the phone and called the *Daily News* City Desk.

The story was written by reporters Vinny Leaman and Joyce White. I was aware of Vinny's reputation as a "Fire Buff" and he was the number one man covering anything to do with the NYFD. I didn't know the name Joyce White but when I asked to speak to Vinny about the story in question, Joyce answered the phone.

I don't recall my exact words to her while voicing my objection to the fabricated pack of lies I read in print, but I do recall her response. I'm so sorry, Officer, I'm so sorry, Officer, over and over until I finally calmed down and took a deep breath. I apologized for my verbal assault and then I explained why I was so outraged.

"Miss White, allow me a moment to calm down. My name is Police Officer Fitzgerald and I am one of the four officers reportedly saved by the fireman at Greenpoint Hospital yesterday. If you have a moment I would like to tell you exactly what happened because the story I read ten minutes ago is a total fabrication to the nth degree. No, the word fabrication is inappropriate. That fireman is a bold-faced liar."

As calmly as possible I told her exactly what happened. She listened without interruption and when I was finished she apologized again. She said there was nothing she could do now. There was no way the *News* was going to print a retraction, but she promised she would tell Vinny when she saw him.

Several hours later I received a 10-2 (respond to) the SH.

As I walked in the door, the D. O. told me to call Vinny Leaman at the *Daily News*. I found a quiet office and made the call. Vinny picked up right away, I introduced myself and told him we met at the last PBA Convention, but there was no way he would remember me. I wanted him to know I was a PBA Delegate and that position came with a certain amount of credibility.

Before I had a chance to begin he told me he had spoken to Joyce White and she filled him in on my grievance regarding the fireman's interpretation of the hospital incident. He continued by explaining how he came by the information that resulted in the story they wrote.

He told me that he received a call from a fireman who claimed he saved the lives of all the people in the Greenpoint Hospital emergency room after a cop had his gun taken by a psycho. He added that he single-handedly disarmed the man and while doing so received a gash over his eye, which required several stitches to close the wound.

I could not believe what I was hearing and told Vinny the person who told him that story was a lying piece of crap.

I asked him to contact the doctor who was speaking to Officer Beady when the psycho took his gun. Talk to the hospital security officer who witnessed the entire scene and ask them to confirm my story.

I told him the only truth in the fireman's story was that he was struck with the barrel of the revolver. He said he was sorry, but there was nothing he could do about what was already on the streets.

I had the fireman's name, but not his firehouse. I asked Vinny where the liar worked, but he refused to give me that information.

I definitely wanted to tell that fireman what I thought of him in front of his coworkers and his boss. I was pissed. Eventually I calmed down. I knew I could have found him if I worked at it, but if that meeting took place it would have been very confrontational. I didn't want to get arrested for beating the crap out of a fireman so I let it go.

Several years later I received the Greenpoint Lion's Club "Cop of the Year" award. That award was presented at a sit-down catered luncheon in one of our finest restaurants in the Nine Four Precinct. My wife and children were invited, as was my commanding officer, several sergeants and two lieutenants who I worked with and they had submitted my name for consideration for that award.

As we waited for the festivities to begin, a lady came over to me as I was speaking to my commanding officer.

"Officer Fitzgerald?"

"Yes, how can I help you?"

"My name is Joyce White, do you remember my name?"

It took me a few seconds, but finally that name came back to me. How could I forget?

"Yes, I do remember you, Miss White. It's nice to meet you and what has brought you here today?"

"As you will recall, my name was added to that story written by Vinny Leaman about the fireman who saved you and the other officers. I'm still very sorry about that. Our conversation regarding that false report by that fireman is what brought me here today.

"I happened to be in our office yesterday when our editor told us he was sending a reporter to cover your award ceremony here today. When I heard your name and your precinct I told him I had to cover this story. I want to make up for not verifying the facts given to us by that fireman. I promise, you will be happy with the story I will write today. I have a photographer with me and he would like to take a few shots of you with your family and of course with your commanding officer."

I had been told I could invite up to six guests, but I had three, my immediate family. I asked Joyce and her cameraman if they would like to join us for lunch and they accepted my invitation.

It was a very enjoyable afternoon. I felt honored with the award given me by such a prestigious organization. I was extremely proud and humbled to be selected as the Cop of the Year from so many great police officers in the Nine Four Precinct.

Joyce White fulfilled her promise. She wrote a great report of what took place that day, which took a full half page in one of the top newspapers in NYC, including a great photo of me surrounded by my wife and two children. Thank you "Joyce White," wherever you are.

18

MY FRIEND MIKE ROGERS AND HIS VW CONVERTIBLE

During my two years assigned to the Seven Five Precinct I worked with and became friends with many fine police officers. One of those officers was Mike Rogers. I never actually teamed up with him during a tour, but from time to time, after a hot-busy four to twelve, our squad would stop for a pint in a pub in Queens to unwind.

As common as Volkswagens were, parked near the SH, that's how rare they were everywhere else in the ghetto; Chevys, Fords, Caddies were everywhere, but VWs, fagedaboutit. No self-respecting ghettoite would be caught dead in a Volkswagen.

Mike had the rarest of them all with his bright yellow VW convertible. One evening while working a four to twelve tour, I was typing a report in the 124 room (precinct clerical office). Mike came in and said, "Jack, someone stole my car." He had worked a day tour, made an arrest, returned from court at about nine p.m. and signed out. When he went to get his car it was gone.

I stopped what I was doing and was joined by my partner. Mike jumped in the backseat and we searched the entire neighborhood, but no VW. After about an hour we gave up and returned to the SH. I completed my report and Mike reported his car stolen.

I'll fast-forward three weeks to our next set of four to twelve tours. At about nine p.m. my partner Hank Steward was behind the wheel, patrolling our sector. We were on Pitkin Avenue, a main road in the Seven Five. It was an unusually quiet evening, so I took advantage of that rare opportunity to sit back while observing the street urchins.

Hank was cruising at about ten miles an hour when I saw a bright yellow VW convertible parked at the curb. WHOA!!! . . . WHAT THE . . . As we passed the car I looked at the plate and sure enough it was Mike's car. I couldn't believe my eyes; I got so excited I told Hank to stop the car as I bailed out on the roll.

I drew my revolver as I ran to the car, which was occupied by three men. One was sitting in the front passenger's seat and the other two were in the backseat. I ordered them out of the vehicle with their hands up. Hank had backed the RMP to where I was holding the three at bay and we did a superficial search before putting handcuffs on them.

"Where is the driver of this car?"

"He went to see somebody. We're waiting for him. Why did you arrest us?"

Hank called for backup to transport the prisoners to the SH and I drove Mike's car. As soon as we arrived at the SH, Hank gave Mike a 10-2 (respond to the station house) and I brought my three prisoners in front of the desk officer for the booking process.

Two of the perps gave their names, but had no proof of identification. They each had about ten dollars. The third prisoner, the guy I found sitting in the front passenger's seat, had ID and over seven hundred dollars cash in his wallet.

"Wait a second, what's your name?"

"My name is Raymond Garcia."

"Raymond, how come your ID I found in your wallet says you're Jose Rivera?"

"Oh yeah, that's my other name."

"How much money do you have in this wallet?"

"About two hundred dollars."

"Two hundred dollars, two hundred dollars, you have seven hundred dollars here. What's up with that?"

"Oh yeah, I forgot, my cousin gave me the money he owed me. I have seven hundred dollars in my wallet."

Another enigma often referred to as a "Puerto Rican mystery" by police officers working areas populated by Hispanic citizens. No disrespect meant.

Hank and I took our prisoners to the second floor detective's squad room for fingerprinting.

As a detective was printing the prisoners, the desk officer called and asked me to return to the desk.

"What's up, Lou?"

He walked me into his side office.

"Jack, you see that guy standing in front of the desk?"

"Yes."

"He just walked in and told me a man with a gun robbed him of his wallet containing seven hundred dollars. He also told me the perp was Puerto Rican. I asked his name and would you believe it was Jose Rivera, the same name as one of your prisoners."

"Wow. What a coincidence. Lieutenant, I do believe this party is about to get interesting. Do you mind if I take his report?"

"By all means and I think I know where this is going."

I walked the robbery victim into the Muster Room and began the UF 61.

"What is your name?"

"Jose Rivera."

"Can you tell me what happened to you this evening?"

As he was walking down Pitkin Avenue, a guy stopped him and demanded money. The guy had a gun. He went on to describe the robber and sure enough his description fit my prisoner also named Jose Rivera. What a small world.

I told the DO I was cutting this short. I was taking the robbery victim to the squad room where he could view an impromptu lineup.

As I escorted him to the second floor he told me he needed to catch a flight to PR in the morning. He asked if he could get his money back from the people we arrested.

No doubt he didn't spend much time planning his visit to the station house. How on earth could he know we arrested the guy who stole his money? He was making this too easy. I told him we did have three people under arrest.

"Mr. Rivera, I want you to wait outside this office. I will have the detectives get the prisoners ready for a lineup."

I had no intentions of going through the proper lineup procedure with this bogus robbery. The results were crystal clear.

I asked the detective to put the three prisoners in the lineup room and I had my complainant view them through the one-way glass.

"Mr. Rivera, do you recognize any of those men?"

"Yes, that's the man who robbed me."

"Are you sure?"

"Yes, that's him."

"Have you ever seen him or the other two men before?"

"No, never. Can I get my money and go now?"

"Mr. Rivera, calm down. You must be patient. I think I'll be able to wrap this up in a few more minutes."

"Thank you, Officer. I really need to get my money and wallet so I can go to Puerto Rico in the morning. My mother is very sick and she needs me."

I sat him down at a desk in a corner of the room and returned to the lineup room. I brought the three prisoners into the main office and put them in the detention cage.

Now the fun begins.

"Mr. Garcia, I have some bad news for you. I am adding a charge of armed robbery and possession of a gun to the grand larceny charge."

"What? What? . . . Officer Fitzgerald, what the f**k are you talkin' about robbery? You're goin' to put a robbery charge on me? No. No . . . No robbery. Who did I rob? Who the F**K did I rob?"

Raymond was very, very upset. I mean upset to the max. I told him someone identified him as the person who robbed him of a wallet containing $700. "The complainant's name is Jose Rivera, he described the wallet you had in your pocket and he knew it contained seven hundred bucks."

"Where is that guy?"

I told my complainant to stand up. As soon as Raymond saw Jose he went wild in the cage.

"Officer, that's my cousin Jose. I lied. He stole the car. We were with him tonight and he wanted to buy some beer at a bodega on Pitkin. He gave me his wallet when he left the car in case he got robbed. You caught us while we were waiting for him to come back with the beer. I swear I'm telling you the truth."

Hank took the "real" Jose Rivera and cuffed him to a cold water pipe. No way could we put him in the cage with his cousin.

Within a few minutes Mike arrived and did a great job of maintaining control of his emotions. I'm sure he wanted to engage in a little street justice, but he didn't.

As Mike went to check on his VW, I brought Jose to the desk and informed the lieutenant I had another criminal under arrest. I searched Jose, but I did not return his wallet or his seven hundred dollars. That was being vouchered as evidence.

Jose never fessed up to stealing Mike's car and he never admitted to fabricating his robbery accusation. As far as I was concerned, this was a case for the Brooklyn DA's office.

Mike returned and was really pissed off. After finding his convertible top sliced open he was looking for payback. Good thing he was a very easygoing cop. Jose had cut the top, allowing him enough room to reach in and unlock the door. He hotwired the ignition and took the car, which was parked a half block from the station house. Talk about balls. Later that night he taped the top from the inside making it almost impossible to see the cut.

The final score for this fiasco is: The real Jose Rivera took a plea to grand larceny and falsely reporting an incident, to wit, the false robbery. Garcia and the other two prisoners were given a conditional discharge for possession of stolen property. They didn't steal the car, but they knew it was stolen, so their plea deal was fair.

My man Jose never made it to PR. He had several prior arrests for grand larceny auto and a couple of drug arrests, so he was sentenced to nine months in the Iron House. Oh, and one more thing: He was ordered to pay for Mike's new convertible top, which was $700. He had just enough to pay that tab.

19

TAXI TRUCK SURVEILLANCE PART ONE:
THE CASE OF TWO DOPES BUYING DOPE

On February 11, 1971, I was transferred from the Seven Five Precinct to an undercover/decoy detail, Taxi Truck Surveillance Unit. Our primary objective was to focus on the increase in crimes against Yellow Taxi Cabs as well as truck hijackings, but taxi robberies were our number one concern.

We wore street clothes, drove in decoy yellow cabs donated by the taxi industry as well as unmarked Highway Patrol pursuit vehicles. Those highway vehicles were in great shape, but were recently replaced with new cars. The NYPD dressed them up to look like gypsy cabs with easily identifiable gypsy cab company decals.

We were assigned to areas in the city where most of that crime was committed. Manhattan, from the East and West Village right up into Harlem. The Bronx and the high-crime areas in Brooklyn. Our roll call assignment was a guide. If we came upon a suspect getting into a cab we followed him to the end of the ride. If we came up empty, which was usually the case, we would continue our search from that location. When we observed other criminal activity we had carte blanche to make any quality arrest anywhere in the city. A sweet detail.

My partner was a very sharp, streetwise cop named John

Konefal. John was assigned to TTSU at its inception, which was about eight months prior to me joining him. He was the senior man with more experience, so I watched, listened and learned; I definitely learned a lot from John.

One evening, while assigned to lower Manhattan in the East Village, we happened upon two men who fit the description of a stickup team. We followed them to the end of their ride and watched as they paid the cabby and exited the cab at 125th Street and Lenox Avenue.

We were about to resume our hunt when we saw a car with New Jersey plates pull up in front of a building on 125th. Both occupants were white. The passenger got out and walked toward a black guy who was standing in the doorway. The white guy had a brief conversation with the black guy and handed him something.

We watched as the black guy went into the building. He came out a few minutes later and handed the white guy a brown paper bag. The white guy returned to the car and they drove away.

It didn't take Sherlock Holmes's powers of deduction to figure out what had taken place. Ninety-nine percent of the white people in Harlem, at that time, were cops, firemen; other city employees assigned there . . . or drug buyers; that other 1 percent was lost. We followed the car as it went west and watched them stop in front of a diner at 125th and the river.

As the two got out, we jumped them before they could enter the diner. We showed them our shields and I said, "Excuse me, guys, we're police officers. Driver, can I see your license and regis- tration for the vehicle?"

"Yes, here it is. It's my car, I own it."

"Thank you. Now passenger, can I see your ID?"

"What do you want my ID for? We didn't do anything wrong. I don't even have any ID with me."

John walked over to the passenger's door and looked in the window. He said, "Passenger is that your brown bag on the front seat?"

"What brown bag?"

"The brown bag right here on the front seat. Come over here and look at what I'm talking about."

The passenger walked over, looked into the car and said, "I never saw that bag before. It's not mine."

"Oh. Driver, it must be yours, right?"

"What brown bag?"

"Okay, you come over and take a look."

"I have no idea how that bag got in my car."

"Let me get this straight, that bag is sitting on the front seat, in plain sight, between you two guys and it doesn't belong to either of you. Is that right?"

"That's my car and I know you don't believe us, but we have no idea how that bag got in the car."

John and I responded in unison, "You're right, we don't believe you." John went on.

"So if it doesn't belong to either of you two, maybe somebody put it in your car by mistake, right?"

"Yeah."

"Okay, let's see what's in the bag. Jack, you won't believe it; guess what I found in the bag?"

"Grapes."

"No, guess again."

"I give up, what's in the bag?

"I found four plastic bags containing some sort of white powder. I wonder what that could be."

We placed both drug buyers under arrest for possession of narcotics with intent to sell. Both serious crimes.

While John was processing the criminals I took the drugs to the lab, where it was determined each bag contained one ounce of pure, uncut, heroin with a street value of five thousand dollars, total value about twenty thousand dollars. The following evening we returned to that building on 125th Street.

20

TAXI TRUCK SURVEILLANCE PART TWO: THE GREAT CHASE

When we arrived at our new target on 125th Street, we noticed a NYC Public Library across the street and about a half block away. I parked our gypsy cab in front of that library and we went looking for the person in charge.

We identified ourselves and asked him if it would be possible for us to gain access to the roof. The guy never asked why nor did we volunteer that information.

As he showed us the way John asked if he would have a problem with us returning to the roof the next evening. He said it was a City owned building and we were city employees. There would be no problem. We thanked him as he left us alone on the roof.

The next night we returned with binoculars. The same fat man with a big Afro was working the door. We decided the best way to approach this two-man stakeout was for one of us to remain behind the wheel of our car while the other made observations from the roof. We used our portable radios to keep in contact.

When the roof man saw a car with out-of-state plates pull up and a white guy, it was always a white guy, get out and approach the fat guy, he would run down the four flights of stairs, jump into our car and we would wait for the target car to pull away from the curb.

During the four days we spent at that location, over a two-week period, John and I made a total of ten good felony drug arrests, including a possession of a loaded firearm added to one of those arrests. That gave us two weeks to hunt for taxi robberies or other non-drug-related street crime.

(Remember, our number one target was crimes against taxi drivers and truck drivers not drugs.) This drug location provided us with the required arrest quota as well as plenty of time to go after our primary objective.

Our commanding officer wanted at least five felony arrests per man per month. John and I never had a problem with that but there were times when members in our squad would have a bad month and a little help wouldn't hurt.

We didn't want to go too far over that established "quota," so we told our lieutenant we had a sure thing going. We explained that we wanted to share with some of the people in our squad who were low for the month. He thought that was a good idea and the first person he put in the car with us was John's former partner, Neil Brodski .

Neil hadn't done very well without John and didn't have a steady partner. He worked with whoever needed a partner for that tour. On the evening he was assigned with us he was going to take any arrest we made. We returned to the library and I took Neil to the roof while John remained in the car. We had our "Highway Patrol" gypsy cab with a big four-forty Chrysler Hemi engine.

It didn't take long before we had our first customer. A Chevy, with Connecticut plates, pulled up and the passenger from the front seat bailed and approached Mr. Fats in the doorway. Neil and I booked down the stairs and jumped into our car. We waited for the Chevy to pull away from the curb. Finally the white guy returned to their car with a brown bag. He got in, the driver pulled away and we followed them as they worked their way south to Ninety-Sixth Street.

At Ninety-Sixth. the driver made a right turn going west and stopped at the red signal light just prior to the northbound entrance to the West Side Highway. We knew they were going to get on the highway, so Neil and I got out; I approached from the passenger's side as Neil went to speak to the driver. As soon as they saw us closing in, the driver went through the red light and onto the WSH. John pulled up while placing our red magnetic FBI light on the roof of our vehicle, Neil and I got into the rear seat and the chase was on.

Allow me to set this stage: John was driving an ultra-fast Highway Patrol vehicle, so it didn't take more than ten seconds for him to catch up to the Chevy. This all happened on a Sunday evening at about eight p.m. and the traffic was light, resulting in a chase. Maybe the word chase didn't apply because we were side by side from the moment we caught up to them. John was in the right lane and as he motioned the driver of the Chevy to pull over, the guy rammed us with the side of his car, forcing our vehicle into the very high curb on the right shoulder. John maintained control and I knew what was coming; He was not going to give up, so he rammed the Chevy and that's the way it went. Back and forth, ram, ram, ram for about a half mile.

As we passed 125th Street, the front seat passenger open his window and emptied the white powder contents of about five good-sized plastic bags onto the roadway, which created a white cloud. I realized something had to be done before we crashed, so I moved over to Neil's side, pointed my .38 caliber snub-nosed off-duty S&W revolver out the window and fired three shots into their right rear tire.

I knew I hit my target, but we were going so fast the tire didn't deflate. But the occupants of their car got the message: The party was getting rough and we had no intention of giving up. The driver slowed to a stop, right there in the middle of Manhattan's West Side Highway.

All the vehicles behind us had slowed as they saw our vehicles ramming each other and we did have our FBI light displayed on top of our car. They knew we were the police.

We ordered the four occupants out of their car and after a superficial search handcuffed them. Neil called for assistance to transport our prisoners to the Two Eight Precinct and I called for Highway Patrol to close the highway and to assist with a search of the roadway. We were hoping to find at least one of the plastic bags containing residue, but unfortunately that didn't happen.

We did get lucky because when the passenger was cutting the bags before dumping the contents he spilled quite a lot of the powder onto the seat and floor of their vehicle. That powder was recovered with the use of a special handheld vacuum. We recovered enough white powder to charge them all with felony weight and it was heroin. We also charged them with attempted murder of three police officers and resisting arrest.

Upon further investigation and after identifying all four prisoners, we discovered they were in the military and assigned to a base in Connecticut. They were held overnight and arraigned the next day in Manhattan Criminal Court, where they were held without bail with a short return date. I contacted their commanding officer to inform him of their arrest.

He was not a happy camper or, I should say, a happy colonel.

He said, "Officer, the four people you arrested are suspected of being the primary source of heroin and cocaine to a major drug ring here on Base as well as in our local town. I won't go into details on the phone, but I will add that they are the tip of the iceberg as far as our investigators are concerned."

"Colonel, I understand your concern. I may be able to help you, but I can't make any promises. I'm not the arresting officer, but we work together. I know the ADA handling this case and I will tell him what you have told me. Considering we weren't injured I don't believe the attempted murder charge will go anywhere.

They dumped ninety-five percent of the dope, so even though

we still have felony weight it's not that much. For your information, I estimate they had at least two and a half kilos. One pound in each bag and our lab stated it was ninety percent pure. Estimated street value one hundred seventy-five thousand dollars. I strongly suggest you have your investigators contact that ADA. His name is Joseph Greenberg. He's a sharp guy and he's also someone you can talk to. I would say they have a good chance of Joseph going along with a plea deal to reduce their charges if they cooperate in your ongoing investigation. If we can be of help, you know how to contact us."

When I ended my conversation with the colonel, I told John and Neil what was said.

They both agreed with my solution. We weren't injured and what we recovered wasn't that much, so what happened in court was a nonissue and Neil got his four numbers for the month.

We continued making arrests at that location for several weeks, but there came a time when we realized most of our monthly activity was drug related. That wasn't what we were paid to do. We spoke to our lieutenant and told him we were going to contact the Narcotics Bureau via an Intelligent Report. One afternoon, two undercover detectives from that unit met with us and we gave them all the info we had.

Over the next few months we each received letters of commendation from the commanding officer of the Narcotics Bureau. We also received a letter from the colonel to our CO. John Konefal enjoyed telling the story about the night he almost lost his hearing as my gun was about six inches from his ears when I fired the three shots. I can assure you, the sound of a .38 being fired inside a vehicle is deafening.

21

WAYNE SHIRLEY

I had been assigned to the Taxi Truck Surveillance Unit for about three weeks. My partner John Konefal was well respected by our commanding officer and our three squad supervisors. That made it easy when requesting a change in assignment, as was the case one Sunday morning in March 1971.

On that day we were assigned to Manhattan South. After roll call, our sergeants invited everyone to breakfast at a diner near our office. John and I decided to accept their offer as did about five other teams. I discovered those gatherings occurred about once a month, at which time our bosses held a "rap session." They brought us up to speed regarding TTSU stats and current events within our zone of influence, to wit, taxi robberies and truck hijackings.

That breakfast would pay off in spades. We learned the Ninth Precinct, in Manhattan South, had more than its share of taxi robberies, so after our breakfast meeting John said, "Jack, let's take a ride to the Ninth Precinct and check out the unusuals on the taxi robberies."

Every reported crime generated a UF 61 (crime report), but some crimes generated an additional report. At that time, taxi robberies were given special attention and an unusual was required for every taxi robbery.

That report was also prepared for all out of the ordinary happenings in a command. To wit, large fires, all homicides in fact all very serious crimes would require an unusual.

The information recorded on those reports went into fine detail and that is what John was looking for. He spoke to one of the detectives in that squad, who then gave us copies of every report related to a recent taxi robbery.

We received twelve unusuals going back six weeks. It didn't take long for John to zero in on the MO (method of operation).

Prime time was between seven and ten p.m. The location of occurrence was always Tenth Street between avenues C and B. The description of the perpetrator was always: A black man about twenty-five years old, medium build, about six feet tall, with a knife. The perp would hail a yellow taxi somewhere on Fourteenth Street near Third Avenue. He would tell the driver he wanted to go to Tenth Street between Avenue C and B. (Tenth ran one-way from C to B.)

As the cabbie approached the middle of the block, the passenger would tell him to stop. The passenger-turned-robber would reach over the front seat and put a knife to the cabbie's throat and demand money. When he got his money he would exit the cab and run through the vacant lots going south.

We drove to the crime scene and got the lay of the land.

For those readers not familiar with that area in New York City: The Ninth Precinct's East Village runs from Houston Street on the south to Fourteenth Street on the north end. From West Broadway to the East River.

Back in the late fifties, it was home to the artists and poets who couldn't afford the expensive upper-class "West Village,", also known as Greenwich Village.

Their bohemian unconventional lifestyle did allow them to find affordable housing on the Lower East side of Manhattan.

Hippies, also young and unconventional joined that "beatnik" culture in the mid-sixties but hippies were less productive and more into drugs, especially marijuana and heroin.

John felt we had enough information to call one of our sergeants to request a change of assignment. We were scheduled to work until six p.m. It was now twelve noon. The plan was we would return to our office and sign out. At six we would sign in again and use a yellow cab for this special assignment. Sergeant Peters gave us the okay. We returned before six, took the keys to a yellow cab and drove to the Ninth Precinct.

We identified ourselves to the desk officer and informed him as to what we were doing. Taxi Truck Surveillance Unit was under the direct supervision of the First Deputy Commissioner's office. We had carte blanche and I don't recall ever having a problem, with supervisors, in any command.

It was nearing prime time so we drove to Avenue C just off Tenth Street and parked. John was driving and I was the passenger in the rear seat. Two cops in street clothes in a yellow taxi cab in Manhattan . . . We were invisible!

Now for Part A of the plan: We would wait for a yellow taxi to turn onto Tenth Street, at which time we would follow that cab. If he went past ground zero, midway up the block, we figured it wasn't our boy. We would follow the car until he turned off Tenth, then return to the roost.

Part B of the plan: We knew the robber used a knife. We also knew he would lean over the front seat and put the knife to the throat of the driver and demand money. When he got the money he would exit the cab and flee south through vacant lots to Ninth or Eighth Street. When our suspect cab stopped midway we would bail out of our cab and approach that car. If we saw the passenger reach over the front seat we knew he was our robber. I would approach from the right side and John from the driver's side.

We waited and we waited some more.

"So, John, how about we take our wives out for dinner next week?"

"Sounds good, where do you want to go?"

"How about that nice Italian restaurant . . ."

As we were into our small talk a yellow cab drove up Tenth. That was the second cab since we began our surveillance at seven. It was now nine. John followed and sure enough the driver stopped midway. We left our car and approached the target.

Our boy reached over the front seat and I was close enough to see the knife in his right hand. John and I opened the rear doors at about the same time, but the perp got out on John's side.

He still had the knife in his hand as I raced around to help John disarm him. John didn't need much help because as the perp got out he tried to stab John, at which time John clocked him with the barrel of his Colt revolver.

Now the robber is a prisoner. I cuffed him and put him in the rear seat of our car while John spoke to the cab driver/victim. He told the driver how to get to the Ninth Precinct SH and that we would follow him.

The driver knew his shift was now over. He would be spending the next few hours with us. He would also spend the next day and many other days as a complainant in the criminal justice system. If our robber/prisoner got chump change for his efforts, the driver might have written it off in lieu of losing many paydays. John wasn't going to allow that to happen. We followed him to the SH.

John escorted the prisoner to the desk and I walked in with the complainant.

"Good evening, Lieutenant, we have one under arrest for robbery."

"Don't tell me you caught the elusive taxi robber."

"Yes sir that is exactly what I am telling you."

"Good work and who will be the arresting officer?"

"Police Officer Fitzgerald."

"What? What the f***. No, that ain't right. No, John, I can't take this arrest. I did nothing but watch you do all the work. You made this happen. I can't take this arrest."

"Lieutenant, Fitzgerald is the arresting officer."

John wouldn't talk about it. He told me this was my collar and that was that.

Now allow me to identify the magnitude of that arrest: Our Taxi Truck Surveillance Unit was created with one primary objective: to arrest criminals who preyed on taxicab drivers. In 1970, there were so many taxi-related homicides, robberies and assaults, the NYC taxi industry demanded our Mayor John Lindsay do something about it. Lindsay ordered Police Commissioner Bratton to do something about it, ergo TTSU was created.

Back to this arrest: Remember that fateful day when Reggie Jackson hit three home runs in the sixth game of the 1970 World Series? This arrest, as far as the NYPD and the taxi industry were concerned, was a tad more consequential.

This arrest was written up in several newspapers. It was on Channel Five news. This was B.I.G. Big. Of course everyone in our unit knew who really made the arrest. The CO and our squad lieutenant and two sergeants knew John was the mastermind behind this great collar, but I was the arresting officer on paper. I made my bones in TTSU.

We lodged our taxi cab robber, Wayne Shirley in the Seventh Precinct SH because he had a one-hundred-dollar-a-day heroin habit and he was definitely going to be sick. The Seventh was where all male addicts, arrested in Manhattan, were lodged overnight.

John and I would work on this arrest together. He had prior experience with the follow-up investigation required to close as many previously reported taxi robberies as possible. While our prisoner slept, John and I got on the phone and called every robbery victim/complainant on our list of unusuals.

We worked through the night and by eight a.m. we had four cabbies willing to appear in Manhattan Criminal Court to view our prisoner at arraignment.

The way that process went down was as follows: John met with the victims in the lobby of One Hundred Centre Street (Manhattan Criminal Court). He then took them to the arraignment part and told them if and when they saw the person who robbed them go before the judge, they should tell him.

I went into the bowels of the tombs in the lower level of the courthouse and escorted my prisoner to that arraignment part. I didn't get a chance to bring Wayne before the judge before John gave me the high sign. He joined me in the "bull pen" (pre-arraignment waiting area).

"Jack, I have four positives. No doubts, all four one hundred percent sure."

The ADA informed the judge that the defendant would be rearrested immediately after being arraigned.

"Judge, the officers just informed me they have four additional robbery victims/complainants present in this room who have identified the defendant Wayne Shirley as the person who robbed them in the recent past. The reports of those crimes are on file with the NYPD."

The judge ordered the defendant be remanded into the custody of the arresting officer, to wit, me.

I put cuffs on Wayne, again, and we returned to the Ninth Precinct SH. We prepared all forms needed for four new arrests. The good news was our robbery complainants weren't at all becoming complaining complainants, as in: "Why do I have to come back to court? How long is this going to take? Yada, yada, yada." The taxi industry decided it was only fair to compensate the drivers/complainants for time lost during the arrest process as well as time lost with future court appearances

That evening Wayne Shirley was arraigned on four separate robberies and held without bail. When the mayor's office gets involved in a criminal matter, everyone in the criminal justice system is on notice, even the judges.

The end result of that one arrest was that we eventually cleared a total of nine UF 61s for taxi robbery. Wayne was indicted for all nine and he took a plea deal in Supreme Court. He spent between seven and ten years upstate in Attica . . . Oh and there were no more reported taxi robberies in that precinct.

Footnote: I want to make it clear the arrest John and I made would have been made by the detectives in the Ninth Precinct if they had the time and resources we had. The Ninth Precinct cops and detectives were and still are outstanding and we appreciated their help with our investigation.

22

THE SURPRISE PACKAGE

As my partner and I were winding down from a busy midnight to eight tour in the always busy Eight One Precinct, we received a call in our neighboring Eight Three Precinct. They had no one available, so we got their job. That doesn't happen often, but it does happen. It was seven thirty and we really didn't want to get involved in anything that would take us past our eight a.m. end of tour.

As we approached the location it looked like a simple two-vehicle collision. One car and one truck dented each other = one accident report and we're signing out on time. Whoa, wait a minute, why does one of the drivers have a gun in one hand and a badge in the other?

Uh oh, that doesn't look good. As we approached, the guy with the badge identified himself as a correction officer and asked if he could borrow a set of handcuffs. He also told us he was arresting the other driver.

Okay, so now we have an accident report and an assist with an off-duty arrest for DWI, right? Ummmm, no. Wrong! I looked at the prisoner and he didn't appear to be intoxicated.

"Officer, what are you charging your prisoner with?"

"Take a look in the cab of the truck."

"Officer, just tell me what you're charging him with."

"Please just look in the cab of the truck."

He had a strange look on his face, so I opened the door to the cab and expected to see a bag of dope or maybe a gun? No. I could see a large cardboard box on the passenger's side floor. As I climbed into the cab I could see red hair sticking out of the box. Then a woman's head followed by the rest of the body, a dead body, what the F**K! Now this job was getting interesting.

My partner cuffed the prisoner and led him to the rear seat of our RMP. I told the arresting officer I would call for a sergeant and precinct detectives and we would need to await their arrival.

The correction officer asked me how long this was going to take. It was Sunday and he had plans to take his family to a pool party at his brother's house on Long Island. His wife and kids were really, really looking forward to having fun and he didn't want to disappoint them, yada, yada, yada. I did my best not to allow my few adverse incidents with correction officers to sour my interaction with this guy, but his whining was starting to get to me.

After listening to him whimper for about five minutes I finally had enough.

"Listen up; you are definitely not going home anytime soon. Is this your first arrest?"

"Yes." (Correction officers rarely made arrests outside the prison.)

"My friend, you certainly jumped into the deep end of the pool on your first try. You will be spending the better part of this day with the detectives. Your prisoner is the primary suspect in a homicide investigation, which is just about the most serious charge in the penal law. I suggest you call your wife and tell her you won't be home in time for the pool party."

While waiting for the responding units, I had time to ask the officer exactly what happened. Here's his story:

He was driving home from Rikers Island correctional facility when the truck, driven by the prisoner, went through a stop sign, striking his car. Both drivers exited their vehicles, but the truck driver was very nervous.

He promised to pay for the damage, but he had to leave right away to take his mother to the doctor. Ummmm, a doctor's appointment on a Sunday morning? Very suspicious, as in "I don't think so." The officer went to look into the cab of the truck expecting to find drugs, maybe a gun, as I did, definitely not a dead body. He told the truck driver he was under arrest and obviously someone called 911 to report the accident and that's the end of that part of the story.

The sergeant and detectives responded to the scene and interviewed the correction officer. My partner and I were asked to transport the prisoner to the Eight Three station house and a sector from the day tour transported the truck and the body to the Eight Three Precinct garage, where they awaited the arrival of the medical examiner.

While waiting for the Eight Three detectives, I asked the prisoner, I'll call him Bobby, for his side of the story. I wasn't conducting an official, on the record, investigation, so I didn't advise him of his rights.... . . . . This is his explanation of how he got involved in this sad bad situation:

It was Saturday evening and his friend Jimmy called and asked him if he wanted to go to their local neighborhood bar. He had nothing else to do, so he agreed and off they went.

They were having a few drinks, enjoying themselves, when they found a couple of friendly girls to enjoy a few more drinks with. After a while Jimmy suggested they all go to his apartment where they could have more drinks, listen to music and just enjoy each other's company without the crowd. Sounds like fun, let's go.

Jimmy broke out a bottle of rum and some coke and they all had a drink. He also put a Sinatra tape on and now they were all getting comfortable while drinking their rum and coke while chatting and listening to the music.

Eventually Jimmy's new squeeze began singing to the music.

She had a terrible voice so finally Jimmy told her to shut up. The singer, who by now was totally wasted, took offense to his rude response to her attempt at a new career in show business. She decided to let him know by calling him every name she could think of and she wasn't using her indoor voice.

Bobby, also a tad intoxicated, got pissed and decided to shut her up, but Jimmy said it was his apartment and he would handle it. He walked over to the singer and forced her into the bedroom where he tied her to a chair and gave her a few punches to the face before returning to the party. Jimmy got another drink, joined Bobby and the new Mrs. Bobby. Before he could get comfortable, his former girlfriend began yelling and screaming and calling him more nasty names from her chair in the bedroom; she wanted back into the party.

By now Jimmy was over the top pissed off. Why didn't we just stay at the bar? He went to his toolbox, got a roll of duct tape, and returned to the bedroom where he put several layers of tape over her mouth. As he walked out of the bedroom she really started to freak out, but at least he didn't have to listen to her whiney voice anymore.

A short time later Bobby's new girlfriend said she wanted to go home and told Jimmy to untie her friend so they could leave together. The boys realized the night was a bust anyway, so Jimmy returned to the bedroom to free the singer. He found her sleeping. He untied her and went to help her up, but her body fell to the floor. She wasn't sleeping. She was dead.

He could see blood around her nose which was bent to one side, clearly broken. With a broken nose and her mouth taped, she suffocated.

The good news, well as good as it was going to get, was the other girl didn't know her friend was dead. They told her that her friend wanted to stay the night and Jimmy would take her home later that day. She bought the story and left. The bad news was they had a dead body on their hands.

Bobby, a truck driver, used his truck to dispose of the body, but on the way to whatever secluded body-dumping area he was driving to, he ran a stop sign and hit the correction officer's car.

The end result of this bright and sunny Sunday morning is: I got to go home to my family with four hours of overtime and the correction officer seemed to go into shock after the conversation he had with Pete Knudtson , the assigned detective.

As I was about to ask the detective to keep me informed as to his progress with his case, I was interrupted by Mr. Correction Officer.

"Detective, it's eleven thirty already, how much longer is this going to take? All I had was an accident with that guy and now I'm in the middle of a big deal murder case. It's not fair. Why is it taking so long?" I could see Detective Knudtson was getting a little impatient with the officer. He wasn't present when I spoke to him earlier, but his message was similar.

"Officer, allow me to give you the cold hard facts with regard to where you are in this very serious matter: You are not going home until we have completed this homicide investigation. You are the arresting officer, so you're here with us until the end. The very end. I want you to understand I am assisting you with 'your' arrest.

Make all the calls you need to make, but you're not leaving this room any time soon. And now for the really bad news: When you do get to leave, YOU are taking your prisoner to Brooklyn Criminal Court where YOU will be introduced to the NYC criminal justice system from a totally different perspective than you are used to."

A few weeks later I decided to call the detective to ask what happened to the homicide investigation. He began by telling me that after I left, he spoke to the desk officer and considering the correction officer didn't have a clue about what was going on, he was assigned to help him

He told me Bobby the truck driver agreed to cooperate and he took them to Jimmy's apartment. They woke him up, at which time they read him his rights. Neither Bobby nor Jimmy had any prior arrests.

Jimmy was charged with criminally negligent homicide and Bobby was charged with attempted disposal of a dead human body. I never called again to find out what the final result was, but considering we were in Brooklyn, I figure Jimmy probably got . . . maybe a year in the can with probation and Bobby got a very short time plus a couple of years' probation.

23

THE MOST HEART-WRENCHING
ASSIGNMENT DURING MY CAREER

While working an eight to four tour in the Eight One Precinct, we were given an assignment in the Eight Three Precinct. There were no Eight Three sectors available, so we were it. Eight One Charlie, 10-54 (sick or injured person), investigate a child out a fourth-floor window at 835 Bushwick Avenue.

Upon arrival we saw a small crowd gathered on the sidewalk. As we approached the scene we could see a small child lying on the sidewalk bleeding from a head wound. She was unconscious. I picked her up and was about to get back into our vehicle when the Eight Three sector arrived. The passenger/recorder took her from me and said they would take her to Wyckoff Heights Hospital.

My partner told them we would escort them to the hospital, so we led the way with lights and siren blaring. The Eight Three sector had Central notify the hospital to have doctors ready as they were bringing an unconscious child to their ER.

We arrived at the hospital and a nurse had a gurney waiting. The recorder bypassed her and went directly into the emergency room with the child. Two doctors took her into a room and began doing all they could for the little girl. As I looked on I could see by their expressions it wasn't going well.

Thirty minutes from the time they began, a doctor came out to where we were waiting and told us the little girl was dead. The Eight Three sector requested their sergeant respond to the hospital and asked my partner and I to return to the scene to notify the family of the child's death and prepare an aided card (a post card size card used to record the pertinent information needed to identify the aided person.) Finally, we needed to know how the child ended up on the sidewalk.

We got the name and apartment number of the 911 caller and returned to the scene of this catastrophic incident. I did NOT want to be the one making this notification. I knew this was going to be bad, very bad. (This is another one of those incidents when I must ask you, the reader, to try to put yourself in my shoes.)

When we arrived at the address the crowd was gone, but the blood was still visible. As I looked up to the fourth floor where the caller had her apartment, I could see an opened window.

The front door was open, so we entered the building, climbed the stairs and knocked on the door. A Puerto Rican woman about sixty-five years old answered the door. My partner and I went into the apartment and had her sit down.

She was extremely hyper and had a look on her face I will never forget. Her facial expression was: Please God please tell me my granddaughter is okay . . . Please.

I was not an emotional person. Police work does not allow for emotion. You get cold and before long you lose all feeling, it's just a failsafe part of being a cop. (After many years in retirement, that inner core began to defrost.)

This was different. I could feel my cold heart melting as I looked into the eyes of this poor grandmother. That knot in my stomach was now the size of a boulder. I held her hand and put my other hand on her shoulder and said, "I am very sorry, but the doctors weren't able to save your granddaughter."

I don't have words to describe the next ten minutes. I'll leave it up to your imagination, but whatever you can imagine, it was worse. Much worse. There came a time when she fell to the floor in exhaustion. Totally spent, sobbing, and praying. That was undoubtedly the most emotional experience during my twenty-six-year career as a police officer.

As we waited with her the telephone rang. I answered and it was the child's mother. She was crying and speaking in Spanish. I waited for her to take a breath.

"This is Police Officer Fitzgerald. May I have your name, please?"

"My name is Maria. How is my daughter? What happened to my daughter? Is she okay? Where is my mother? I want to talk to my mother."

"Where are you now?"

"I'm at work."

"You need to come home . . . now."

"I want you to tell me what happened. I need to know how my daughter is."

"Maria, I will wait for you to come home. Please come home now."

I called the Eight One desk officer and told him where we were.

"Lieutenant King, this is PO Fitzgerald calling to inform you that Bob and I are at 835 Bushwick Avenue. We're still assisting the Eight Three sector with a job we got about an hour ago. I want you to know we need to stay on this one and we may go past four p.m."

"Jack, you can't have an Eight Three sector take over?"

"Not now. I'll explain when we come in."

"Keep me informed."

As much as we didn't want to be where we were, we wouldn't pass this job off to another sector. There came a time when the grandmother stopped crying. We needed to find out what caused the child to end up on the sidewalk.

Bob helped her up from the floor and walked her into the kitchen. She sat at the table as I gave her a glass of water.

"My name is Police Officer Fitzgerald and this is Police Officer

Tighe. What is your name?"

"Carmella Sanchez."

"Carmella, can I get you anything? A cup of coffee, tea, anything?"

"No, thank you."

"Carmella, we need to know what happened here today."

"My daughter works, so I watch my granddaughter all day. There is something wrong with our buzzer so when someone rings the doorbell, I open the window, put the key in a bag and throw it to them. That's what happened. The drugstore delivery man rang the bell to deliver my pills. I opened the window and threw him the key. I left the window open and went to my door to get the pills and that's when Rosa fell out." On that afternoon that's exactly what happened. The grandmother opened the window, dropped the key, and opened the apartment door for the delivery guy. Before she could return to close the window, her four-year-old granddaughter ran to the window, which had a very low sill, and fell the four stories to the cement sidewalk.

We had what was needed for the aided card. As Bob called the Eight Three Precinct with that info, the child's mother arrived home. As soon as the mother entered the room she asked where her daughter was. All I could do was look her in the eyes . . . for what seemed like an eternity. I just couldn't find the words to tell this poor woman her daughter were dead.

"No, no, no. Please God tell me my daughter is all right."

"I am very sorry, Maria, but your daughter is not all right. The doctors at the hospital did everything they could for your little girl, but they couldn't save her."

I must say again: I don't have the words to describe the ultra, ultra-extremely emotional scene that took place in that small apartment that afternoon. It was indescribably horrific.

We calmed the mother and grandmother down and I called the hospital and asked the Eight Three sergeant if he wanted us to bring the mother to the hospital and he said yes. Of course the grandmother wanted to go with us, but we wouldn't allow that.

We were concerned for her health and we knew what would happen when she saw the child.

We arrived at the hospital and escorted the mother into the emergency room where the sergeant and the sector car team were waiting. I told them that my partner and I were going back to the Eight One. Our relief was waiting for the car and their clerical staff had the required info necessary for the paperwork.

The mind photo of that little girl lying on the gurney in the emergency room stays with me to this day. As hard-hearted and calloused as I had become, nothing prepared me for that experience on that day. Sitting here now, typing on my computer, I can still see that poor child's face and the agony that followed with her grandmother and her mother. That was, without a doubt, the worst day in my life as a police officer.

24

JOHN AND AL'S

A t approximately six p.m. on Friday, January 19, 1973, a call came over the Fourteenth Division radio; 10-30, robbery in progress at John and Al's sporting goods store. That store was located at the corner of Broadway and Stockton Street in the Nine O Precinct, just outside the Eight One Precinct boundaries.

It wasn't unusual for available sectors, from an adjoining precinct, to back up on a robbery in progress job. That radio run resulted in one of the longest standoffs in the history of the NYPD.

Four criminals entered the store to steal guns and ammunition that would be used to begin their "holy crusade" or Jihad. The store manager hit the silent robbery in progress alarm, causing the police response. At that time there were a total of twelve hostages in the store, including the manager, Gerry Ricardo.

In 1973, I was assigned to sector C in the Eight One Precinct. On that day I had a tour change and worked an eight to four, due to a court appearance. If it were not for that court appearance I would have been in the thick of that deadly incident.

My partner worked our scheduled four to midnight tour and was one of the responding officers. As the sector crews arrived, the four men opened fire and two police officers were shot within a short time. The officers returned fire, but after realizing there were customers/hostages in the store they held fire and in fact never fired another shot.

The criminals armed themselves with twelve-gauge shotguns and high-power magnum rifles. They also had an unlimited supply of ammunition. To make a bad scene worse, they turned the lights off so the store was dark. They could see out, but the officers couldn't see into the store. The gunmen would fire their weapons at anything that moved.

The first responders found themselves pinned down and forced to find cover behind their RMPs as well as vehicles parked at the curb in front of the store.

Broadway is a main artery in Brooklyn and the elevated train ran overhead. The El structure blocked most of the sunlight during the day and made it very dark at night. The numerous overhead lights made good targets out of the responding officers.

Finally an emergency service unit arrived with their bullet-proof vests. They took up positions as close as possible to the front of the store. One officer, Steven Gilroy, made it to the El pillar directly in front of the store. Those supports are made of thick steel and are about two feet wide on all four sides and could easily hide an average size person.

Gilroy was safe behind the pillar until he tried to look from around the structure. One shot fired from a magnum rifle struck him in the head, killing him instantly.

The officers that were pinned down began shooting at the overhead lights, bringing an even playing field to this standoff. Now everyone was in the dark.

There came a time when our NYPD armored personnel carrier was transported from our hanger at Floyd Bennett Field, in Brooklyn, to this crime scene and put into action.

When the APC moved, the criminals began shooting at it. (Nothing they had could put a dent in that heavily armored vehicle) While under fire the driver made his way from one officer to the next until all police officers were safely inside and out of harm's way.

I was scheduled for a midnight to eight a.m. tour, but after hearing of the ongoing incident in the Nine O on the news, I called the precinct and was told to report as soon as possible.

As I walked in the door I was ordered to change into uniform. I wasn't alone in the locker room. Just about everyone scheduled to work that late tour had called and we were all ready to do what needed to be done.

I was assigned to my sector C with special attention to be given to crowd control at the corner of Broadway and Myrtle Avenue. That corner was one short block from the store.

My partner was still at the scene, so I worked with Joe Carbone for that tour. After roll call, our sergeant ordered us to respond to Broadway and Myrtle to relieve the men who had been there since six p.m., and he added that we were to remain at that location until given an assignment by Central.

Upon arrival I met with my partner. He and everyone else being relieved were happy to see us, as we were the first of several relief sectors. They were very cold and exhausted. The stress they endured for almost six hours took its toll.

"Bill, a tough tour, right?"

"Jack, tough is not the word, but I'll give you the blow by blow tomorrow. Right now all I want to do is go home, take a hot shower and have a hot meal." It was now almost midnight. This was a Nine O crime scene, but several sectors from the Eight One were assigned to give special attention for crowd control. I parked our RMP on Myrtle Avenue and we walked the two hundred feet to our assigned post on Broadway.

The sight/crime scene was surreal. Total darkness with the elevated structure framing the scene. I could see the outline of the armored personnel carrier parked across the street from John and Al's about one hundred and fifty feet away. The RMPs were still double-parked in front of or near the store as they were abandoned by the first responders.

Then we had the press and media to contend with. Every TV and radio station as well as every newspaper in the NYC and surrounding area had at least one reporter present. Our corner was ground zero for the media because we were as close to the store as anyone could get.

Every street adjacent to the crime scene was closed off for two blocks, a "no-go zone." Our part of Broadway as well as Myrtle Avenue had to be kept open to allow access to NYPD personnel as well as emergency vehicles.

Back to the media: Most of that group knew enough to give us room to maneuver. They kept their distance, but the cameramen were another story. Those guys made their money by getting action shots. That night it was John and Al's and they all tried to jockey into position as close as possible to the store.

They wanted that once-in-a-lifetime shot or video of violence that was sure to come. That shot that would bring them fame and fortune. John and Al's crime scene could make that happen.

To give you a better understanding of "our corner": When we arrived that night, we found an RMP parked on the sidewalk, blocking pedestrian traffic. The rear end of the car was about two feet from the building and the front end was about ten feet from the curb near the corner. That was our cover point.

We were diagonally across from the store and about one hundred and fifty feet away. We couldn't see inside the store, but our view of the front was clear.

As said above, we were as close as anyone could get and the cameramen were crowding us. One photographer even tried to place his movie camera on the roof of the RMP. Of course we weren't about to let that happen.

We ordered them all to back off. We moved them across Myrtle Avenue and now we had some breathing room.

At about twelve thirty, two POs from the Nine O precinct joined us and they were assigned to the corner for the entire tour. When we were given an assignment we left. Upon completion, we returned. It went like that most of the night.

A command post/temporary headquarters was established across the street in a bank where an official NYPD log was maintained. Radio communications was set up and a ranking supervisor above the rank of captain was in command. The bank was warm; they had restroom facilities and hot coffee.

At about three a.m. our PBA mobile canteen arrived and set up just out of range of gunfire. Our PBA union has a large van they use to provide sandwiches, coffee, doughnuts, and water at scenes like ours that morning. It was manned by members of the board.

At about four a.m., I went to the canteen and found two of the four board members were men I knew from our Brooklyn North. There was no line, so I had a moment to chat.

Ray Lonagan said, "Hi, Jack, how have you been?"

"Okay, Ray, how about you?"

"We were doing well until Steve was murdered and God only knows how this debacle will end."

"Yes, and I don't want to tell you how I hope it ends."

"I can read your mind and I'm sure every cop in the city is hoping for the same ending. Now, what can I get you?"

"I'll have the bologna sandwich and a container of coffee, please."

"We don't have bologna. We have turkey, ham and cheese, and roast beef. All on a Kaiser roll. They're all delicious and we had everything catered by Junior's." (A famous restaurant on Flatbush Avenue in Brooklyn.)

"Thanks, Ray, I needed that. I'll have the bologna."

"Jack, I'll give you a turkey sandwich. How about your partner?"

"He'll have the roast beef."

I thanked Ray and returned to my post with the sandwiches and coffee. Lo and behold I had a delicious turkey sandwich and my partner enjoyed his roast beef. Even the coffee was hot and tasted like fresh brewed coffee. The canteen was a constant presence for the duration of the siege at John and Al's.

At eight thirty that morning we were ordered to return to our command.

End of tour.

During the afternoon of that second day, our hostage negotiators arranged for a trade: Three hostages for a doctor, a nurse and medical supplies to treat the injured criminal who had been shot in the abdomen.

Fourteen and a half hours later I returned to work the first platoon. Same assignment, same corner, same temporary partner, and same RMP on the sidewalk.

The four men from our Eight One who responded to John and Al's the previous day were assigned to duties inside the station house as were the men in the Nine O. My partner was one of those men.

The NYPD was very conscious of stress-related incidents. The John and Al's standoff was a nine on that scale, resulting in those first responders getting the change of assignment. I'm sure the Borough Commander decided it was a reasonable and prudent decision.

We answered our jobs, but always returned to our corner. At about three a.m., the driver of the APC moved the tank closer to the front of the store. I have no idea why, but he must have received orders from the command post and it did generate a response from the criminals.

They opened up at the APC with their high-powered rifles. Whack, whack, whack. That vehicle could take a lot more than they could deliver. Then they turned their fire on the buildings and storefronts across from their location. Shooting holes in the large glass windows and taking chunks of brick and concrete from the buildings. (Some of the damage is visible to this day.)

Eventually their bullets came closer to our corner. When that happened, several photographers made a mad rush to our RMP, but as the bullets began smacking against the buildings about fifty feet from where we were, they ran for cover.

The 12-gauge shotgun slugs were very loud as they hit the

façade and the sound of those high-powered weapons being fired from inside the store was like cannon fire. It must have been deafening to the hostages. The barrage lasted several minutes and then total silence . . . again

At about four thirty, a man approached us from across Broadway. He lifted the yellow "Crime scene tape" and just walked right up to us and identified himself as a fireman assigned to a Queens firehouse. I could see he had been drinking and most certainly should not be driving a car, but he was here and out of respect for firemen we decided to listen to what he had to say.

"Officers, my name is Jimmy Johnson and I'm a NYC fireman. I've been watching this go down for the past two days and I want to offer myself as a hostage if they will release all the other hostages. I'm sure they would rather have a fireman over civilians, right? I want to talk to the boss in charge."

After hearing what he had to say I was happy the media people were out of hearing range because there is no doubt they would have jumped all over Jimmy the fireman. There wasn't much else going on and they would at least have a human interest story to report.

I said, "Jimmy, how about a cup of coffee and a nice sandwich?"

I took Jimmy over to the canteen and got him a container of coffee, a turkey sandwich, and several doughnuts. I watched as he enjoyed his snack. He seemed like a nice guy who just got caught up in the moment. No doubt he envisioned himself as someone who would risk injury or death for the recognition he would receive. If he had his way, the name Jimmy Johnson would go down in history as the fireman who sacrificed himself to save ten innocent hostages.

The NYPD and the NYFD have had a long, friendly, but sometimes adversarial relationship. The Finest vs the Bravest was, is, and will forever be, but we respect each other. That morning I took care of Jimmy the fireman.

"Jimmy, how you feeling?"

"Good. When can I talk to the boss?"

"Unfortunately the boss left for a while, how about another cup of coffee and another sandwich?"

"No thanks."

"Where are you parked?"

"Down the block on Myrtle Avenue behind those police cars."

"Okay, let's go back to your car. You take a nap and as soon as the boss gets back, I'll wake you."

"Okay and thanks. I am a little tired."

"Jimmy, I want you to do me a favor. You don't have to, but I would really appreciate you giving me the keys to your car."

His first reaction was to give me a look of "No way and why do you want my keys." I just kept looking at him and finally he went into his pocket and gave me the keys.

"Thank you, Jimmy, when the boss returns I'll wake you."

I returned to the corner. About an hour later Jimmy returned.

"Officer, can I have my keys back?"

"How you feeling, Jimmy?"

"Much better, thanks. Can I have my keys, I want to go home."

"You ARE going home, right?"

"Yes. Thank you for the coffee, the sandwich, and the doughnuts."

There was no more talk about wanting to see the boss. I walked Jimmy to his car. I could see he was sober enough to drive. He made a U-turn and I watched as he drove down Myrtle Avenue toward Queens.

The remainder of that tour was uneventful. We returned to the station house at eight a.m., End of Tour.

At about two the following afternoon, forty-four hours after the onset of the longest siege in New York City history the criminals were distracted by noise from an adjacent building. The store manager, Gerry Ricardo, took advantage of that time and was able to tear a hole in the half-inch plasterboard covering an old stairway. He led the seven men and two women to the roof. Our boys in blue, who were on the roof, escorted the ten former hostages to safety.

At approximately four forty-five p.m. the criminals emerged from the store with their hands up. Without their hostages they had lost their ability to bargain. The end was inevitable.

After a trial in Brooklyn State Supreme Court, the recently converted to Islam gunmen were found guilty of forty-one counts including murder of a police officer, kidnapping and robbery. They were sentenced to twenty-five years to life in prison.

25

MY EXPERIENCE AS A VICTIM OF ATTEMPTED ROBBERY

As a police officer I learned early in my career to expect the unexpected.

While working a day tour we received a call from Central: Eight One Charlie respond to a 10-53 (motor vehicle accident) Ralph and Chauncey.

It didn't take long to realize this was a simple accident. No injuries, minimal damage. I asked the drivers for their documents, after which I spent a few moments interviewing them to gather the information needed to write the narrative on the accident report.

As I began writing I looked at the license the driver of vehicle number one handed me. James Brown gave me a forged driver's license. A good forgery, but not good enough.

"Mr. Brown, would you mind telling me where you got this driver's license."

"From the Department of Motor vehicles."

"No really, where did you get this license?"

At that moment his eyes gave him away. He knew that I knew it was a phony license. He admitted he bought it from a friend. I told him he was under arrest, handcuffed him, and placed him in the rear seat of our RMP. Bob told the other motorist to meet us at the Eight One Precinct SH where we would complete the paperwork.

When I arrived with my prisoner, another member of the command, Charlie Irig, had a prisoner in the cell, so we shared the arrest processing room. By three thirty we were ready to transport our prisoners to Brooklyn Criminal Court.

The desk officer was a good boss who never forgot how it was to be a cop, so when we asked if we could change into our civilian clothes he said yes. We would be more comfortable during the many hours required to arraign our prisoners in night court.

Fast forward to seven p.m. We completed what needed to be done in the "Complaint Room" and our rap sheets (fingerprint record) came back, so we were ready to proceed to Part AR Two. (The evening/night arraignment part.) We delivered our folders to the Bridgeman (court officer) and waited to be called. At eight thirty the judge recessed for dinner.

On a Saturday evening that area is very quiet. We had one crummy greasy spoon restaurant to choose from, but they served a pretty good cup of coffee.

As we neared the front door we were engaged in light conversation, but noticed two men standing in the doorway. They were standing side by side about three feet in front of the door. As we approached I noticed one had a knife in his hand and the other had a belt, with a large buckle, wrapped around his hand, dangling the buckle in a menacing manner.

The guy with the knife said, "Give me your money." I could not believe it, we were being robbed. This was a new experience. What was I supposed to do? I could give him my money, but then how was I supposed to pay for my coffee? I think I'll go with plan B. I punched the knifeman in the face several times; he was shocked and didn't expect my response. He went down, hard. Charlie did the same to the other guy and now we were able to unzip our jackets to get to our guns. Surprise . . . You're under arrest. No doubt that wasn't the way Mo and Jo expected this caper to play out.

We handcuffed the stickup team and took them into the restaurant. Charlie called 911 requesting a sector and a sergeant to respond to our location. When they arrived we told the sergeant what took place and asked the sector to transport our prisoners to their precinct, the precinct of arrest.

We returned to Part AR Two, found a court officer in a rear office and explained what had occurred. I told him we needed to have our prisoners arraigned by an assigned officer. After providing him with our list of available return dates, we drove to the Seven Eight Precinct SH where our prisoners were waiting for us. I arrested the guy with the knife and Charlie took the guy with the belt. After I completed the paperwork and while finger-printing my prisoner, he said, "Listen, can we talk somewhere private?"

"Sure, let's finish the fingerprints, and then we can talk all you want."

I took him into the restroom so he could wash his hands. He kept looking around and seemed nervous.

"How would you like to make fifty thousand dollars?"

"I would like that just fine. How am I going to make that kind of money?"

I knew where this was going and I needed time to make a call to the Internal Affairs Division (IAD).

"The guy I cop from always has a lot of money and shit in his apartment. You and your friend have guns; I'll take you to his place and get him to open the door. You get all the money and we get the shit."

"I need to talk to my partner before I can make any deals."

I took him back to the cell and found a phone in an adjacent room. I called Internal Affairs and told the detective I was in the Seven Eight Precinct SH and in the process of being bribed. I wanted to record the offer. He said he would meet me in twenty minutes. I brought Charlie up to speed and told him we needed to stall our arrest processing to give the IAD detective time. I returned to the desk officer and explained where I was with this new development.

"Lieutenant, while fingerprinting my prisoner he offered me a bribe. I called IAD and a detective is on his way with a recorder."

"Good work, Officer Fitzgerald. I'll call you when he arrives."

An arrest for bribery was not something I would need to clear with the DO before calling IAD. In the early seventies, the Knapp Commission exposed extensive corruption in the NYPD, ergo bribery arrests were given high priority and very appreciated by the department. He told me to do what I needed to do and if he could be of assistance just let me know.

I returned to the squad room and my prisoner.

"I have to get the lieutenant on the desk to allow me to cut you both loose and that's not going to be easy. I'll need to give him something."

"I don't care what you do with the money as long as we get out of here."

As I was ending my conversation, Charlie asked to speak to me and I joined him in the hall. He introduced me to the detective from IAD and we went into that adjacent office where he explained the procedure for bribery arrests.

The person making the bribe/offer needed to do so of his own free will. It had to be a clear offer of money or benefit in return for release from arrest. The detective then taped a recording device/wire to my chest under my shirt.

We returned to the squad room, unlocked the cell door, and took the two prisoners to the restroom. I was the person being bribed and I would be the lead when accepting the offer.

Once we were in the restroom, Charlie closed the door and I got very close to my new friend. I said, "Now that my partner is here you need to go over what you told me before, especially the part about us getting money." He didn't miss a beat and went right to the offer, explaining that he knew this drug dealer who always had a lot of money and drugs in his apartment.

"I'll take you guys to my guy. I cop from him every day so I won't have a problem getting him to open the door. When he opens the door we go in and rip him off."

"Does he have a gun?"

"Yeah, but I know where he keeps it and he won't have it when he opens the door. You guys get all the money. We get cut loose, we get the shit, and I want the gun."

"Don't even think about it. You get the dope, no gun. We get the cash and the gun. Now about the cash, how much did you say we will walk away with?"

"At least fifty grand."

"You expect me to believe your dealer will have fifty thousand dollars in his apartment."

"At least. He is big and does a lot of work in the whole neighborhood. Everybody cops from him, He can do keys if you want that much product. When you see his apartment you'll know what I'm talking about."

"So he has a nice place?"

"Yeah. It's like super cool. It used to be a factory by the river, but now it's all big apartments."

"Where is this super cool big apartment?"

"You'll know when we get there, but it's not very far and you can see the bridge from his window."

"What bridge?"

"The Brooklyn Bridge. You can see the Brooklyn Bridge from his window."

"Why is this big-time dope dealer, living in a super cool apartment, selling shit to a street punk ass like you?"

"He's my cousin." With that last answer I knew I wasn't going to get the exact location, so I ended the conversation. I thought we had enough for the bribery charge. We returned the prisoners to their cell and told them we were going to talk to the lieutenant about cutting them loose.

We rejoined the IAD detective and confirmed we had enough to make the arrest for bribery. The recording was perfect. Then I asked if he knew the penal law charge for attempted bribery, because considering we weren't actually going to receive the promised benefit, to wit, the money, we couldn't charge them with bribery.

That's when I learned something new. He explained there is no such charge as attempted bribery in the penal law. Once the offer was made the crime was committed, end of story. We could now add bribery to the attempted robbery, possession of weapons and resisting arrest charges.

The detective told us he would make a copy of the tape available when needed in court. We thanked him and returned to speak to the desk officer. I told him that the bribe offer was recorded and we were going to add that charge.

He reminded me that our prisoners required medical attention and he asked if we were ready to transport them to Brooklyn College Hospital. I said yes and he told the TS operator to have a sector respond to the station house. Both criminals were injured during the arrest and they would never have been arraigned without the "treated and released" forms signed by a doctor.

We returned to the squad room and told our prisoners we were ready to go. They were both happy because they were about to be freed. Then they were going to get high on the dope we were going to get from the robbery. Their attitude changed when we put handcuffs on them.

"Let's go, we're taking you to the hospital."

"We don't need the hospital, we need to get high."

"I got some bad news for you. You are going to the hospital and then you're going to a cell for the night. Tomorrow you're both going to court. More bad news; I added the charge of bribery to the other charges."

His response: "You ****** *** ***** ****** ******* ."

You will need to use your imagination to fill in the stars.

My prisoner tried to kick me and then he tried to head butt me, so once again . . . necessary force was required. As he tried the head butt, I caught him with a short left hook just above the right eye, resulting in a deep two-inch gash at the eyebrow. The wound was bloody, but I found a rag that I used to stop the bleeding.

Of course the desk officer wanted to know why my prisoner was in worse shape on the way out than he was on the way in.

"Officer Fitzgerald, what happened to your prisoner?"

"Lieutenant, when I told him he wasn't going home he tried to assault me . . . again . . . I did my best to stop that assault and I was successful. I wasn't injured, he was. Now we're ready to take them to the hospital."

He accepted my explanation. The sector arrived and transported our prisoners to Long Island College Hospital. My guy received twelve stitches over the right eye and the other mope was treated for his superficial injuries.

We got the medical forms needed at arraignment and transported them to the Eight Four Precinct. Night court was closed and they would be lodged there until their trip to see the judge the next day. Charlie and I returned to the Eight One, showered, and got a few hours' sleep. By eight a.m. we were on our way to the Eight Four Precinct and then on to Brooklyn Criminal Court with our prisoners. They both had extensive criminal records. The ADA requested high bail, but ten bucks was high enough. Between the two of them, they didn't have the price for a pack of gum.

Three days after arraignment we were testifying in the Grand Jury, where they were both indicted as charged. Now we were ready for trial in Brooklyn Supreme Court.

We were assigned to the Brooklyn DA's office for several days to assist our prosecutor as he prepared this case. As I wrote earlier, bribery arrests were very high on the priority list, so the NYPD as well as the Brooklyn DA's office wanted a conviction on this one.

Transcribing the recorded bribe offer to paper was labor intensive. The DA wanted the jurors to be able to read along with the recording as it was played at trial. It was not unusual to have words lost or hard to understand when listening to a tape.

What we thought would be about four hours' work took almost two days before it was perfect. Upon completion there was absolutely no loss in translation and every word could be followed and understood.

We were notified to appear for trial in Brooklyn Supreme Court. As we entered the courtroom we saw the two defendants sitting with their lawyer. The judge took the bench and the court officer called the docket. Their lawyer requested a sidebar.

A sidebar was an off-the-record meeting, at the bench, with the judge, the prosecutor, and the defense attorney. Sidebars often resulted in a plea bargain. After a few minutes the court officer called for a short recess, allowing the ADA time to bring us up to speed with this new proposed resolution.

He found an office and we had the following conversation:

"The defense attorney wants to make a deal."

"What's the deal?"

"They will take a plea to attempted robbery to cover all charges and be sentenced to five years in prison. How does that sound?"

"Not good. You know we want a guilty to the bribery. I don't care how much time they do inside, but they must plead guilty to the bribery."

We returned to the courtroom and another sidebar. This time we could hear every word.

"Judge, unfortunately we can't accept the plea offer."

"What is the problem?"

"We want a guilty plea to the attempted robbery and the bribery. There is no issue with the five years, but if the defense can't agree to those terms we are ready to proceed to trial today."

The Legal Aid lawyer took ten seconds to say, "We'll take the deal."

Even though this was a done deal it had to be entered in the court records, so the Legal Aid lawyer began his spiel. "The defendants wish to plead guilty to attempted robbery and bribery to cover all charges." The judge asked the DA if that was acceptable to the people and he responded, "Yes." Now it was the Legal Aid attorney's turn to speak.

"Before sentencing I would like to inform the court that even though the two defendants have a prior history with the criminal justice system, until this arrest neither of them has been in trouble for over seven years."

That's when the judge gave me my first good laugh in court.

"Councilor, have you taken time to review their criminal history?"

"I did scan it, but only briefly."

"Councilor, the reason they have been able to stay out of trouble is because they both spent the past seven years in Attica prison after being convicted for another armed robbery."

Everyone in the room laughed and the judge finally said, "Nice try, Councilor."

The end result was the criminals received room and board for another five years and I received a letter of recognition for my arrest for bribery.

26

THE TRIPLE HOMICIDE

A s I entered the Eight One Precinct SH to drop off a report, the precinct receptionist asked to speak to me away from her desk. She was a civilian member of the department and told me the man sitting in front of her desk came in to report that he thought he might have committed a crime the night before. She told him he had to speak to a police officer and that's when I just happened to walk in.

We walked to her desk and I introduced myself to the man. He told me his name was Wayne Johnson. I asked if I could help him and he replied yes. He wanted to talk to me about a possible murder. With that statement I took a long hard look into his eyes. There was no sign of emotion. I took him into a side office and asked the receptionist to have my partner join me as I began questioning Wayne.

"Wayne, you want to talk to me about a possible murder, right?"

"Yes."

"I'm having difficulty with the 'possible' part of that statement. Can you give me more information about the murder?"

He began in such a matter-of-fact manner; it was like he was telling me about going to a ball game with his friends.

"Officer, I went to see my girlfriend last night, she lives with her grandparents. When I got there her grandmother didn't want to let me in. She told me she didn't want her granddaughter seeing me anymore. We started arguing and I got mad because she was nasty, she had no right telling me I couldn't see my girl-friend. We're both grown people.

"Then her grandfather came out of the bedroom and pushed me into the kitchen. I hit my head on the wall. He's a big man and I was afraid so I grabbed a knife sitting on the table. My girlfriend tried to take the knife away from me and her grandma and grandpa were beating me all over and that's when I think I killed them."

I asked why he "thought" he killed them and he said he wasn't sure. He remembered leaving the apartment and walking home and going to sleep. When he woke up that morning he found the clothes he wore the night before had blood on them.

He took a shower, put on clean clothes, and came to the precinct to speak to a police officer.

This issue was clearly beyond my zone of influence. I walked him up the one flight so he could tell his story to the detectives.

My partner had requested four hours' lost time, so he left for the day. There were two detectives working and I knew both very well. James Wilson was a lazy do-nothing and I never understood how he got a gold shield. The other detective, Bob McGovern was a very sharp guy and without a doubt the more competent of the two.

I introduced Wayne to them and asked him to repeat his story, which he did, in detail. They asked him questions and he gave them answers. The interview went on for about fifteen minutes. Finally James got up and with a look of disgust on his face told me to call for a bus, as there was no doubt I had a psycho on my hands. I could see he thought I was wasting his time, so he went back to reading his newspaper.

After listening to Bob question Wayne, I began to believe he actually did kill his girlfriend and her grandparents. I told Bob we should at least try to find the crime scene. He agreed. He called the Seven Seven Precinct and spoke to the desk officer.

During their interview, Wayne was able to give us the name of a street and a description of the house. He said it was next to a vacant lot and there was a tailor shop on the ground floor. Bob gave that info to the Seven Seven DO and asked him to have his sectors canvass their zones looking for the house.

I asked Wayne if he would mind waiting in the cell located in the squad room. He said no and I brought him a cold drink. (I want to make it clear; up to that moment Wayne was as calm as calm could be. I didn't see the need to cause him to be alarmed by forcing him into the cell, but if he decided he didn't feel like going in . . . He was going in one way or another.)

About thirty minutes later, the Seven Seven Precinct DO called and told Bob the sectors completed the search for the building. No luck. Bob thanked him and said, "I guess it's time to take Wayne to KCH "G" building." (Psych ward.)

I thought it would be best to have Wayne stay in the cell awaiting the ambulance. I called down to the TS operator and asked him to call for a bus as I began preparing the forms required for this aided case. James gave me an "I told you so" smirk.

About forty- five minutes later the TS operator called to inform me the ambulance had arrived. I took Wayne out of the cell and escorted him down the stairs to the bus. I was just about to assist the now-handcuffed, possible psycho, into the ambulance when Bob yelled out the window: "Jack, bring him back up here." I told the ambulance driver to wait a minute and I returned to the squad room with Wayne.

Bob said, "Jack, put your prisoner back in the cell and tell the ambulance driver he can leave, Wayne will be with us for a while."

I returned him to the cell and asked Bob what happened. He told me that as I was walking down stairs, the Seven Seven DO called again and said their sergeant found a building that fit

Wayne's description. He rang the bell and finally someone from the first floor let him in. He went to the second floor where the incident was reported to have taken place. After pounding on the door with no response, he kicked it in and found the three murder victims.

Their DO wanted to speak to me.

"Officer Fitzgerald, I want you to bring your prisoner to the Seven Seven Precinct. Our Brooklyn North homicide detectives will assist you with this arrest."

(At that time the NYPD had what was called specialization units and the homicide unit for Brooklyn North was at the Seven Seven Precinct.)

I took Wayne to their office and handed him over to Detective Joseph Campizi. He lodged our prisoner and asked me to accompany him to the crime scene.

I have seen more than my share of bloody homicide scenes, but that one was way over the top. The girlfriend and the grandmother were lying dead on the kitchen floor. Both covered with blood. The grandfather was also dead and on the living room floor in a pool of blood. There was a small dog in the apartment and he too was covered in blood. The dog had had at least twelve hours to explore the five rooms.

He rolled around in the massive pools of blood, causing his white fur to turn blood red. He left a blood trail in every room, on every piece of furniture; the entire apartment reeked of blood. That was a surreal experience.

After a short while I returned to the Seven Seven Homicide Squad with Joe. I prepared the arrest forms. I was the arresting officer and Joe was the assigned detective. We eventually took our prisoner to BCB and on to Brooklyn Criminal Court where, after arraignment, Wayne was held without bail. The judge ordered a psychiatric evaluation for him at Kings County Hospital.

I never saw Wayne Johnson again, ever. I didn't give that arrest much thought, but one day about six months later I met Joe Campizi in court and asked him if he had heard anything about our Wayne Johnson case. He told me that he sent a message to my command notifying me of the disposition, which I never received. He told me that Wayne Johnson was admitted to a psychiatric hospital for the criminally insane and the chances for his release were nonexistent.

Postscript

I have been asked why someone didn't respond to the victims' screams that must have been part of this horrendous murder. The only answer I have is the one I received most of the time when I asked that same question at so many crime scenes: "I didn't want to get involved and it was none of my business." That was life and death in the ghetto.

27

JUST ONE OF THOSE DAYS

I t was a sweltering Sunday in August and I was working a four to midnight tour in Sector Frank-Henry with Billy Correa. Our first job out of the box was a 10-53 collision on Guernsey Street. Guernsey was exactly one block from the SH and a very narrow street. When we couldn't find a parking space for our private vehicles, Guernsey was always a last resort. Thank goodness not on that Sunday.

(For you to truly appreciate the scene I'm writing about, I must provide more information: The zone is Guernsey from Norman Avenue to Meserole Avenue. One block, about three hundred and fifty feet long. Maybe fifteen five-story walk-up tenements on both sides of the street for the entire length. Each building had ten apartments. That's a lot of people crammed into one narrow block.

On any given Sunday, in the summer, we could expect between one and two hundred people/kids hanging out on the stoop or playing on the block.

There was parking on both sides of the narrow street, which allowed for one vehicle to drive through the passageway created by the always present cars.)

We drove the one block to Guernsey and Norman and discovered the street was backed-up to the scene of the collision, a good three hundred feet away. Bill got out and walked to the job-site and I took the RMP back to the SH. Now it was my turn to walk.

As I approached the scene I could see Bill engaged in conversation with about six people. Six very unhappy people and they all wanted this one Polish guy crucified; my words, but you get the picture. That one man had everyone really pissed off.

"Bill, what's going on?"

"Jack, I'm still trying to find someone who knows."

As I was talking to Bill, a guy I knew from the neighborhood came over and said, "Jack, you ain't gonna believe what happened."

"Hey Lenny, how have you been? Did you witness what went down?"

"Yeah."

"So I'm waiting, give me the blow by blow."

"See that woman over there? Well, she was driving the Chevy. She pulled up to the parking space and tried to back in. You know how tough it is to park on this block. It's a tight space, so it took forever and she just couldn't park her car. Now it's takin' at least ten minutes and the block is backed up to Norman, but she won't give up. The horns are beeping, the people are yelling, but she won't give up.

"Then the driver of the car behind her got out and walked to her car. He said something to her, opened her door, and then he pushed her over and got behind the wheel. When he tried to park her car he hit the gas and as you can see, he struck three cars on the right side, then he bounced off and hit two more on the left."

Bill had several owners of the damaged cars identified and he began trying to locate the rest. I went to the woman who was now sitting behind the wheel of her car.

"Good afternoon, my name is Police Officer Fitzgerald; may I have your driver's license, registration and insurance card?"

"Yes. Here's my license and registration. I'll look for my insurance card."

"Your name is Elizabeth Jablonski and I see you own this Chevy."

"Yes."

"Elizabeth, can you tell me what happened here today?"

"Yes. I came to see my friend, she lives at One Seventy-Seven Guernsey and I had trouble parking my car. I always have trouble parking on this block. So the cars were honking and then a man, who I don't know, came over to me and said he would park my car for me. I said no, but he opened my door and pushed me over and got behind the wheel.

"As he tried to park my car he stepped on the gas instead of the brake and he smashed into all those cars. I don't even know how many cars he smashed. Officer, I also think he's been drinking. I could smell alcohol on his breath."

"Okay, Elizabeth, I want to help you, but I need to know what you want to do here."

"What do you mean?"

"There are five cars that were damaged by the guy who took control of your car. Let me explain your two options: Option number one, we prepare the accident report and that will make you responsible for all the damage to the five cars. I don't know how that will affect your insurance, but I wouldn't be surprised if your company raised your premiums."

"Officer, that's not fair. I wasn't driving when he hit those cars."

"Then you have option number two and listen to me, Elizabeth, you really must consider that option. You told me you don't know that man. He opened your door, got in your car, forcing you from the driver's seat and took control of your car. As you described what happened, you did not give him permission to take control of your car. Am I right?"

"That's right. I did not give him permission."

"So according to the penal law, that guy stole your car with you in it. It's called carjacking / robbery . . ."

I knew what I was saying was a stretch and going to the edge of that crime as described in the penal law. I also knew it would never be prosecuted as such. But at that time I was 100 percent correct with that charge.

"Okay, Elizabeth, we'll arrest him on your complaint, which will free you from liability in this accident."

"What do I need to do now, Officer Fitzgerald?"

"You must find your insurance card and then we will go to the precinct where we will continue preparing the forms."

I asked Bill how he was doing locating the owners of the damaged vehicles. Mission accomplished.

"Jack, I have everyone and I think we should take this into the house."

"I'm with you, Bill, let's go. Oh and one more thing: How would you like a collar for robbery and grand larceny auto?"

"What robbery? What GLA?"

"I'll explain everything when we get to the SH. You get all the car owners and take them to the precinct and I'll take care of the prisoner."

I parked Elizabeth car in the still available space and then found a space for the prisoner's car. As I escorted the guy who caused this debacle he asked me why he needed to go with me. He had plans to visit his friend at a party. As we walked in front of the desk officer I informed him he was under arrest, I also advised him of his rights. He had great difficulty understanding why he was being arrested but quite frankly, I really didn't care.

Bill had the five owners in the muster room when I arrived with Stanley. I told the DO what I had and when he asked who would be the arresting officer, I told him I needed to talk to my partner.

I brought Bill up to speed with this unusual incident.

"Bill, this collar will begin as one under arrest for robbery and grand larceny auto. It will be reduced on the first return date or before, to unauthorized use of a vehicle. I doubt you will need to appear in court a third time. If by chance it does go to a hearing, I'll have the ADA subpoena me, because I interviewed the complainant and I'll interview the prisoner with you. There will be overtime involved, so unless you just don't want this, it's yours. If not, I'll take it, but Billy, a robbery and a GLA collar will look good on your activity report."

"Thanks, Jack. I'll take it. I could use the arrest activity and I most certainly can use the OT."

I told the desk officer that Bill was the arresting officer. We prepared the accident reports and I told Elizabeth she would need to meet with the district attorney later that day. I also told her I would make sure she got a ride to Central Booking.

When Bill and I began the arrest process, Stanley was reasonably cooperative. It was obvious this was his first time in the criminal justice system. He may have consumed alcohol earlier in the day, but he was not toxed now.

"Stanley, what happened today?"

"Officer this is crazy. That woman couldn't park her car. She tried for about fifteen minutes and I could see she was never going to get the car in the space. I tried to help her. I opened her door, told her to move over and I got behind the wheel. As I tried to park her car my foot slipped off the brake and onto the gas and I hit those cars. I'm sorry. I didn't mean to do it. It was an accident and now I'm under arrest."

I did feel a little sorry for Stanley. I'm sure every word he said was true. There was no criminal intent, but the police are not permitted to do the judging. Our discretion goes only so far. It wouldn't have been fair for Elizabeth to suffer the consequences for Stanley's impulsive act.

I asked Stanley for his documents, to wit, his license, registration and insurance card. I made copies of his driver's license and his insurance card and gave them to the five owners of the cars that were damaged. I also gave Elizabeth a copy for her insurance company as they would most certainly want to pass this on to Stanley's company.

Postscript

My prediction, regarding the outcome of this arrest, was close. I asked Bill to tell the ADA exactly what Stanley told us. He also told the ADA we followed the letter of the law when charging him with robbery and GLA, but we, the arresting officers, didn't think Stan was trying to steal her car.

The ADA agreed. Stanley had no prior arrests, so the charges were reduced at arraignment to unauthorized use of a vehicle. The ADA conferred with the Legal Aid attorney and Billy's prisoner was given an ACD (adjourned in contemplation of dismissal). As long as he stayed out of trouble for the next six months, this arrest would be stricken from his record.

Stanley was happy, Elizabeth was very happy, and Bill and I were happy. Justice was served.

28

THE IDIOT MOTORIST

After spending all morning testifying at a robbery trial, I returned to the Nine Four Precinct and asked to be assigned to summons enforcement in my unmarked RMP.

As I was monitoring the signal light at the corner of Meeker and Graham avenues, an accident-prone location, I observed the driver of a Mercedes-Benz go through a dead red light at that intersection. I followed the driver as he made a left onto east-bound Meeker Avenue, which was a heavily traveled road. I put the small FBI light on the dash, pulled up alongside his vehicle, and motioned him to the curb. I was in uniform, so there could be no doubt that I was a police officer.

As I approached, he was exiting his vehicle. I had him join me on the sidewalk away from traffic and asked to see his license, registration, and insurance card. His response was, "Why, what did I do wrong?" I again asked for his documents and he said he didn't have the registration or insurance card, but he handed me his license. I asked where his registration and insurance card were and he said his wife had them. It was her car and he forgot to get them from her.

I told him that I stopped him because he went through the red signal light at Graham and Meeker avenues. I also told him he could sit in his car as I returned to my RMP to run his plate number to see if it was stolen. Eventually Central gave me a 10-17, not stolen.

As I began writing the summonses, I saw him approaching my car. He was walking in an oncoming traffic lane, so I got out and said, "Mr. Green, return to your vehicle. I don't want you to get hit by a car. I'll be with you shortly."

"What's your name?"

"I'll write and print my name at the bottom of the summonses, but I want you to return to your car."

I could see he was annoyed. I wrote him for the signal light, no registration and no insurance card. As I approached his car, he got out and was waiting for me. He was about two feet from the many cars and trucks driving by on that three-lane major artery. I told him to join me on the sidewalk away from traffic. I handed him his license as well as the three summonses. I read my name as written on the bottom of the summonses.

I explained that if he had the registration and insurance card, all he needed to do was plead not guilty, make copies of those documents and send them with the summonses as proof of his not guilty plea. I then told him he could plead not guilty on the red light summons and he would have his case heard before a judge in traffic court.

I'd met his type before. He was probably a wealthy businessman and not at all used to being told what to do. His position in life was at least five steps above that of a lowly cop who had the audacity to stop and detain him for the fifteen minutes it took to write the summonses.

In a very condescending tone he again demanded my name and my shield number. He rambled on about how he paid my salary and he spends more on lunch than I made in a week yada, yada, yada. I'd heard it all before. What he was actually trying to do was get me to do or say something foolish, allowing him to make a civilian complaint. He wanted payback.

There was no way on earth he was going to get me to react to his rants. I responded to his abuse as a professional police officer. Yes sir no sir, I was very good at that. Finally he took a pad out of his vehicle and demanded I write my name and shield number for him. I thought to myself, come on, bozo, you're making it too easy, just get back into your car and drive away. But no, this guy had to have his pound of flesh.

He could not comprehend that he wasn't going to get me to do or say anything stupid.

I pointed to my shield and name tag and said, "Mr. Green, you have a pen and paper and unless there is a reason why you can't write, you can note that information yourself."

"No, I want you to write it for me, unless YOU don't know how to write."

As I returned to my vehicle I saw him following me. This guy wouldn't give up. I really didn't want this issue to escalate into an arrest, but I could see it was going in that direction. As I opened my door he was right next to me, yelling in my face. Now he was desperate.

He couldn't allow me to just drive away. I'm sure he treated his underlings with the same nasty aggressive attitude he tried using on me. That was Mister Green's personality and he was comfortable with it because I'm sure he was usually successful with that approach.

It wasn't working. In my most concerned voice I said, "Mister Green, I can see you are upset, but I don't want you to get hit by a car or truck, so please either return to your vehicle or stand on the sidewalk. I have work to do, so I'm leaving."

I got into my RMP, closed the door, and with that he ran around to the curb side. I could see out of the corner of my eye he moved his foot as though he was putting it under my front tire. Now I knew there was no way anyone in their right mind would make such a stupid move. He was bluffing. I told him I was leaving, end of story, right? Wrong!!!!!

Folks, you can't make this stuff up. That idiot actually thought he would stop me from driving away by placing his foot under my front tire.

The best part of my story is he did call the Civilian Complaint Review Board and he did give me a civilian complaint. This was one of the complaints that did not require a visit to Manhattan to be interviewed by a sergeant and a lieutenant at CCRB.

I was interviewed by our Nine Four Precinct Integrity Control Officer. Lieutenant Korchinski was an honest, fair-minded supervisor. If I was wrong, he would have done what needed to be done.

As I walked into his office he handed me a copy of the complaint and said, "Jack, I'm sure you'll want to keep this for your records." Just before he turned his tape recorder on, he said, "I don't believe this one."

He read the allegation for the record and almost every word on the complaint was true.

The ICO asked me to respond to the complaint; I told him that with the exception of me seeing Mr. Green put his foot under the front tire, every word he wrote was true. I then asked the lieutenant if he felt I could have handled that incident more discreetly. His response: "Based on this complaint, as written by the motorist, I only hope I could have been that discreet. I am sending this back to CCRB as unfounded."

I still have a copy of that civilian complaint.

29

THE DOBERMAN PINSCHER

While on patrol in the Nine Four Precinct, my partner Bill Correa and I received an assignment to investigate a man trapped in his apartment. As we arrived, the caller was waiting for us at his opened window one flight up in a building that was once a factory but had been converted into lofts/apartments.

"Officers, thank goodness you're here. I can't get out of my building, there's a vicious dog under my car. Every time I try to leave, to open the gate, he growls. I'm afraid he's going to bite me."

The building he lived in was separated from the adjacent building by a common driveway about thirty feet wide, which was secured by a chain link fence. A large Doberman pinscher had been able to squeeze between the locked gates and enter the yard, but he couldn't find his way out.

He found shade under the guy's car, but when I called him he came out and approached the gate where I was standing . . . I want to add that I have been bitten by dogs, in the line of duty, twice and this dog didn't look very friendly to me. I asked the caller if he had food I could use to lure the dog back to my side of the gate. He said all he had was a can of sardines.

I knew that wouldn't work. As I was about to tell him we were going to call the ASPCA, his two friends showed up in their pickup truck. The caller asked them if they had food with them and the driver said yes, they had cold cuts which they just purchased for lunch. I asked what they had . . . Ham.

I asked Bill to get the rope we kept in the trunk of our RMP. I then asked the guy with the food to give me some ham. He peeled off one wafer-thin slice and handed it to me.

I called the dog. He came to me and I fed him the tiny piece of ham through the fence. It was such a small piece that when he took it he almost bit my fingers. This dog was hungry. I told the guy I need more ham, so he tried to give me another sliver of meat.

On a good day I have very little patience. I usually start off, on a scale of one to ten, somewhere between a one and a two, but this cold cut guy was taking me down to ZERO very fast.

I grabbed the ham, rolled the entire pound into a wad and used it to lure the dog close enough to the gate to allow Billy to put the noose around his neck. Finally I was able to lead him out through the small opening and onto the sidewalk.

Now our caller could leave his building. One problem solved one to go. I didn't trust this dog, but we needed to transport him to the SH and secure him until the ASPCA arrived.

There was no way I was going to put that large Doberman in the backseat of our RMP. My only option was to walk him the five blocks to the SH. I petted him and he responded. Nice dog!

As I began walking away with Rover, the guy with the ham asked me what was going to happen to the dog. Now this was a purebred Doberman, a beautiful animal that probably got away from his owner.

There was no collar or identifying tags; I told him I was going to take him to our precinct station house, put him in a cage that we had on hand for that purpose, and I would then call ASPCA. I went on to tell him ASPCA would take him to their facility and if no one claimed him, he would be euthanized.

"Officer, he seems like such a nice friendly dog, can I

keep him?"

"I would hate to see this dog put down, so I'll let you have him, but you must agree that if anyone reports a missing Doberman and this is that dog, you will give him up. Or, if you decide you no longer want this dog, you promise to call me at the precinct and I will return and take him to the ASPCA."

He agreed, gave me his identification so I knew where he lived, and off he went with the dog.

About a month later, while parked not far from where the dog incident took place, a man approached our RMP.

"Hi, do you remember me?"

"No, should we?"

"Remember that Doberman you said was a friendly dog and would make a nice pet?"

"Oh, right, you're the guy who asked us if you could have the dog. I do remember you, but I don't recall saying anything about that dog being friendly or a nice pet. I definitely remember you wanting the dog and I said you could have it, but if there came a time when you didn't want him you should call me and I would pick him up. How is the dog and is there something we can do for you?"

"You see my face? You see my Fu**** scar. That Fu**** dog did this to me."

"Wow, the dog did that to you? What happened?"

Then he told us his very sad story: He took the dog home where he lived with his boyfriend Bruce. They both liked the dog, but Bruce let Rover sleep with him in his bedroom. The dog was great company and became very attached to his new owner. Then one night "Stitch" went into Bruce's room and got into bed with him.

The dog went wild and bit his face, causing a severe gash requiring seventy-nine stitches to close the wounds. He called the ASPCA, they came, took the dog, and put it down.

I didn't have the heart to remind him that he promised to call me if he decided he no longer wanted the dog.

30

TWO SHORT STORIES ABOUT INCIDENTS ON THE KOSCIUSKO BRIDGE

Story number one

One night, while working a midnight to eight tour, my partner Bill Correa and I received a call regarding a motor vehicle accident on top of the Kosciusko Bridge. Now before I go further I want to identify the conditions we were working under that night: It was raining, storming, wind blowing like crazy, in fact we were working in a hurricane. The winds on the ground, according to the weather report, were measured at seventy-five MPH, which meant the wind at the top of that bridge had to be in excess of one hundred miles an hour.

The two vehicles were traveling westbound into Brooklyn from Queens, so we needed to drive into Queens and come back over the bridge to aid the motorists. It had been raining all day and I was not familiar with the lay of the roads in Queens, but a road is a road, right? As I drove our RMP on the eastbound Long Island Expressway service road, I saw a puddle that went the entire width of the road.

I slowed and proceeded through the puddle until the water came into the vehicle through the door. Lo and behold Billy and I found ourselves sitting in the puddle that was about three feet deep. I must admit I am not a mechanic, but I am a quick study. I learned when a car motor is submerged in water it stops running.

Great, now we're sitting in a puddle in our RMP, wet up to our seat and I couldn't move the friggin' car. We were truly "dead in the water." I asked myself, "Can it get any worse?" We sat there and called for department tow. Calling for another RMP to push us out would result in another sector car team sitting in the puddle. Then considering it was three fifteen in the morning, I figured department tow would arrive just in time to get us back to the precinct for return roll call.

As we waited I got the answer to my question; yes it could and did get worse. A city bus drove by and had no problem going through the water. We tried to stop him to ask for a push, but he just went through and while doing so he created a wake that brought the water level in our car even higher.

UMMMMM let's review: A NYC bus driver comes driving down the road and he comes upon a marked blue and white NYC police car half underwater just sitting there and he just goes barreling through. What would you think? Maybe he didn't like cops, right?

As we continued sitting in the friggin' lake waiting for the air and sea rescue helicopter to arrive to save our sorry asses, a NYC sanitation truck pulled up behind us. No doubt the driver of that truck liked cops more than the bus driver because he gently pushed us out of Lake L.I.E.

I waited a short time and hoped against all hope the engine would start. I turned the key and after a few cranks the motor started and we were on our way to the collision.

I caught up to the driver of the sanitation truck and thanked him, I also gave him my name, my command phone number, and told him if there was ever anything I could do for him to call me. He never called, but I was ready to return his good deed.

As we approached the scene we found the two vehicles with drivers. There was no need to even try using flares because the wind would have blown them out, but there really wasn't much traffic anyway. Neither car had much damage and both were drivable. Why didn't they just drive the quarter mile to the next exit where they would have been off the bridge and safe?

Billy ordered them to drive to that next exit and we returned to our RMP. I had parked away from the lanes of traffic and as close to the bridge guardrail as possible. While walking back to the car a gust of wind caught my rubber raincoat, which wasn't completely closed, and it became a sail. I was blown against the guardrail with such force that I had to grab and hold on until it died down.

As I hit the rail I looked down. I was a long way from Newtown Creek. A fall that far (exactly one hundred and twenty-five feet) into the polluted water would have been worse than hitting the street.

We had the motorists follow us to the station house, where we prepared the accident reports after changing into dry uniforms.

Story Number Two

I wasn't present for the onset of this job, which occurred on the midnight to eight tour, but one of my close friends was. I aided him by interviewing the sole survivor of this very sad incident.

I was working an eight to four day tour and talking to Lieutenant Cohen, the desk officer, before roll call. He was telling me about an incident that took place on the Kosciusko Bridge an hour ago. Four of our local residents, all young men, had a terrible accident. Three of them are dead and the driver is on the way in.

As he was telling me about that incident, Louie Payton walked in with Carmine the driver of the vehicle.

"Lieutenant, my partner and Sergeant Levine will remain at the scene awaiting the arrival of Highway Patrol, CSU and the medical examiner. No doubt they'll be there a while. I have the parents due any second, so I could use some help."

The DO said, "Jack, Bill took the day off, so maybe you would like a break today. If you want to give Louie a hand, I'll cover your seat."

"That sounds like a good idea. I'll help Louie."

Louie and I took Carmine into my youth office and before he had a chance to say another word the parents of the three young men arrived. Louie asked me to interview Carmine and make out the UF 61 while he met with the parents.

"Your name is Carmine, right?"

"Yes."

"My name is Police Officer Fitzgerald and I need you to tell me what happened last night causing you to be here this morning. Can I get you a cup of coffee or a soda?"

"No thank you. I'm good for now."

This is his story:

It's Saturday evening; Carmine and his three friends decided to visit a club in Queens they visit once in a while. They went to the club for an evening of dancing, drinking, and all-around partying. They had a good time, met some foxy ladies, but didn't score.

At about three thirty, they decided to leave that club to try their luck at an after-hours social club, also in Queens. They drank a little more, they danced a little more, but still no luck and by six-thirty they were ready to call it a night. The four amigos returned to Carmine's big Buick station wagon. Carmine and Anthony got in the front and the other two jumped in the backseat.

As they drove back to Brooklyn on the LIE, Anthony came up with a really cool idea.

"I got a really cool idea. Let's climb out the windows and ride on the roof."

Vito said, "Good idea."

Sally Boy said, "Let's go."

Carmine the driver said, "What are youse guys crazy? Don't be stupid."

So Anthony, Sally-boy and Vito, being young, foolish, and a

little drunk, went out the windows and onto the roof. Onto the roof of a car doing exactly fifty-five miles an hour according to Carmine.

"Officer Fitzgerald, I swear, as I came around that turn going onto the Kosciusko Bridge I lost control of my car. The front went to the rear and I began to go around and around until I hit the rail on the edge of the bridge and that's when my friends flew off the roof."

I could see Carmine was very upset. I believe it was at that moment he finally realized the consequences of that evening. No more Anthony, no more Vito and no more Sally-Boy. His three best friends since childhood were dead and all because of a stupid stunt.

I prepared the scratch copy of the 61 as well as the accident report. My report read as follows: At time and place of occurrence and while driving his vehicle over the Kosciusko Bridge, the driver of the vehicle lost control due to the actions of his three passengers.

Those passengers had climbed out of the vehicle onto the roof. The added weight on the roof caused the driver to lose control of his car. As he lost control, all three passengers were thrown off the top of the car and off the bridge.

Louie told me they found one kid splattered on the ground/side of a factory wall, a second kid on the roof of another factory, and the third kid on the ground about ten feet from Newtown Creek.

I went as far as possible with the required forms. I would need to wait for Highway to complete their on-site investigation before I could complete my work. Our NYPD Highway Patrol was without a doubt the ultimate expert investigators when it came to accident investigations. Especially when those accidents resulted in death.

Lieutenant Cohen asked me to take a ride to the scene to check on their progress.

I told Louie I was leaving and he was in charge of Carmine.

When I arrived I met the Highway Patrol Delegate, who I knew for many years.

"Billy, how are you doing?"

"Good and you?"

"My lieutenant would like to be brought up to speed on your investigation."

"What can I tell you? This is a bad one. The medical examiner was here. The bodies will go to the morgue. Crime Scene is on the way to take pictures and we still need to finalize our sketch of this scene. That will take a while."

He asked me for the back story. I gave him an audio replay from what Carmine told me. I knew he would eventually ask me the one question I didn't want to answer.

"Jack, you know I'll need to give him the Breathalyzer, right?"

"Yeah, but is there a rush? This thing happened at about six-thirty and it's now almost ten. You're over the two-hour limit anyway and believe me Bill, I've been with that kid since a little before eight and he wasn't toxed then and he isn't toxed now. He admitted in his statement they all had a few drinks, but that kid will live with this morning for the rest of his life and I really don't think it was his fault. His dumb friends did something really stupid and they paid the ultimate price."

"Okay. I can't leave here now anyway because we still have a lot to do. You're right, by the time I take him to the Seven Eight precinct for the test I'll be way past the workable time frame."

"Thanks Bill. Believe me, if I thought that kid was guilty of anything, I would tell you."

"Tell your DO we'll be in with the paperwork when we complete what needs to be done here."

I had a brief conversation with Sergeant Levine: "Sarge, Lieutenant Cohen wants to know when he can expect you to resume patrol. "

I was just about to go ten-ninety eight (resuming patrol)

I returned to the precinct and reported to the DO: "Lieutenant

Cohen, I spoke to the Highway Patrol officer handling the bridge incident and he will be in with the paperwork upon completion."

"Jack, see if Louie needs any more help."

I went into our muster room, where Louie was still speaking to the families awaiting my return with news from the scene. I asked Louie to join me in my office.

"Louie, I spoke to the Highway Patrol officer in charge and I know him for a long time. The three kids are on their way to the morgue. He also told me it was bad, so their families should be prepared for the worst when they need to view the bodies at the morgue."

"What about Carmine? Do I have a possible prisoner?"

"No. There won't be any test."

The only other possible charges would be criminally negligent homicide, reckless endangerment or vehicular homicide and none of the above came into play. The bottom line is Carmine did nothing more than drive his car with three foolish friends.

There wasn't much more I could do, so I asked to be assigned to my unmarked RMP with a shotgun.

I resumed patrol!!

End of a very sad story.

31

OUR NEW TOOL TO DEAL WITH OUT OF CONTROL PRISONERS

In the 1980s, we received a new tool to be added to our tool belt, to wit, Mace. While attending our firearms training at the outdoor range we received a canister of Mace, a Mace holder, and about fifteen minutes of training in the use of this new tool. We also received instructions as to what we needed to do if and when the time came we used it.

There were established procedures in place and in a nutshell, after using Mace we were required to transport that person (the Macee) to the nearest hospital where he/she would have their eyes flushed with a special solution. Unless the person was an EDP (psycho), the next step was to take the prisoner to Brooklyn Central Booking for processing.

The procedure was clear: If we Maced someone, who under normal circumstances would have received a universal summons for a violation and then been released at the station house, that person went to BCB and into the criminal justice system. End of story.

One cold Friday evening at about five thirty p.m., we received a call of two men fighting in front of a bar at Greenpoint and Manhattan Avenues The reason I identify the time and day is because on Friday, at that time, that corner is a beehive of pedestrian traffic. There is a subway entrance as well as a bus stop at that location, so we wanted to respond quickly to bring the combatants under control before an innocent bystander was injured.

When we arrived we found the two drunks wrestling on the ground while throwing punches at each other. We tried to pull them apart, but they were both large, very drunk, men. I knew we would need to use "necessary force" to end this violence, but the last thing I needed was another civilian complaint for excessive force, aka alleged police brutality.

My nightstick would have been my only weapon available, but very often when you used a baton there was a bleeding heart cop-hating liberal who would call CCRB or the precinct to make a complaint. The cop hit the poor innocent man for no reason whatsoever . . . The guy wasn't doing anything wrong . . . Why did the cop have to hit him so hard? I've heard them all and been accused of them all. And then there was the guaranteed prisoner's trip to the hospital.. Considering the size of our combatants, there would have been a lot of stitches.

On that afternoon at that location, the guy who invented Mace couldn't have hoped for a better scenario for the use of his product. Perfect. No nightstick, no blood, no CCRB . A simple press of the button and psssssst. Ummmm, make that psssssst again, and again. What the hell? This stuff doesn't work. The two drunks kept fighting. Now Bobby and I were kneeling on their chests spraying Mace directly into their eyes from about six inches away.

Finally, FINALLY they stopped fighting and began screaming as they rubbed their eyes. The more they rubbed the more they screamed because rubbing made it worse, but thank goodness the fight was over. We were able to handcuff our prisoners and stuff them into the backseat of the RM.P. Wow, that Mace finally worked and we didn't need to use a "Bat."

Now we're off to Greenpoint Hospital for the washing of the eyes ceremony. Remember, it was cold out, so we had our windows rolled up. Our Mace instructor never told us about was going to happen next: As I drove I began to feel the effect of the Mace circulating around the inside of our car. My tear ducts were responding to the irritation in my eyes and they began talking to me: Jack, what the **** did you do to us?

I was crying, Bobby Mack was crying, and our two prisoners were definitely crying up a storm because we maced the ever-lovin' shit out of them. I couldn't see, so I pulled the car to the curb. Bob and I got out and used the box of tissues we kept in the car. Don't rub, just dab. We opened all the windows, were good to go.

Greenpoint Hospital wasn't what you would call a cutting-edge facility. Yes they could treat just about any emergency, but mace was a relatively new item and they weren't ready for us when we rolled in.

There was no need to prepare all the forms required to have our prisoners treated because this was a simple procedure. Or at least it should have been.

"Good afternoon, Officers, how can we help you?"

"Good afternoon, Nurse, we all need the mace eyewash treatment."

"What's mace?"

Now we knew we were in trouble. I found a hospital security officer that I knew and he was familiar with mace and the required treatment.

"Griff, maybe you can help. We just maced these two guys and we all need to have our eyes flushed with the mace-flushing stuff."

"Okay Jack, I know exactly what you need, follow me."

He took us to the doctor who was familiar with the "Mace treatment "and he did what needed to be done. Thank you Griff, thank you Doctor, our eyeballs are squeaky clean and we're ready to move on.

We were good to go to BCB with our two combatants, who were under arrest for disorderly conduct. (A violation)

(Now a few words about BCB: Every person arrested in

Brooklyn for a felony crime was processed at BCB. Most misdemeanor crimes and violations are handled at the precinct of arrest with a desk appearance ticket or a universal summons and released. The felons are processed and held for arraignment in Brooklyn Criminal Court.)

BCB was usually a simple process. Everyone knew exactly what they needed to do. We logged our prisoners with their names, what they were charged with, followed by photos. Easy, right? Maybe not so easy tonight.

On that evening, the sergeant working admissions would make an easy process very difficult. That sergeant resembled Fred Sanford from the comedy series *Sanford and Son*. He looked, walked, and spoke like Fred Sanford.

When we arrived and signed in, the APO (arrest processing officer) assigned to that desk asked what our prisoners were charged with. Disorderly Conduct. Sergeant Fred stopped what he was doing, which was usually nothing, and now we had his undivided attention.

"Officer, how long have you worked in Brooklyn?"

"Most of my fifteen years on the job, Sergeant."

"I guess you don't come to BCB often, right, Officer?"

"Wrong, Sergeant, in fact I am a very active member of my command and spend more time here than most."

"Then why did you bring' those two men charged with disorderly conduct, a violation, to my BCB?

"Because we needed to use mace while making this arrest."

I guess Fred never read the amendment to the Patrol Guide related to arrest procedures. He immediately caught an attitude and yelled "OUT, GET THOSE MEN OUT OF HERE. THEY DON'T BELONG HERE. GO . . . NOW."

I couldn't believe my good fortune. I didn't like Fred, the officers assigned to BCB hated Fred, and now I was going to have the opportunity to mess with him like he messed with so many good cops over the months he was assigned there.

I knew exactly how to play this guy and in my, rarely used,

mild-mannered persona I informed him we were there because we used Mace to bring our prisoners under control.

"Sergeant, my partner and I didn't come here to create a problem; we are following the guidelines . . ."

"What is your name, Officer?"

"Police Officer Fitzgerald."

"Officer Fitzgerald, maybe I didn't make myself clear. Get the **** out of here. Take your prisoners back to your command."

"Okay Sergeant, sorry to bother you, we'll take our prisoners back to the Nine Four as ordered."

By now every cop assigned to BCB as well as every cop there with a prisoner was listening to or watching this scene. The cops assigned there knew me and Bobby and they knew I was definitely right. They also knew I was up to something because this was not the Jack Fitzgerald they knew.

I had every right to file a formal complaint against the sergeant, but that would have eventually led to serious repercussions, as in, I ratted the sergeant out. No. I'm no rat, but I knew exactly what to do.

Upon arrival at the Nine Four I gave the desk officer a blow-by-blow description of events, from the initial arrest using mace, to the trip to the hospital, and finally what occurred at BCB, including Fred's verbal abuse.

"Jack, I heard about that sergeant from several other members in our command. The word is he doesn't like white cops."

"Lieutenant, I don't know about that but I can tell you he definitely doesn't like cops who bring violations to 'his' BCB."

"I happen to know his commanding officer. You and Bobby take your prisoners back to BCB and I'll take care of the sergeant."

Our desk officer called his friend as promised. That CO told him to have us return to BCB and he would instruct the sergeant regarding the changes to the Patrol Guide.

We returned to the sign-in desk. This time there was no need to tell the APO what our prisoners were charged with. Sergeant Fred saw us come in and went into a back room.

I couldn't help myself; I had to throw that final punch. I followed him into that room and told him that we were ordered back by our DO, who wasn't happy that we brought our maced prisoners back to the Nine Four in direct violation of the Patrol Guide.

Fred was a beaten puppy. I don't know what his CO said to him, but he wouldn't even look at me as he said, "Officer, do what you have to do." That was the last I saw of Sergeant Fred that evening. We processed our two dis cons and the next day they pleaded guilty to the violation and were given a conditional discharge. No more fighting.

About a week later I returned to BCB with another prisoner. As I signed in, Officer Reyes said, "Jack, I want you and Bobby to know you have an open invitation to our coffee room anytime. You have made every cop assigned to BCB very happy."

"Angel, what happened?"

"Remember that issue you had with our sergeant last week?"

"Of course."

"It turns out that was the final straw for our CO. Sergeant Williams was transferred to motor transport in the Bronx."

32

THE ABSOLUTELY POSITIVELY DUMBEST TWO MEN IN BROOKLYN

The NYPD has a program for people who want to volunteer their time as auxiliary police officers. The volunteers are trained by the NYPD and all of their equipment—to wit, uniforms and handcuffs—are provided by the department. They are assigned in their resident precinct and patrol the streets in their neighborhood.

Their supervisors are promoted from within their ranks, but they are under the direction of a police officer with the title of Auxiliary Coordinator. That program gave civilians the opportunity to play cop for several hours during the evening hours and they usually did a good job. A very good friend and carpool partner, Police Officer Jimmy Ryan, was the Auxiliary Coordinator when the incident I am writing about took place.

Jimmy was a senior member of our command and a well-liked coordinator, which was reflected by the number of hours his APOs spent on patrol. The NYPD is a numbers-oriented city agency and when it came to the Auxiliaries, the coordinator was rated on how many hours his people worked each month. Jimmy was number one in all of Brooklyn North because he knew how to treat people and he made them want to come to work.

Over the years my partner Bob Mack and I requested the

assistance of the auxiliary force when we needed a police presence and there were no police officers available. They had a large retired Emergency Service truck they used for patrol and when we had a large group that needed arresting, Bobby and I frequently called for the APO truck to transport our prisoners to the precinct..

We got to know the APOs and they loved the idea of helping us when we needed them. I can identify many incidents, but I'll simply write that the program was and most likely still is a great addition to the NYPD.

In the late 1980s, the department realized it would be a good idea to provide every police officer with a bulletproof vest. If you ever visit One Police Plaza, Police Headquarters in lower Manhattan, you will see, upon entry, a wall listing every police officer killed in the line of duty and there are far too many names from the seventies and eighties.

It didn't take long to equip every police officer with a vest. Unfortunately, the auxiliary force was not included in that program. They did not receive vests even though they did patrol the streets in uniform. Unless you were close enough to read their arm patch or see their badge, you would never know they weren't the real deal sworn police officers.

There came a time when two of Jimmy's APOs came up with a brilliant idea. I won't identify the two men, but I will use appropriate names. Let's use Mo and Larry. So Mo and Larry came to the conclusion that it is absolutely "not fair" the auxiliaries didn't receive vests. They patrolled the same streets the police officers patrolled and they were exposed to the same assault by firearms as the police officers, but because they were auxiliary POs they were not afforded the same lifesaving equipment.

I agree with their logic and they should have been issued vests, but they weren't. Time for some "self-help." So Mo and Larry gave their dilemma much thought and came up with the following plan:

They will purchase one vest and that vest will be worn by the shootee. Then the shooter will shoot the shootee in the chest. The vest will stop the bullet, saving the life of you know who.

Mo buys a vest and goes on patrol with another auxiliary who is totally unaware of what is about to take place. Mo and Larry needed someone credible who would be a good witness to the dastardly deed, so they had a female APO fill the spot. I happen to know the chosen APO and they couldn't have picked a better witness.

Allow me to set the stage for this caper: Mo came to work and for the first time asked to be assigned with ummmmm let's use the name Wendy the witness. Jimmy Ryan had no problem with his request because Larry took off that evening. Mo and Wendy asked to be assigned to patrol Driggs Avenue, which was a rather quiet area in the evening and rarely patrolled by the auxiliary force. Jimmy did his best to make his people happy so he gave them the green light.

Now what Jimmy didn't know was Larry was waiting for Mo and Wendy with his loaded .22 caliber rifle.

The plan was the vest would save Mo's life, resulting in great publicity for the "Give the auxiliary force bulletproof vests" campaign. Mo and the unaware Wendy approached the predetermined spot on Driggs Avenue where Larry, who was crouched in his car, fired a shot at Mo. Larry is a bad shot and missed.

Mo and Wendy heard the shot, but before they could react Larry fired another shot, hitting Mo in the chest as planned. Wendy went into shock because that wasn't supposed to happen to auxiliaries, then she called a 10-13 officer shot. Mo went down to the ground because what he and Larry didn't realize was that the vest will easily stop a .22 caliber round, but it will still cause injury via blunt trauma to the body.

Larry fled the scene as every available RMP in the Nine Four and the Nine O responded and immediately began a search for the shooter. I can't think of a more serious job than a "10-13 officer shot." Of course, the exhaustive search resulted in no shooter found.

Mo went to Greenpoint Hospital where he was treated for his injury and admitted. Of course it didn't take long for the emergency room to become overcrowded with PD supervisors, to wit, the Duty Captain, the sergeant on patrol, several auxiliary supervisors, the Nine Four detectives, and of course Jimmy Ryan. The Duty Captain called for Emergency Service Units for a more thorough search for the sniper. Still no shooter.

After Mo was moved to the room he would be occupying, the detectives began their investigation. Our Nine Four PDU (Precinct Detective Unit) were sharp, so it didn't take long before Mo cracked under the intense questioning and told the truth. All of the above information was told to me by Jimmy and the two detectives who investigated this shooting incident.

I clearly recall Detective Jefferson telling me the story and when he came to the end he began to chuckle. He said, you won't believe it, but when Larry fired his first shot he missed, so he fired a second shot, which hit the mark. He added that those two clowns had to be the dumbest people in Brooklyn.

Later that night as I was driving home with Jimmy, he told me the kid with the vest really screwed himself. He was high on the list for the NYPD and waiting to be called to begin a new career in law enforcement.

He knew his temporary bout with insanity would put the old kibosh on any hopes he had for that career. Mo and Larry were both arrested, but neither had a prior criminal record, so they both pleaded guilty to a reduced charge and received a conditional discharge.

Obviously they were dismissed from the Auxiliary Force and my friend Jimmy Ryan had to endure a few days of verbal abuse by his peers in the precinct after that entire scenario, with a cartoon, was published in the editorial section of the *NY Post* newspaper.

33

THE EARLY SUNDAY MORNING PURSUIT THROUGH THE NINE O PRECINCT

The NYPD was forever summons conscious; all precinct commanding officers had to meet the required number of summonses every month (as in quota). If they were short they had to answer to the Borough. You would think our primary function, as a police department, would be crime prevention, but no, it was summons enforcement.

In my twenty-six years as a police officer I never heard a commanding officer, or any ranking member of the department, complain about the lack of arrests. The bottom line as far as this subject is concerned is: Summonses generated revenue for the city and the city always needed revenue.

There came a time when the department began a program called "red light overtime." Every precinct was given an allowance of overtime that would be used for the enforcement of the red light traffic regulations. One eight-hour tour (eight to four) on Sundays only.

The boss knew I would always meet the required ten summons minimum, so I was given the green light to make my own hours for the red light detail. Why lose an entire Sunday, so I worked from six to two p.m. I worked in uniform, but I used my unmarked RMP.

That first Sunday I arrived early, changed into my uniform, and reported to the desk officer. Lieutenant Sullivan knew why I was there, so we exchanged pleasantries before I took the keys to the RMP to begin the hunt.

I wasn't satisfied just making the quota, so I doubled down by working an accident-prone location. One red light summons at an APL was equal to five anywhere else.

By seven I was parked near the exit ramp for the westbound traffic off the Brooklyn Queens Expressway, our number one APL. At that location we had three signal lights. Those lights directed the flow of traffic for three heavily traveled streets as well as the exit ramp. I parked my vehicle on Metropolitan Avenue just east of the ramp and waited.

I didn't wait long before I saw a BMW coming east on Rodney Street. I watched as it went through the dead red light at Metropolitan Avenue. Then he went through the red light at Met and Meeker before making a left turn onto Marcy Avenue.

I put the red FBI light on top of my RMP and went after the Beemer. I hit the siren a few times and two heads popped up in the back window. They looked at me and I could read their minds by the look on their faces: Holy shit a cop! The driver took off and the chase was afoot.

He drove west on Marcy far too fast for conditions. (I should add that a few months prior to that Sunday, the NYPD came out with a General Order prohibiting vehicle pursuits for anything less than serious felonies and going through a red light did not qualify.)

I notified Central that I was "following" a vehicle for traffic violations. The word follow was understood by every police officer in the department; this was a friggin' pursuit. I was actually requesting assistance from any sector available to help in my "following."

The car was now entering the Nine O Precinct's Jewish Hassidic community, going through every red light and stop sign. On Sunday morning that neighborhood was alive with people.

Merchants, workers, shoppers, delivery trucks, et cetera– you would think it was high noon with the pedestrian traffic.

This was not good. I decided my pursuit was not worth risking lives. As I slowed I lost sight of the car and I informed Central that I was no longer following the vehicle. I gave her a description of the BMW and as I was on my way back to my accident-prone location, right there, not one hundred feet away, was my BMW.

The two heads from the rear seat and the guy on the front passenger's side were in the process of bailing out and were doing a felony run down Lee Avenue like they were on fire.

I pulled my RMP directly behind their car. As I ran to the driver's side I could see him struggling to open his door. It was jammed. He freed the jam and was opening the door as I approached. I was his only obstacle to freedom so he came out swinging. I stopped his assault using minimal force.

He was stunned and collapsed back into the front seat. I pulled him out, cuffed him and called for two Nine O Precinct sectors to 10-85 me (respond to my location). I needed help transporting my prisoner as well as the recovered vehicle to the Nine Four SH. (I should have taken this arrest to the Nine O Precinct, the precinct of apprehension, but I was sure no one would complain if I took it home to the Nine Four.)

As I awaited their arrival, a group of about ten Hassidic Jews returned with the other three passengers. I had written them off as "gone in the wind." That scene was surreal. I'll do my best to describe what took place: I'm standing next to my RMP with my handcuffed prisoner as the "Lee Avenue Hassid gang" returned with the three mopes who fled the scene. They were beating the ever-loving crap out of them with their shoes. That gang didn't need knives or guns; their weapon of choice was the shoe.

They couldn't possibly have known what the track stars did or why I was chasing them. All the boys in black knew was they were running away from the police. I learned that in the Hassidic community, you run from the police, you get a Thom McCann shampoo.

(Many years ago, my squad in TPF was assigned to the Nine O Precinct due to a report of hostilities between the Hispanic community and the Hassidic community. The allegation was, a Puerto Rican guy molested a Hassidic child in the elevator of one of the buildings in the projects. He took her to the roof and raped her. While the child was being treated at Greenpoint Hospital for the rape and related injuries, the father, joined by about one hundred of his fellow Hassidic Jews, went after the rapist. That's when I discovered, in that community, if you mess with one Hassid you mess with all of them. The alleged rapist had friends too, resulting in a full-scale riot. The good news for the Jews was that we arrived, because their weapon of choice was a shoe and the Puerto Ricans had knives.) With the help of my Hassid deputies, I now had all four car thieves in custody. My posse stayed with me because I had one set of cuffs. It didn't take long before three Nine O sector cars arrived and they transported my prisoners and the recovered vehicle to the Nine Four Precinct SH.

I took a few names and phone numbers from my deputies, just in case I needed to explain how three of my prisoners had been tuned up and may be in need of medical attention.

As I drove to the Nine Four, I called Central to check to see if the car was reported stolen. She ran the plate and it came back 10-17, not stolen. That's not good.

When I arrived at the Nine Four, the desk officer asked me what I had.

"Jack, I heard your 'following a vehicle' transmission. I'm sure this is going to be good. I can't wait."

"Lieutenant, would you believe at this moment I'm not sure?"

"Yes, I do believe you, but I also know you will find a way to justify this arrest, right?"

"Absolutely."

Lieutenant Sullivan had the station house Security Officer assist me with the search and detention of my "possible prisoners" while I used our computer to run the plate on the car. It was owned by a man who lived in Stuyvesant Town, an upscale neighborhood on the lower east side of Manhattan. I got his phone number and made the call.

"Mr. Jones, my name is Police Officer Fitzgerald and I would like to know if you are the owner of a 1985 BMW, NY registration ABC 1234?"

"Yes, I am."

"Do you know where your vehicle is at this time?"

"Yes. It's parked in front of my building."

"Did you give anyone permission or authority to drive your vehicle?"

"No. Give me a minute officer let me look out my window . . . My car is gone, my fu**in car is gone. Someone stole my fu**in car. What do I do now?"

"Mr. Jones, the good news is I have recovered your car and I don't see any damage. The not so good news is you will need to meet me at Brooklyn Central Booking in about three hours to speak to an assistant district attorney and sign a complaint."

This was a new experience for me. I had never recovered a stolen car before the owner knew it was stolen. Not unheard of, but unusual. I was expecting a "Thank you, Officer Fitzgerald, for recovering my expensive two-year-old BMW. I will do whatever you need me to do."

Silly me. What was I thinking?

"Officer Fitzgerald, today is Sunday and I made plans to take my family to see our friends in Riverdale. Can I talk to the district attorney on the phone?"

"No, Mr. Jones, that's not possible. You must speak to the DA in person and sign the affidavit. You must also produce proof of ownership for the vehicle. A registration in your name will do."

"How long will that take?"

"There is no way I can give you an answer to that question. It is seven forty-five and I am just now being told that the car I recovered was stolen. I have four prisoners to process and that will take at least two hours, that is, if no one needs medical attention."

"Medical attention, what medical attention. Did they wreck my car?"

"No, Mr. Jones, I told you I didn't see any damage to your car, but three of the car thieves did resist arrest and suffered minor injury when apprehended. Then I won't know how busy Central Booking is until I get there."

"Why can't I go to see the DA now?"

"Mr. Jones, do you have any prior experience with the criminal justice system in NYC?"

"No."

"Let me tell you now, there are established rules that we all must follow. You, me, everyone. I promise I will do my best to make this experience as painless as possible, but we must begin at Brooklyn Central Booking and we must do that today."

I gave him the address of BCB and told him where to go when he arrived. I gave him the phone number of the Nine Four Precinct in case he had any additional questions.

I returned to the desk and gave Lieutenant Sullivan the good news.

"Lieutenant, to answer your previously asked question, I am happy to inform you that my possible prisoners are now officially under arrest for grand larceny auto and resisting arrest. There was no alarm on the car because the owner didn't know it was stolen . . . Now he does."

"Jack, I had faith in you good work.

The desk officer told me he didn't have anyone to help me with the vast amount of paperwork. He was down to "minimum manning," the rock bottom number of police officers needed to patrol our precinct.

I knew this was going to be a long day and probably go into the late evening hours. I called my wife to let her know I was not coming home and she needed to spend this Sunday without me.

I was about thirty minutes into the paperwork when the desk officer told me I had a call.

"Police Officer Fitzgerald, may I help you?"

"Hi, Officer Fitzgerald, this is Robert Jones calling to tell you I'm not feeling well. I think I have food poisoning and I can't meet with the DA today. I am very sick."

Wow, did this guy think this was my first rodeo? Okay, so now this party is getting interesting.

"I'm so sorry to hear that, Mr. Jones. I hope you feel better. I have to go now."

"Wait, wait, what about my car? When can I come to get my car?"

"Unfortunately there is a problem with that. As soon as I end this conversation I will inform my lieutenant that he must void my arrests. He won't appreciate that. I will then release my four prisoners and tell them I am sorry I arrested them. I can assure you I will not enjoy doing that. Finally, if you think you're sick to your stomach, I can assure you I will be very sick to my stomach as I watch them drive off in THEIR beautiful, like-new, two-year-old BMW."

"What are you talking about? You can't do that. It's my car."

"Mr. Jones, would you believe that is exactly what the driver I arrested told me when I stopped him."

"I'm leaving in a few minutes; I should be there in about an hour."

"No need to rush, if you could be there by noon . . ."

Of course, most of what I told him was not true, but I did need him to meet with the DA and sign the complaint. His vehicle hadn't been reported stolen and I needed his registration, as proof of ownership, to prepare the UF 61.

The arrest process took about two and a half hours. I had a sector transport my prisoners to BCB. I changed into civilian clothes and drove my private vehicle. By eleven thirty I was signed in, my prisoners were lodged, and their fingerprints were being sent to the proper authorities.

Sunday mornings were usually very busy in BCB. Saturday evenings and early Sunday mornings were prime time. It could be even busier when there was a raid by our narcotics units during the early morning hours.

That Sunday was unusually quiet, so all I needed to do was wait for their rap sheets (criminal history) before proceeding to the DA's side of the building. I had plenty of time, so I walked over to that area where I met my complainant.

Again, no "Thank you, Officer."

"Good morning, Mr. Jones."

"Good morning, Officer, can you tell me when I can speak to the DA and get my car?"

"Mr. Jones, I understand you have plans with your family today. I also understand this is a grave inconvenience for you. I am sorry the people I arrested chose your car to steal but they did. If it makes you feel better I too had plans with my family for this afternoon. I did what I had to do; I recovered your stolen car. Now you must do what you need to do. To answer your question; I have done all that I can do. I'm waiting for their criminal records. When I receive those documents, we're ready to meet with the ADA."

I took his registration and completed the UF 61. I then returned to the BCB side to await the results of their prints.

As I waited I decided to write summonses for all the red lights the driver went through during the time I was "following" him. He didn't have a driver's license and of course he didn't have the registration or insurance card for the vehicle. The end result of that exercise in futility was that I issued eleven red light summonses, four summonses for failure to stop at stop signs, speed not reasonable or prudent, reckless driving, driving without a license, registration or insurance card.

Yes it was an exercise in futility, but the summonses would be added to the charges at arraignment and as I stated earlier; I would receive credit for a lot of summonses and that was the name of the game.

It was now almost twelve thirty, so I went to the sergeant in charge, who I knew from my time in the Seven Five Precinct.

"Sarge, how are the prints running?"

"So far we're on time, but it will be at least another two hours. Jack, you have plenty of time to get a bite to eat. No need to rush."

With at least a two hours' backlog, I drove the three miles to the Nine Four Precinct and spent my meal hour in the boxing gym. A good workout always left me relaxed and stress free. After a shower I felt like a million bucks. I called the sergeant to check on the prints.

"Sarge, Jack Fitzgerald here, any word on my prints?"

"Yes. Bad news, there was a sweep in Coney Island and you won't be getting out of here soon. You can figure on at least another couple of hours. More bad news. Your complainant is driving the ADA crazy. "

"I'm on my way back. Is there anything I can bring with me?"

"We have coffee, so a few rolls for me and the boys would be nice."

"Consider it done."

Sergeant Kennedy knew me well. He knew that with as much time as I had for a meal, I would probably spend time in the Nine Four gym. On my way back I had to pass the bakery on Rodney Street where I usually bought a dozen of their extra special rolls and buns for the PD staff at BCB.

I arrived with my package, gave it to Sergeant Kennedy and before I could ask for a cup of coffee he told me the supervising ADA wanted to talk to me.

"Mr. Roberts, I'm PO Fitzgerald. You want to speak to me?"

"Yes, what's with your complainant?"

"What now?"

"He's ready to leave. He's sick and he wants to talk to you 'immediately'!!! He didn't look very sick to me."

"Yes, I know, Mr. Jones seems to think he's special and we're stupid. He has, or I should say he had, plans for today and my arrest of his car thieves has ruined his day. I'll talk to him."

I found Mr. Jones trying to solicit help from the ADA who would be drawing up the complaint, Linda Davis. Linda was an experienced ADA, but she went by the book. Mr. Jones was wasting his time.

"Mr. Jones, I was told you were looking for me."

"Yes, OFFICER FITZGERALD, I've been looking for you for over an hour."

"Mr. Jones, you will be pleased to know I was acting on your behalf that entire time."

"How so?"

"You will recall earlier this morning there came a time when you told me you were too ill to precede with the arrest process."

"Yes."

"You eventually said you would meet me here, but I didn't want to take a chance with your car in case you couldn't make it. I decided to voucher the car for safekeeping. I added an 'investigate auto' request because the driver I arrested didn't have proof of ownership. Bottom line; it was taken to our NYPD auto pound in Whitestone, Queens.

"After meeting you this morning I needed to have your vehicle returned to our station house. It is Sunday and it took quite a while to contact the supervisor in charge of that facility. He did us a favor and thank goodness your vehicle has been returned to the Ninety Four Precinct.

"I did what I had to do, now I must ask you to be patient. The minute their criminal records arrive we can speak to ADA Davis. She will draw up the complaint, you will sign and swear to it, and hopefully she will release your car to you today."

"Officer, do you understand I am sick. I have food poisoning and I must get out of here. Please let me sign the form, let me get my car and go home. Please!"

"If you can give me a few minutes I may be able to help you with that."

I had eye contact with the ADA and she read my mind: Linda, I have this covered!!!!!

I went to a phone and went through the motions as though I was making a call. He watched me but he couldn't hear what I was saying. Finally I returned to where he was still talking to Linda.

"Mr. Jones, I just got off the phone with Dr. Andrews at nearby Long Island College Hospital. I told him you had food poisoning and asked if he had something he could give you for that malady. He told me to bring you in to the emergency room. He has a sure fix waiting for you. I have a car ready to take us, let's go."

"Officer Fitzgerald, you win. I guess I have no choice but to stay until this ordeal is completed."

"If you're well enough to stick around, I'll do my best to have your car released to you today."

Linda said, "Mr. Jones, I don't see any reason why you won't be able to drive your car home today, but if you feel you need to see the doctor, I'm sure Officer Fitzgerald will take good care of you."

"Thanks. Do I have time to get a bite to eat?"

With that question Linda and I looked at each other and burst out laughing. My man Robert Jones was taken aback with our response but it didn't take long for him to realize he had given himself up.

Linda told him where he could get a decent meal, in that almost deserted area, on a Sunday afternoon.

I returned to the BCB side and had a cup of coffee with Sergeant Kennedy. By four thirty I had my rap sheets in hand and I was on my way back to the DA's side.

I found Linda Davis and told her I was ready to go. This was a simple felony affidavit for grand larceny second degree. Mr. Jones had to swear that he parked his car in front of his apartment building at a given time and he did not give anyone permission or authority to drive it.

My part in this saga was a tad more involved: I explained what led to the arrest of my four desperados. All the additional information, to wit, the foot pursuit and apprehension of three of the perps by my self-appointed posse as well as my struggle with the driver, would come out at a hearing. If there was a hearing.

I found Robert in the complainant's waiting room and took him to meet with Linda. He signed and swore to the affidavit. Linda signed the DA's release for his car and explained there might come a time when he would need to appear in Brooklyn Criminal Court to testify. She added that considering all four defendants had numerous prior convictions for similar offenses, she didn't think we would go to trial.

With his release in hand, I said good-bye to Robert Jones.

"Mr. Jones, do you have anyone you can call for a short ride to the Nine Four Precinct?"

"No, aren't you going there now that this ordeal is finally over?"

"Remember I told you I had plans with my family for today? Well, now my plans have changed. I must now take my prisoners to the courthouse where I'll spend the rest of this day and possibly into tomorrow completing this arraignment process."

"I'm lost and I don't know Brooklyn. Can't you call a police car to drive me to get my car?" (Wow; talk about balls.)

"No, Mr. Jones, that's not possible. I gave you the address of the precinct. If you walk to the corner of Tillary and Adams Street, I'm sure you will get a cab. It's not very far. There is nothing more I can do for you. Now I'm off to night court with your car thieves."

The final tally of this arrest was: I was credited with four felony arrests and numerous summonses, including my required ten red light summonses. My prisoners were arraigned later that evening in night court. I returned to the Nine Four Precinct and signed out at eleven with seventeen hours' overtime. All four defendants pleaded guilty to attempted grand larceny and received six months at Rikers Island Iron House.

34

MY TATTOO AT CCRB

In the Nine Four Precinct, I worked in civilian clothes while assigned to the Youth Car/Gang Car. One day in July and prior to going in for a four to midnight tour, I went to see a friend who had a calzone stand at a local Italian feast.

While I was visiting Joey A., he asked me if I would like to get a temporary tattoo. His friend had a tattoo stand and he could see he wasn't busy. (A temporary tattoo is applied with special multi-color pens and will last until they are scrubbed off. If the artist is good you would never know they were painted on.) I said why not so off we went to see Angelo the tattoo artist.

Angelo gave me a book with about 150 photos, including a rugged looking American eagle. I went with the eagle. In twenty minutes I was inked up with a beautiful eagle on my left bicep.

I left Joey, drove to the Nine Four Precinct, and went to work with my partner Bobby Mack. At about nine p.m., there was a call for assistance (10-13) from a Nine O Precinct sector. We responded as a civilian clothes backup unit. We donned our colored head-bands identifying us to other members of the department as police officers.

As we pulled up to the scene I realized we were walking into a riot in an adjacent precinct where we were not known by many of the officers. This was not good.

On this sweltering summer evening and while following a citywide directive, a police officer shut down a fire hydrant used to give the locals a break from the heat. The entire city suffered from low water pressure due to thousands of opened hydrants, creating a severe fire hazard.

This predominantly Hispanic neighborhood depended on the cool water that gushed out of the hydrants to beat the heat. When the hydrants were turned off, they were turned on, resulting in the riot we found ourselves in the middle of.

In a riot everyone gets hurt. We were punched and kicked, but nothing that took us out of the fight. Finally, there came a time when the bad guys had enough and took to the hills, leaving their wounded to the law. I don't have a clue as to the number of arrests that were made, but I do know the responding Duty Captain kept calling for more ambulances as we returned to the confines of the Nine Four Precinct.

About a week later I was handed a notice to appear at CCRB (Civilian Complaint Review Board). I was told to bring my PBA attorney as General Order 15 was in effect. That meant that the allegations being made could result in criminal charges. I called the PBA office and informed them that I needed a lawyer at CCRB. That was nothing unusual, so no big deal.

CCRB was a unit formed under the Lindsay administration in the mid '60s.. It gave the public a venue for making complaints against members of the NYPD. In reality it became a way to allow the public to air their grievances. A way to vent.

Ninety-five percent of the complaints were closed out as either unfounded or unsubstantiated. The remaining 5 percent went to the trial room where the recipient of the complaint became a defendant in an internal department trial that could result in dismissal. Due to my aggressive/proactive style of policing I was not a stranger to CCRB and, as they say, I knew the ropes.

Upon arrival I located the PBA board member assigned for the day. He had a copy of the complaint and we reviewed it together. That was usually the first time the member of the service got to see what he/she was accused of.

In a nutshell, the civilian complaint read: For no reason, the police turned off the hydrant. Someone threw a bottle at the cop who shut the hydrant and then a big fight started. More cops came and then more people came. Finally a cop, not in uniform but with a badge around his neck, hit me on the head with his stick. I had to go to the hospital where I got eleven stitches.

He described the cop and as Bob and I were the only "known" responding members out of uniform it didn't take long for the CCRB investigators to track me down. I definitely fit the description; ergo I was the chosen one. (Other precinct civilian clothes members may have responded, but they wouldn't have informed Central as we did.)

When the PBA attorney arrived he read the allegation, after which he joined me and the PBA rep in the hall for a brief conference. When I was called, we entered the room and met the lieutenant and sergeant responsible for my case. The entire interview was recorded. The lieutenant read the allegation and asked me if I had responded to the call for assistance on the evening in question.

The question and answer part of the interview continued until the lieutenant asked me to expose my left bicep. I rolled up my sleeve and could see a look of disbelief come over his face. He reviewed his notes and then asked me to roll up the other sleeve; now both biceps were exposed. He looked at the sergeant and stated for the record that my left and right biceps were clean and free of tattoos. He ended the session and turned the recorder off.

I returned to the waiting room, leaving the lawyer, my rep, and the two bosses in their office. I had no idea why I was asked to roll up my sleeves, but that seemed to be a turning point in this interview.

As the lawyer and rep returned to the waiting room, they were both smiling. The lawyer said, "This case is officially over."

"What's the story with the rolling up of my sleeves?"

Your complainant was arrested, treated and released from Greenpoint Hospital. He was charged with second-degree riot and pled guilty to disorderly conduct (Appropriate in Brooklyn Criminal Court for this less then extremely violent melee)

He made the CCRB complaint and had a vague description of the person who caused his injury except for one unmistakable detail. He was absolutely positive; no doubt about it, the person who hit him had a tattoo of an eagle on his left bicep. When you rolled up your sleeves and there was no tattoo, the lieutenant realized you were not the person who caused his injury. He closed this case by saying, "no tattoo not guilty."

I signed out and returned to my command. It was years later, after being elected to the position of PBA delegate, that I saw the PBA board member I had that day at CCRB. He remembered me and I needed to fess up by telling him exactly what took place , especially the part about my tattoo. We both had a good laugh and he said, "Sometimes the good guy wins."

35

THE LIQUOR STORE CAPER

One Friday evening Bob Mack and I were assigned to our conditions car (We were responsible to address and solve all complaints/conditions the C.O. received from the community) on that day we were to give special attention to the illegally parked cars in the bus stops on Nassau Avenue at Manhattan Avenue. A very busy block for both pedestrians and cars.

The cause of the problem was that one entire block was a bus stop on both sides of the street. There was a pizzeria and a catering hall on one side and a liquor store on the other and no one obeyed the "No Standing BUS STOP" signs.

The buses needed to double-park as the passengers exited and boarded the bus. One day an elderly lady tripped while getting off, breaking her hip. She sued the city for a gazillion dollars and we got this assignment.

We were parked on the north side of Nassau about seventy-five feet from the front door to the liquor store when we heard what sounded like gunshots. Bob was driving, so he pulled up to within twenty feet of the front door just as the owner of the store came running out, being chased by a man wielding a revolver. Bob was out of the car in a second as he was at the curbside and I was a couple of seconds behind. He was wrestling the gun out of the guy's hand when I hit the shooter, causing him to fall to the ground. Bob had the gun and I cuffed the prisoner.

I got in the backseat with the prisoner while Bob spent a few moments interviewing the owner. He told the owner to meet us at the Nine Four Precinct station house.

I advised the prisoner of his constitutional rights and as Bob put the car in motion, he became combative; he didn't like being handcuffed.

Our prisoner was in the extremely violent stage of drunk and caught an attitude as I searched him in front of the desk officer.

This was definitely Bob's arrest. He disarmed the gunman, but had requested four hours off, so I became the arresting officer. We took the prisoner to the arrest processing room; Bob began the paperwork as I tried to fingerprint him.

Stosh was a rather large, very intoxicated man who decided he didn't want to be printed. As I tried to roll his fingers onto the cards, I came to the conclusion I was wasting my time.

Stosh was a construction worker and most likely a bricklayer. He didn't have identifiable fingerprints. Now I must go to plan B. He goes to BCB without prints. I wrote "Prisoner has no fingerprints" on the three print cards.

I interviewed my complainant and this was his story: He did a lot of business with Polish immigrants in the neighborhood, especially those "without papers." They worked as day laborers, off the books, and were paid a fraction of what union workers received. They worked hard and sent most of their money back to their families in Poland.

One of the many issues those men had to contend with was where to cash a paycheck payable to "Cash" when the employer insisted on paying by check. That's where our liquor store owner made it easy. He would cash their checks if they made a purchase.

On that Friday evening, Stosh's friend Erick brought a half-gallon bottle of vodka to McCarren Park, where all Polish workers hung out after work, drinking. That park was one block from the liquor store. Eventually the six men went through the bottle and

Stosh was elected to buy another half G. He needed to cash his check anyway, so off he went.

The owner thought Stosh was intoxicated and refused to serve him. Now Stosh had two problems: He couldn't return without the vodka and he most certainly needed to cash his check. He became belligerent; words were exchanged, resulting in the owner physically removing Stosh from the store. As he was being ejected, he told the owner he was coming back with a gun and he was going to shoot him.

Another idle threat, right . . . Wrong. Stosh did have a gun, which he brought back as promised. As he entered the store he saw the owner at the far end. He fired a shot, but missed. He ran down the aisle to get closer as the owner ran up the next aisle.

It went that way for about thirty seconds with a total of four shots fired before the owner ran out of the store being chased by Stosh. That's when Bob rushed the gunman and put an end to his attempt to shoot the owner.

I transported and lodged my prisoner at BCB. I met with the ADA and my complainant explained what took place that evening. The affidavit was prepared and sworn to, which ended a very traumatic afternoon for the liquor store owner.

I appeared in court the following morning to arraign my prisoner. He was held without bail. A week later, the owner and I appeared before the Brooklyn grand jury. Stosh was indicted for attempted Murder, possession of a dangerous weapon, to wit, a loaded firearm, discharging a firearm, reckless endangerment and resisting arrest.

The end result was Stosh pleaded guilty, in Supreme Court, to attempted assault in the first degree and possession of a deadly weapon in the first degree to cover all charges. He was sentenced to three years in prison with an order to deport upon release. My complainant was happy because he didn't have to return to Brooklyn Criminal Court.

36

THE MURDER IN THE MEEKER AVENUE TAVERN

Date, July 7, 1986. Tour, four to twelve. Assignment: Youth Gang Unit in civilian clothes in unmarked RMP 882.

Bobby Mack and I had two of our informants in the backseat. We were parked in "off-street parking" under the Brooklyn Queens Expressway. Bob was taking notes.

"Officer Mack, me and Carmella got news for you about Lenny Ortiz and his crew from Java Street. They be sellin' dope to the kids in the neighborhood and that ain't right."

Before Julio could say another word we heard a muffled BANG, BANG, BANG from the Meeker Avenue Bar not one hundred feet directly in front of us. As we bailed out of the car, we saw a guy run out of the bar. We identified ourselves as police officers and ordered him to stop.

"STOP . . . POLICE!!!"

He stopped just long enough to say, "If you're the police you better get in that bar. There's a guy in there shooting up the place."

We had to make a quick decision; do we chase that guy or do we go into the bar? There was something about his actions that caused both of us to go with plan B. Bob called for backup as we ran to the front door. I was the senior man, so I was going in first.

That's just the way it was, but he was so close he was pushing me in.

As I entered I could see three men on the floor about ten feet from the door. Two were semiconscious and one was not moving. I caught a glimpse of one guy as he ran away from the bar and into a back room.

There were about ten patrons standing at the thirty-foot-long bar. I yelled, "Police, don't move," and focused on the bar as Bob went toward the three men on the floor. I could see him kick something out of the hand of one of the men, but my undivided attention was on the ten suspects in front of me. I ordered everyone to get down on the floor as Bob checked on the three men. One was dead and the other two were seriously wounded. All three had been shot. That's when Bob retrieved the revolver he kicked out of the hand.

My mind was racing. Where was the other guy with a gun? Three people shot, ten suspects now on the floor and then there was the guy who ran into the back room. My money was on him.

We were outnumbered in this large room, so rather than begin a superficial search or go after the last guy I decided to wait for backup. Within seconds the first sector arrived, followed by the sergeant on patrol, and finally every sector not on assignment.

I brought the boss up to speed and told him I was going after my primary suspect in the back room, which turned out to be a restroom. He said, "I'm right behind you." Before I opened the door I yelled, "Police, come out with your hands up!" With that I heard a voice say, "I'm on the job and I'm coming out." He came out with a police shield in his hand and identified himself as a Housing Police Officer.

At that time the Housing Police were referred to as Housing Guards by the rank-and-file members of the NYPD. They were useless and this guy was a classic example.

Sergeant James relieved the Housing Guard of his revolver as I took him to the front of the bar. He joined the other patrons who were now on their feet. Bob told me everyone had been searched . . . no gun found.

Three people shot, one gun found; the guard had an off-duty gun. This shooting is close to being solved . . . Or maybe not. The boss took the guard's revolver, opened the cylinder; all six bullets accounted for. That gun had not been fired today.

I reviewed this crime scene in my head: Three people shot. So far the only gun that we recovered, that was fired, was found on one of the victims. Did the second shooter have time to hide the gun or toss it somewhere we hadn't had time to search yet?

OH NO! Suddenly I got a knot in my stomach. The other shooter was the guy who ran out of the bar. No sense wasting time looking for him, he's in the wind. It's time to talk to a witness. The bartender will be a good place to start. I asked the bartender to join me in the back room.

"Okay, pally, what's your name?"

"Mike."

"Mike, do you have a last name?"

"Mike Hancock."

"Mike Hancock, how long have you been tending bar here?"

"About two years."

"Good. You saw what happened here, right?"

"Yes."

"We need your help. This is a serious crime scene and we need to know exactly what happened today."

He began by telling me the bar was sold about two months ago. The new owner retained all the help; several bartenders, a cook, et cetera. About three weeks after taking possession, he caught Stanley, the bartender, stealing and fired him. He went on to say Stanley was a real sad sack. He had no life outside the bar, where he worked for about five years. Everybody knew Stanley.

On that afternoon, Stanley returned to the bar for the umpteenth time and tried to speak to the new owner and his son, who were drinking with the other patrons. He begged for another chance. He was sorry, he promised never to do it again please

please please let me work here. Eventually the new owner had enough and told Stanley to leave and he was banned from the bar for life.

In the words of the witness, Stanley backed away from the bar, took out a gun and shot the owner in the back. Then he shot the son. Finally Stanley turned the gun on himself and fired one round into his stomach. We arrived seconds later and Bob disarmed the shooter by kicking the gun out of his hand.

The end result was the owner died; the son was seriously wounded and lost his spleen. The shooter eventually recovered and pleaded guilty to all charges. After a review of his criminal history, which included two prior robbery convictions and three felonious assault convictions, he was given a twenty-five-years-to-life sentence.

37

I HAVE THE RIGHT TO REMAIN SILENT

August 23, 1985, was a typical hot/humid evening. It was nine p.m., Bobby Mack and I just ended our exhausting, hour-long training session in the boxing gym. We showered, changed into a clean uniform, and as we walked to our RMP we were stress free and ready for anything the mean streets of Brooklyn could send our way . . . Or maybe not!

Our first stop was to our friendly greengrocer Abe Greenberg's fruit stand, where we purchased several pieces of fruit. I must confess Abe would never take our money for the fruit, but we always offered. We watched his back and he showed his appreciation with his generosity. On that evening he told us there were a few "Mutts" (the name he gave to the street thugs) hanging out in front of the laundromat on the corner. They were drunk, panhandling, and harassing everyone walking by as well as the people using the laundromat.

"The corner" was one block from his store. It was also one of our known drug location. We left him and drove around the block. We waited several minutes and as we approached we could see the three men, clearly intoxicated, harassing the women doing their wash in the store. They were begging for money and just being drunk and disorderly.

I pulled our RMP to the curb and expected the drunks to walk away. Everyone in that neighborhood knew we did not permit "hanging out" on that corner. These guys were testing us. They didn't leave, so Bob, who was the recorder and closest to the sidewalk, told them they had to get off the corner.

With that, one of them approached Bob's window while holding his almost empty pint bottle of 151 proof rum: F**K YOU!

So much for the stress-free time. Now we had to take proper police action, also known as doing what had to be done.

Mr. Drunked-Up Kamikaze backed away from our vehicle. As Bob was getting out, the guy with the rum moved in and punched him hard in the face, causing him to fall back against the RMP. He never saw the assault coming and I could see he was stunned. I went after that guy and as I got close he began throwing punches at me.

I backed away, avoiding the blows until I finally found an opening. I moved in and caught him with a strong right hand followed by a left hook. Mr. Wannabe tough guy went down. Now his two friends began moving in my direction, but by now Bob was back in the fight. It didn't take much to bring them under control. We called for backup to help transport our prisoners to the SH.

Bob and I transported the guy who assaulted him, because he never stopped with his assault. He was rear-cuffed when I put him in the car and he continued to try to head butt me but I just squished him into the corner of the back seat.

As we pulled up to the SH, I could see he was spent. No more fighting, no more assaulting. As I began telling the desk officer what we had, the sector arrived with the other two prisoners. We searched them in front of the DO and I could see the guy who had assaulted Bob was hurt. He had difficulty speaking while answering questions

After the routine search, the arrest processing officer put them in the cell and I took Bob to Greenpoint Hospital to be checked out, which was SOP. While we were at Greenpoint, the desk officer realized our prisoner was in need of medical treatment, so he had a sector transport him to Cumberland Hospital.

We would never take the officer and the criminal to the same hospital if it could be avoided. After Bob was treated and released, we returned to the SH to begin the arrest processing of the two remaining prisoners in the cell.

A short time later, one of the officers assigned to take my prisoner to Cumberland returned to the SH with the paperwork needed to prepare the arrest forms. After giving me the paperwork he asked, "Jack, what did you hit that guy with?"

"I just used my hands. I hit him twice and that was all it took to bring him under control."

"I have news for you, that guy was admitted and from what I was told he'll be there for quite a while. After the doctor in the ER looked at the X-rays, he said he was going to take them home. He had never seen a face shattered like that before. Then he showed me the pictures. Jack, that guy looks like you hit him with a Louisville slugger baseball bat."

Jose Rodriguez received a bedside arraignment and was admitted for an extended stay. I didn't give that incident much thought until three weeks later when our roll call man called me to his office.

"Jack, I have subpoenas for you and Bobby. You are ordered to appear at the Brooklyn district attorney's office to answer questions regarding an arrest you made. The defendant's name is Jose Rodriguez. You are to appear with an attorney."

I immediately called the PBA office and spoke to our financial secretary, Jimmy Hannon. I told him I needed a lawyer to represent me and Bobby Mack at the Brooklyn DA's office.

I gave him the facts about the arrest. I also told him that the perp was still in the hospital recovering from his injuries. I asked for a specific attorney who I knew was their best in cases like ours and Jimmy told me he would make sure we had the best attorney they had.

When we arrived at the DA's office we met with Brian Daily,

the lawyer I requested. After a brief exchange of pleasantries he went to speak to the ADAs assigned to our case.

About ten minutes later he returned and told us that we had received a civilian complaint initiated by a city councilman named Leonard Omega on behalf of Jose Rodriguez. That complaint was followed by a call to the Brooklyn DA's office alleging that I committed an act of felonious assault on one of his constituents.

We would be interviewed separately, at which time we would be read our rights. He went on to say that he didn't like the ADA's attitude. He added. "That guy never played stickball when he was a kid. He's not streetwise and I personally think he doesn't like cops. I advise you to invoke your constitutional right and refuse to make statements. If he wants to pursue this matter he should take it to the grand jury where you will have the right to testify and tell your side of the story."

As the target of this investigation, I went first and listened while the ADA read me my rights.

"Officer Fitzgerald, you have the right to remain silent. Anything you say may and will be used against you in court. You have the right to have an attorney present during questioning. If you can't afford an attorney one will be provided free of charge. Now that I have advised you of your rights, are you willing to answer my questions?"

I could not believe this was happening. I was one of the good guys, a police officer doing what I was paid to do and now "I" had the right to remain silent.

After being asked that final question, a question I had asked thousands of times before, my answer . . . "NO! On advice of counsel, I refuse to answer your questions."

I could see the surprised look on his face. As I stood up and walked toward the door I heard him tell the stenographer, "He's got something to hide." Bob went in and a few minutes later walked out of the room after giving the same answer.

Brian said, "Jack, how is the case against Rodriguez going in court?"

"We did a bedside arraignment and he's still in the hospital. His jaw is wired."

"I want you to know it is imperative that he either pleads guilty to assault or if he won't take a plea you absolutely positively must go to trial and get a conviction for assault. Jack, your job may depend on the outcome in criminal court. That councilman is really pushing to have you arrested."

The ADA assigned to our case against Rodriguez was an experienced prosecutor. I also had a copy of Rodriguez's rap sheet and he had six prior arrests with four convictions for assault, robbery, possession of a gun and sale of narcotics.

I knew his prior arrest/conviction record couldn't be admitted if we went to trial. It didn't have any bearing as to his guilt or innocence in my case, but I couldn't help wondering why such a violent criminal could be allowed to prowl the streets instead of doing hard time for his numerous crimes. Then I remembered; this was Brooklyn and the criminals were rarely punished for their crimes.

There came a time when we received our subpoenas for the next step. We arrived at the courtroom where our hearing was scheduled to take place and met the ADA assigned. As I began to explain my dilemma, he stopped me.

"Officer Fitzgerald, your PBA attorney, Brian Daily, called and filled me in on what went down here as well as what is at stake. Brian and I worked together before he left our office for the PBA. I promise, you have nothing to worry about. The defendant Rodriguez has a history in the criminal justice system and if he doesn't take a plea today I will present this to the grand jury and he can take his chances in Supreme Court. Believe me; he will take a plea today."

Our case was called and the ADA informed the judge we were ready to proceed with a hearing or we could go straight to the grand jury and trial in Supreme Court. The Legal Aid defense attorney requested a sidebar. The end results: Mr. Jose Rodriguez pleading guilty to misdemeanor assault on Bob. He was sentenced to thirty days in jail and his two codefendants took a plea to disorderly conduct and resisting arrest. They received three days in. We never heard another word about that incident.

About six months after the final chapter in the Jose Rodriguez saga, I was reading the *Daily News*. Lo and behold, there was a report on page three: Councilman Leonard Omega was ordered to appear at the same Brooklyn district attorney's office to answer questions regarding his involvement in criminal activity, all felonies. I don't recall the particulars, but I do know things didn't work out as well for him as they did for me. I know he pleaded guilty to corruption charges and I think he spent time in the Iron House.

38

LORIMER STREET AND METROPOLITAN AVENUE

A s I walked into the station house for a four to midnight tour, the desk officer told me the CO wanted to talk to me.

"Good afternoon, Captain, you want to see me?"

"Jack, take a seat. I got a call from Vinny Abruzzi (the district leader in our Williamsburg section of Brooklyn) and he asked for a favor. You know the group that hangs out in front of the pizzeria on Lorimer and Met?"

"Yes, know them well. Another bunch of wannabe wise guys who watched too many *Godfather* movies. They all think they're Don Corleone."

"Vinny told me the people who live above the stores need some peace and quiet. Most of the people on that block are senior citizens and either don't have air conditioners or can't afford to use them, so they keep their windows open. He also told me he received many complaints about the crowd due to their loud and very bad language. He added that the residents can't watch TV or get to sleep."

"Boss, Bobby and I will correct that condition, but Vinny knows that crew and he knows they all have an attitude problem. He also knows their parents think their little Anthonys can do no wrong. He will owe you big time. Oh and I can almost guarantee you we're going to make a trip to CCRB over this."

"Jack, that's why you get paid the big bucks."

I met Bob in the locker room and told him we would be working in uniform that night.

I brought him up to speed regarding the new addition to our already long list of precinct conditions and added this was a special request (favor) to the CO from Vinny Abruzzi.

Bobby said, "I hope the captain knows Vinny will owe him big time after this one. You know there is no way we're going to take control of that corner without a trip to CCRB."

"Bobby that was the first thing I told the boss. I also told him we would have this condition corrected within a few days." Bobby Mack and I were very good at solving community generated complaints. You name it; we found a way to make it right. Yes, we knew we would correct the Lorimer Street job, but we had no idea we would need to use such an unorthodox method to bring that assignment to a successful conclusion.

I do believe the use of the word "unorthodox" is an understatement. Our motto was, "We'll do whatever it takes to get the job done, within the law." I will admit there were a few times when we danced on the edge, but never over the line. Okay already, maybe once or twice we needed to go a tad over, but we got the job done.

We began that tour by visiting our daylight conditions. We checked the parks and our "no hanging out drug locations." We visited our prostitutes on Kent Avenue, where we picked up several "ladies on the stroll." They went to the SH for universal summonses. Sometimes we made arrests, but today was a "give the girls a break day" because we had bigger fish to fry.

At seven we took our meal hour and by eight we were ready to engage the Lorimer Street Guidos. We made a few passes to scope out the condition . . . Not yet. We'll wait a little longer. By nine it was prime time. We called for a 10-85 (rendezvous) with two available sectors at McCarren Park, which was five blocks from ground zero. We explained exactly what we were going to do and we told them we would need prisoner transportation to the SH.

Bobby and I drove up to the location where we now had about ten mopes just hanging out. They weren't doing anything wrong other than blocking pedestrian traffic and using loud and abusive language. Wait a second; according to the NYS penal law that's disorderly conduct.

The standard routine was: We tell them they can't hang out there anymore. They say, "We ain't doin' nuttin' wrong."

I pulled up to the Pizzeria and Bobby said, "Hey guys, listen up, we received a lot of complaints about the noise and the bad language. You're also blocking the sidewalk and people can't walk by. You can't hang out here anymore."

"But Officer, we ain't doin' nuttin' wrong. We're just hangin' out."

"We know that, but you can do your hanging out a few blocks away in McCarren Park. In the park you can make all the noise you want and no one will complain."

"Why can't we just hang out here, this is our neighborhood and we ain't bodderin' nobody."

"If you weren't bothering anyone we wouldn't be bothering you, but you are and now we are."

Then I said, "Did any of you not understand what my partner just said? We want to make sure you understand us because we are dead serious about this. Listen to my words: When we come back, everyone hanging out here will be going to the precinct. Last chance, does anyone not understand? No . . . Good. Take a hike and do not come back."

Bobby and I waited as the entire group moped down Lorimer Street toward the park. I drove past them and we visited a couple of conditions in that area.

We gave them fifteen minutes to return to the forbidden turf. Fifteen minutes was probably thirteen minutes more than enough time.

I returned driving on Metropolitan Avenue and made a left onto Lorimer. Lo and behold, guess who was back? If you guessed the same jamokes (idiots), you are right. Who would have thunk it.

As we got out of our RMP, four of them ran away. Obviously they finally realized we were serious. The remaining six were way too macho. No way were they going to run.

"Okay boys, it's clear you have decided to test us. Everyone up against the wall."

Bobby got on the radio and requested the two sectors 10-85 us at Lorimer and Met for transportation of prisoners. They acknowledged: "On the way."

As we tossed our prisoners (gave them a superficial search), the owner of the pizzeria came out from behind the counter and walked up to us. He had a heavy Italian accent and said, "Officca, why you bodderin' these boys. They ain't doin' nuttin' wrong. They good boys."

"Excuse me, what's your name?"

"Angelo, why you want to know that?"

"Because if you don't get back inside your pizzeria right now I will arrest you for obstructing governmental administration. Do you understand what I'm saying, Angelo?"

"Yes, Officca, I'm sorry."

As Angelo went into the store, two older men came out of the bar on the corner. They both seemed to agree with the pizza guy and said, "Officers, why you bodderin' the kids?"

"Excuse me, how are you guys related to these prisoners?"

They both said they weren't related in any way. Bobby told them to go back into the bar or they would be arrested. One guy made an about-face and went back into the bar; the other jerk just had to test us. Another test, right?

"What's your name?"

"My name is Ralph and don't think you can push me around like you're pushin' these kids around."

Ralph was trying to build on his neighborhood "Cred." If he

could make us back off from what we were doing he would immediately become a legend. He would be the guy who saved the neighborhood kids from the cops who had nothing better to do than "bodder" the kids. Unfortunately, Ralph didn't know Jack and Bob.

"Okay, Ralph, up against the wall."

As Bobby tossed Ralph, our backup arrived. Now we had enough handcuffs to go around. We cuffed our seven prisoners and they were transported to the Nine Four SH.

I must now identify the sergeant working the desk: Sergeant Melvin Silverman. Mel was a nice man, but a shaky boss. He hated being assigned to desk duty or any other duty when Bob and I were working because according to him: We always caused him stress. Unfortunately for Sergeant Mel, tonight was going to be his most stressful . . . ever.

It didn't take long before Bob and I were standing before the Desk Officer with seven prisoners under arrest for disorderly conduct, which is a violation in the penal law. Dis Con is a summonsable offense and we would not need to take them to court that evening. . Sergeant Silverman watched as we search our prisoners. That search was a "take everything out of your pockets" search.

As our six Guido's began emptying their pockets, Ralph asked to speak to me away from the rest. I wasn't sure what he wanted to talk about, but the first thing that came to mind was maybe he was wanted and was going to offer me a bribe to cut him loose. A long shot, but I wanted Mel to be in on the conversation.

"Sergeant, one of my prisoners wants to talk to me and I would like you to hear what he has to say."

"Bring him into my office."

"Okay Ralph, what's on your mind?"

"Officer I'm very sorry for disrespecting you, I promise I'll never do it again."

"Okay Ralph, is that all you have to say?"

"No."

After he said "no," he began taking everything out of his pockets. What the F**k? I looked at Mel; Mel began to lose color in his face and said, "Jack, what have I ever done to you to deserve this?"

"Ralph, you must be the dumbest man in the neighborhood. I gave you every opportunity to walk away but no, you had to be a big shot, right?"

"I'm sorry, Officer."

Ralph had a pocket full of policy slips. He was a numbers man aka a bookmaker,

I confiscated his paperwork and took him to our muster room. He joined the other six prisoners who were about to be issued summonses for disorderly conduct returnable to Brooklyn Criminal Court. As I returned to speak to Sergeant Silverman, I actually felt bad for what I was putting him through, but this was police work and very unpredictable.

"Okay Jack, now what?"

"Sarge, you and I know uniform doesn't make gambling arrest. So if I collar that idiot for possession of policy slips, the CO will receive a UF forty-nine from the Borough Office demanding an explanation. The CO will come to you wanting to know how you let this happen and who are you going to pass this onto me, right? Look at me, Mel, I know these people. Let me do what I need to do and if it comes back to haunt us, I'll take the heat."

"What do you have in mind?"

"All I have him for is obstructing governmental administration, but I can make that dis con. I keep his slips, and give him a warning and admonishment before cutting him loose. Later, I'll give you the second half of my plan, but is it okay if I cut him loose?"

"Go ahead . . . Jack, you're killing me. You know that, right?"

I returned to the muster room and took Ralph by the arm as I walked him out the front door.

"Okay Ralph, you're free to go. I never want to see you again. Do you understand?"

"Thank you, Officer, if there is anything . . ."

"Ralph, just go . . . now."

I knew what was coming next.

"Officer, can I have my papers back?"

"No, Ralph, and I have more bad news for you. I'm going to let the word out that you don't have the slips."

"Please Officer, don't do that. You know what that means."

"Yes Ralph, I do. You bought your ticket to this show."

I watched as Ralph walked away. He knew what to expect and whatever the criminal justice system could have done to him, it was nothing compared to what he had to look forward to. In a nutshell:

Ralph the numbers man meets his customer Louie the gambler on the corner. Louie says, I want a buck on 123. Ralph adds Louie's wager to his list with all the other names and bets. Now if Ralph is a busy "Book" he probably has way over a hundred steady customers. If Louie's number 123 comes out, he goes to Ralph with his good news. Ralph takes out his paperwork to confirm that win. Ralph pays Louie. End of transaction. The odds on picking the three numbers are nine hundred and ninety-nine to one, but I'm sure the book's payout is probably no more than five hundred to one. I really don't know the exact amount.

Later that evening I went to see a friend who knows everybody in that neighborhood, including Ralph.

"Jamsie, do you know Ralph the bookmaker?"

"Of course, who doesn't?"

"I want you to do me a favor. He busted my balls during an arrest and I need to teach him a lesson."

"Whatever you want, Jack, that guy is a pain in the ass."

"If you could let about ten of his customers know he doesn't have his slips and tell them to claim they picked tonight's number, that would be a good thing."

"Great, thanks. I happen to be one of his steady customers and I never won a dime. This is my lucky day."

Now we have six prisoners. As I was about to write the first summons for dis con, the telephone switchboard operator called my name.

"Jack, I have a call for you."

It was a good friend and member of the Seven Five Precinct.

"Jack, I just got an emergency call from Leo Campeze. He said you have two of his kids and his nephew, Freddy Rocco, in the SH."

"Who's Leo Campeze?"

"Leo Campeze, you know him and he's a good guy."

"I don't know any Leo Campeze and yes, we have a couple of Campezes and a Rocco here, so what about it?"

"Jack, can you give them a break? They're good kids."

"Joey, if they were such good kids I wouldn't be talking to you right now."

"Jack, can you give them a break?"

"I'll get back to you."

Before I had a chance to speak to Bob about the new developments, the TS operator called me again. I knew what it was, another friend looking for a big favor.

As the switchboard operator handed me the phone he said; "It's Angelo Ricardo"…Angelo was a member of our command and a good friend.

"Angelo, what can I do for you? No, let me guess, we arrested your godmother's best friend's three sons, right?"

"Close. You know my wife Maria, right? Well, you got her three stupid nephews in the SH."

"Give me the names."

"Anthony, Joseph, and Peter Riguzzi."

"Ang, let me tell you my problem and I hope IAD isn't monitoring this phone. I have Silverman on the desk and he almost had a heart attack a few minutes ago with another issue related to these arrests. Now you and Joey Armando from the Seven Five want me to cut the remaining six prisoners loose. I want you and Joey to come to the SH. I'll call Joe. You're on your way, right?"

"I'll be there in about twenty minutes."

I called Joe Armando and told him to come to the Nine Four with Leo Campeze.

As we waited for Angelo and Joe, I told Bobby Mack where "we" were with this arrest and the recent developments. The first thing Bobby said was thank goodness there was no paperwork . . . yet.

I returned to the desk and told Mel I had to speak to him in his office, which was adjacent to the desk.

"Sarge, I think this would be a very good time for you to take your meal hour."

"Why?"

"Trust me, you don't want to know. If you're on meal, you can't be blamed for anything that happens during the next hour. If you don't have a relief, Bobby will take the desk, but that's your call."

"Okay, have Sergeant Caruso Ten-Two, no emergency."

Sergeant Caruso was the direct opposite of Sergeant Silverman. He understood there were times when Bobby and I worked "outside the box," but we had a way of getting the job done and that's why we had our detail . . . WE GOT THE JOB DONE!!!

Sergeant Caruso arrived and relieved Mel. I waited a few minutes, allowing him to get settled, and then asked to speak to him in that side office.

"Sarge, earlier today the CO called me into his office and gave me a special assignment. Vinny Abruzzi asked him for a favor and you know who Vinny is, right?"

I brought him up to speed. I told him about Ralph and how I adjudicated that issue and I explained my plan for the remaining six.

"What we have here are six dumb 'neighborhood' Guidos who refused to obey the 'no hanging out' zone given to us by the boss. That's why they're here. Three of the six are friends of my friend from the Seven Five and the remaining three are related to Angelo Ricardo's wife.

"I have Angelo and Joey coming in to speak to these idiots. I think I can bring this condition to a successful conclusion tonight if you will allow me to use professional discretion. I promise I won't do anything until I get your okay."

"Jack, now I know why I'm relieving Mel early, right?"

"Right."

As I asked Bobby to join me in our Youth Office, to explain what my plan was, Angelo arrived, followed by Joey. I asked them to join us.

"Ang, Joe, you want me and Bobby to cut your people loose, right?"

"Yes."

"Yes."

"Our CO got a call from Vinny Abruzzi, you both know who and what he is, right?"

"Right."

"Right."

"Vinny has received so many complaints from the people living above the stores on Lorimer between Conselyea and Metropolitan that he came in to see the captain. Vinny doesn't ask for much, so the boss promised him that condition would be taken care of.

"The CO called me into his office and when he gave me this assignment he said, 'Jack, I want you and Bobby to make this problem disappear. I don't care how you do it, just do it.'

"Okay, this is the deal: Bobby and I are going to give you both as much time as needed to talk to those six morons. No, allow me to correct myself, Silverman returns from meal in forty-five minutes. You have thirty-five minutes to give us a solemn promise they will never return to that block. We don't even want to see them buying a slice at the pizzeria. If they're on the block and their two feet are not moving, they are hanging out. If and when you give us that commitment, we'll talk to them."

Bobby joined the conversation. He said, "We want them to know if they give us their word and agree to our proposal they will probably go home tonight with a warning."

We gave Angelo and Joey time to speak to their recently acquired goombas. A short while later Angelo came out of the room and told us they all understood.

Now it was our turn to seal this deal. We entered the room and I said, "Okay, allow me to review what Officers Ricardo and Armando told you all. Please stop me if I say something you don't understand or can't agree with.

"You were taken into custody because you failed to comply with our lawful orders. You can't hang out on either side of Lorimer Street between Conselyea Street and Metropolitan Avenue. Do you all understand that?"

"Yes."

"If you want to buy something from the pizzeria, go inside. If you are on Lorimer Street and your feet are not moving, you are hanging out. Do you understand?"

"Yes."

"Do you all understand that if you break your word to us you will be spending more time with me and Officer Mack than you spend with your mothers?"

Bob went to each punk and waited for the yes response.

The commitment was made, now all I needed to do was convince Sergeant Caruso to go along with our agreement.

"Sarge, I don't want to bore you with the entire story, but the bottom line is we have six neighborhood kids in custody. We brought them in for dis con. If we issue universal summonses, I believe Bobby and I will be spending a lot more time on this condition than necessary.

"If you will allow us to use discretion by giving them a warning as well as an admonishment, we feel confident this problem can be closed out as 'Condition Corrected.' The father of two of the mopes is also the uncle of another and he is happy with and understands this arrangement. Angelo's wife is the aunt of the other three and he will make sure they comply."

"Jack, this is your call. I have faith in you and Bobby. Do what you think is best to get the job done. Just do me a favor, get them out of here before Mel gets back. Oh and I know when he returns from meal he'll ask me about the six prisoners. My response will be, 'Don't ask. It's all on me.' I'm depending on you to make this disappear, do you understand?"

"Yes Sergeant, I certainly do. Thank you."

Looking back, Bobby and I got lucky on that evening. If Sergeant Silverman had made an entry into the official desk blotter when we brought the prisoners in, there was no way we could have gotten away with our "unorthodox" solution to this problem. No way on earth.

But he didn't . . . If Sergeant Silverman didn't allow me and quite frankly himself to take a walk on the edge of the penal law and the Patrol Guide by allowing me to cut Ralph a break, I could never have done what I did. Sergeant Caruso had confidence in me and himself, so that worked out well.

Any active cop will agree that police work is never cut-and-dried. Good cops and good bosses know how to think and sometimes work outside the box. Most people don't have a clue how difficult police work is. The old saying, "You're damned if you do and you're damned if you don't" is so, so true.

The end result of this Vinny Abruzzi complaint is: The kids kept their word most of the time and if we drove by and a few of them were not moving their feet when they saw us, they got into high gear. Vinny came in and personally thanked the captain for correcting the problem. The people who originally made the complaint came in to thank the CO and I'm sure Vinny had something to do with that.

Bobby and I got the opportunity to come back and do it all again the next day, but we did feel very good about the way this worked out.

Postscript

Our commanding officer, Captain Darcy, was one of the best bosses I ever worked for. We both had the same approach to policing: Get the job done. I trusted him implicitly and I know he felt the same about me.

One evening he invited Bobby and I to have coffee with him at a local coffee shop. He asked how we were able to resolve the Vinny Abruzzi complaint so quickly while avoiding CCRB.

"Captain, this conversation is not happening, right?"

"What conversation?"

I gave him the blow-by-blow details as I have written here. He thanked us for "Another job, well done," his words not mine. As we were leaving the shop, he said, "I know Caruso has balls, but Silverman, I didn't know he had it in him. I am pleasantly surprised."

39

MY INTRODUCTION TO SANTERIA

One very busy evening and while working in uniform Bobby and I received a call from Central: 94 conditions car investigate animals being mistreated in "The Back House" at Sixty-Three India. A back house is unusual for most areas in New York City. It's actually a house that was built on a large property. Eventually that land was subdivided allowing for a second house to be built in front of it. Ergo a back or second house built on the same lot.

The people living in the back house needed to walk through a narrow alleyway to get to the street. That house was not visible from the street and if you didn't know it was there, you wouldn't know it was there. Brilliant statement, but that pretty much identifies the layout.

Upon arrival we found the alleyway. As we entered the front yard of the back house we could see a fenced-in pen containing several goats and chickens. We also observed a well-lit first floor apartment. As I walked up the few steps to the front door I could see into the large front room, which was void of furniture except for about fifteen chairs lined up along two walls facing toward the center of the room. The chairs were occupied by men and women just sitting looking straight ahead. It was, to say the least, an eerie sight.

I was first into the house. As I entered the vestibule I heard the flapping of wings, which startled me. I looked up and saw a pigeon with one of its wings nailed to the upper door frame. What the F**k? I immediately went into "on guard" mode. My many years of experience kicked in and I knew when something didn't seem right . . . it wasn't.

A man approached us wearing a long white shirt that went down below his knees. He also wore white pants. I'm sure there is a name for his garb, I just don't know it. I ordered him to free the bird, which he did, and then we walked into what was obviously the living room.. The chairs were neatly placed side by side along two of the three walls and I didn't count the front wall with the two large windows. Then there was the fourth wall to the right of the doorway.

The far right corner was set up like a stage. They had a white sheet attached to the ceiling and draped like a canopy. Both corner walls were floor-to-ceiling white sheets and the floor was covered with a white sheet. Sitting on the floor in the middle of the sheet was a dark-skinned man dressed in white, pretty much like the guy who answered the door.

He was just sitting there with his hands and legs crossed. The people sitting in the chairs were looking straight ahead and didn't acknowledge our presence. Eerie to the max. They all appeared to be in a trancelike state. In front of the chairs were bowls containing what appeared to be blood and chicken feathers. I couldn't tell if there was anything else in the bowls.

It took a few seconds to come to terms with the images my eyes were sending to my brain. I had never seen or even heard of anything like what we walked in on.

We heard noise coming from the second floor, so we climbed the stairs and walked into a kitchen where several women, dressed in what appeared to be African style robes, were boiling meat in large pots and it smelled disgusting.

I went into a small side room, possibly a bedroom without a bed, and found goat parts that I won't expound on. Finally, there was a dead goat on the floor. Bob called for a sergeant and I asked Central to have the ASPCA respond to the address. I ordered the women to go downstairs to the living room and now we had everyone in one place.

The stench was so vile that I had to go outside onto the stoop to get some fresh air. That's when the guy who opened the door came out and asked me why we were there. I asked him what was going on and he told me they were performing a ritual according to their Santeria religion.

I had never heard of that religion. I didn't want to sound uninformed, so I said,

"What is your name?"

"My name is Mobuto; people call me Mo."

"Okay, Mo, can you tell me the purpose of this ritual?"

He told me the man sitting in the corner was in need of healing to rid him of the demons that caused him to seek out other men for sex. The people sitting in the room were there to pray for him. Mo, the priest, was conducting the service.

I inquired about the animals and he told me the goats and chickens were part of the ritual and were sacrificed as an offering. The bowls, containing goat blood and chicken feathers, were all part of the ritual. I asked about the meat being cooked and he said it was the goat and they would all eat after the service.

As I was speaking to the priest, our sergeant arrived, followed by the ASPCA police a few minutes later. The sergeant had no knowledge of the Santeria religion or their rituals and other than the animals being slaughtered, we couldn't think of a crime they had committed. The ASPCA police knew exactly what we had and issued several summonses to the priest, who was also the home owner, for violations including cruelty to animals.

Now that I knew we had at least one house in our precinct where the practitioners of the Santeria religion gathered, I decided to learn more about that religion, so I did some research. I learned a lot, but I will be brief and to the point as it relates to our involvement that evening.

Santeria is a system of beliefs that merges the Yoruba religion, which was brought to Cuba by West Africans, with Roman Catholicism.

Eventually it was brought to the Northeast by Cuban refugees. They don't have a central creed for their religious practice and their rituals and ceremonies take place in what are known as house-temples or houses of saints. Most of these houses are owned and run by initiated priests or priestesses, as was the case that evening.

The priest builds a shrine as a space for worship. On that evening, the man they were trying to heal took center stage. Animal sacrifice is a big part of their religion and the issue of animal sacrifice was taken to the Supreme Court of the United States. The court ruled that the animal cruelty laws targeted specifically at Yoruba were unconstitutional, which probably resulted in the summonses that were issued by the ASPCA police being dismissed.

Bob and I did have one more assignment at that location about six months later. We were called to investigate a violent dispute at that address. When we arrived, the same man/priest greeted us. There was no ceremony or gathering of people this time, just two men, excluding the priest, in need of medical attention.

Neither of the men would answer questions, such as why they both needed an ambulance to transport them to a hospital to get stitched up. In fact, neither combatant seemed to want the other arrested, but we couldn't just walk away, considering the physical damage they had inflicted on each other. This was a typical "Tell it to the judge" scenario.

The priest had no problem telling us what happened. I began, "Good afternoon, my name is Police Officer Fitzgerald and this is my partner Officer Mack. Your name is Mo, right?"

"Yes, that's right; you are the officers who came during our cleansing ritual a while ago."

He asked if we remembered the last time we were called to his house. "How could I forget?" He pointed to one of the men and said, that's Carlos, he is the man we held the ceremony for. We tried to free him from his homosexuality devil. It didn't work.

The priest continued, saying that Carlos caught his boyfriend Ramon cheating on him and he confronted him with a knife. Ramon responded with his own knife and they cut each other.

None of the wounds were life-threatening, but they would both be charged with felonious assault with weapons. The incident occurred in their apartment and we never recovered the knives, so there were no additional charges.

Our first stop was Greenpoint Hospital, where they spent time with the needle and thread man, Doctor Stitches. Then it was off to BCB.

This incident was treated as a domestic violence dispute with weapons and injuries. They were both held without bail. My partner was the arresting officer and he told me they both dropped all charges on their return date. The possession of weapons charges were dismissed because we never recovered the knives.

40

THE WESTIES

Bob Mack notified Central that we were 10-98 (resuming patrol) from our meal hour. That hour was usually spent in the gym hitting the heavy bag or each other while sparing, followed by a shower and finally some stress free time on patrol. Our routine was the same most of the time: It was August and the city was into the third day of a heat wave. At about three a.m., it would cool down to about 90 degrees, but during the day we're talking 95 to 100+. We usually wore street clothes, but due to the massive workload, we were assigned to our unmarked Plymouth in uniform, which allowed us to answer jobs.

"Nine Four Youth Car, no other units available, respond to shots fired. Two men shot, front of 437 Skillman. Be advised numerous calls at that location."

We pulled up to that address and saw what appeared to be an unoccupied Mercedes Benz parked in the middle of the street. The driver's door was wide open, so I went to that side and found four bullet holes in the door. Then I saw another bullet hole in the center of the steering wheel. Finally I could see blood on the seat and on the street just outside the door. Bobby checked the backseat; no one hiding there.

This was our Williamsburg section, which is predominately

Italian American. I am a transplanted Brooklynite, so I know both cultures identified here. In the middle-class suburbs, we hang out on the patio or by the pool, usually an aboveground pool, enjoying a beer or glass of wine. In middle-class Williamsburg and many other areas in the city, people hang out "on the stoop" or on the corner enjoying the same beer or glass of wine. That's the way it was that hot summer evening and it's still that way today.

That evening was no different from any other until the shoot-out in front of 437 Skillman.

We knew a lot of people in that neighborhood, so it didn't take long before a friend named Ralphie approached and said, "Jack, you and Bobby better be careful wit' this one. Me and Annette were sittin' on the stoop havin' a cup of coffee and the Benz pulls up and stops right in the middle of the street. Then this other guy pulls up behind him in a Ford, gets out, runs up to the driver and fires four shots into the car. The guy in the Benz shoots back and I think he hits the guy and that guy runs back to his car. He backs out of the street and drives away toward the BQE." (Brooklyn Queens Expressway.) "Ralph, what happened to the driver of the Benz?"

"He ran down Skillman, about a half a block, and went into a house on the right side of the street. I don't know what house, but we've been watching and we didn't see him come out and you guys got here fast, so I think he's still in that house. I see Vito down there; he'll tell you where the guy went."

"Thanks Ralph, tell Annette I said hello."

Bobby got on the portable.

"Nine Four Youth Car to Central, K."

"Nine Four Youth Car go."

"Central, be advised that shots fired job is founded. Can you have a Nine Four unit and a sergeant respond to front of 437 Skillman when available? We're searching for one of the shooters on Skillman. We'll keep you informed."

"Nine Four sergeant responding, Nine Four Anti-Crime on the way. Nine Four Edward on the way."

As we ran east on Skillman, the people on the block pointed farther down the block. About halfway down, I saw Vito Bavona who, before I could say a word said, "Bobby, Jack, the guy you're chasing went into the house two doors down. We heard the shots from down the block and I think that guy was shot. You better be careful, I saw a gun in his hand."

"Thanks, Vito. How long has he been in there?"

"Maybe a few minutes. But be careful."

Allow me to set this scene: As we entered that well-lit vestibule, we saw a man trying to crawl up the stairs toward the second floor; he was about halfway up. Every resident home at that time, about ten people, was watching. As I approached the man I could see he had been shot. He still had his gun in his hand as he struggled to crawl up the stairs.

I went up to where he was and took the revolver out of his hand and asked where he was hit. He looked me in the eyes and said, "F**k you cop." Here I am trying to help this guy who is most certainly in need of help and he says F**k me. Not very nice, right? It was at that moment I came to the conclusion he didn't like cops.

As we waited for the ambulance, I was about to tell Central to cancel the responding units when our Anti-Crime team arrived.

The first thing Joe Stremmel said was, "Jack, are you or Bobby taking this collar?"

"Good evening to you, too, Joe. Let me guess, you're in a dry spell, right?"

"You have no idea, I can't get myself arrested."

Bobby and I didn't have a quota. Our special assignment always generated more than enough activity and we knew Joe could use this one. On occasion, Anti-Crime needed a little help and this gun collar was a home run. If he could find the other shooter and that person was indeed shot, this arrest would go from a gun collar to an attempted murder collar. A grand slam home run. As we were about to give Joe this arrest, our sergeant arrived.

"Jack, Bobby, what do you have here?"

"We have this very rude foul mouth criminal under arrest and awaiting the arrival of a bus. He was shot on his left side and his left leg. You probably saw his Mercedes-Benz in front of 437 Skillman.

"If it's okay with you, Joe Stremmel will take the arrest. Bobby and I didn't witness anything and there were no statements made, so I can't think of a reason why Joe can't take it. I did recover the gun and if that becomes an issue, we're not going anywhere."

"Okay Joe, it's your collar. Jack, Bobby, take the Benz to the station house and put it in the garage. Let the DO know it must be safeguarded until Crime Scene does their thing."

As Bob drove the Benz into the garage I went to the desk and brought the lieutenant up to speed.

As the TS operator was making the notifications, a detective from the Eight Four Precinct called, requesting to speak to the DO. The lieutenant had a brief conversation with him and then handed the phone to me.

"Police Officer Fitzgerald, can I help you?"

"This is Detective Roberts from the Eight Four; I was told you had a shooting in your precinct a little while ago. Can you give me the particulars?"

"Yes, the guy we have was in his Mercedes-Benz when the driver of a black Ford pulled up behind him. The driver of the Ford got out and fired four shots into the Benz. Our driver/perp was hit and returned fire and I have been told by witnesses the driver of the Ford was hit before fleeing the scene."

"Can you give me any additional information about the one who got away?"

"All I have is he is a male white driving a black Ford."

"I think I have the other shooter. I'm at Cumberland Hospital with a man shot. He pulled up to the ER in a black Ford. Do you have anyone who can identify the shooter that got away?"

"I'm sure there were several witnesses who could finger your guy, but will they? That's the question."

"Who is taking your guy?"

"One of our Anti-Crime officers, Detective Stremmel."

"Okay, when I have more information I'll call back."

"Detective Roberts, don't call me, call Joe Stremmel."

Bob and I resumed patrol.

I didn't give that arrest more thought until about six months later, when I was notified that I had to report to the Federal Prosecutor's office in Manhattan. I was to meet with a prosecutor regarding the Skillman Avenue shooting.

"Officer Fitzgerald, I'm Special Prosecutor Walker and I am currently gathering information for a Federal Racketeering (RICO) case against a group of criminals known as the Westies. Have you ever heard of them?"

"No."

"You will. I am near the conclusion of my fact-finding process and that's why you are here. You were the first officer on the scene and you recovered the weapon from the hand of Mr. Murphy, correct?"

"Correct."

"Allow me to give you this story in a nutshell: The Westies is an Irish American gang from the west side of Manhattan. The Hell's Kitchen section to be exact. They are responsible for contract killings; drug trafficking, murder, racketeering, loan-sharking, bookmaking and extortion.

"They number between twelve and twenty members, depending on how many are in jail. We know they have murdered at least one hundred people since 1968. The Westies are a notoriously bad crew. There came a time when they hooked up with the Brooklyn Genovese crime family. There is a book written about the Westies that will hit the bookstores in a few days, but we're here to discuss your interaction with James Murphy." (Not his true name.)

"God was with you that night, Officer. Murphy has a long rap sheet and is a suspect in several contract murders. Is it true you actually took a .38 caliber revolver from his hand?"

"Yes. I must add that he didn't resist in any way. It was no big deal. He was trying to crawl up the stairs and I don't think he saw me approach."

"That's good for you because if he did I'm sure he wouldn't have hesitated shooting you. He is definitely a cold-blooded killer."

"Mr. Walker, there is one thing I am sure of; he doesn't like cops."

I hadn't prepared any written documents regarding my involvement in this incident other than a brief memo book entry. It wasn't my arrest and we had no way of knowing this was going to become a "Major Case" with the Feds.

"Officer Fitzgerald, I was told you spoke to several witnesses immediately after the shooting. Is that correct?"

"Yes."

"We would like to interview those people. Could you contact those witnesses and ask if they would be willing to speak to us?"

"Yes, I'll speak to them, but I'm not sure they will want to speak to you. That is a tight-lipped neighborhood. What I will do is ask them if they will talk to you. If they say yes, I'll give them your number. If they say no, which is what I expect, maybe I can act as a go-between for you. You ask me and I'll ask them. If they have info that will help you with your prosecution, I will do my best to get them to testify."

"Thank you, Officer Fitzgerald; I appreciate you coming in today. You've been a great help. I'll be in touch."

That was the last time I had anything to do with Prosecutor Walker or the Westies.

About three weeks later, the *Daily News* began an exposé on the notorious Irish gang known as the Westies. Their report included the ongoing trial in federal court and the prosecutor was none other than my new friend Mr. Walker. They exposed their heinous criminal activity, including the names of the gang members charged with those vicious violent crimes. One of the names at the top of the list was Jimmy Murphy.

In the book there was a reference to the incident I was involved in: There was a long-standing feud between a capo from the Genovese crime family and a few members of the Westies. Jimmy Murphy agreed to meet with a member of the Genovese family at a well-known Italian restaurant in Williamsburg to iron out their differences. Jimmy waited, but the Italian mobster never showed.

Jimmy returned to his car and began driving down Skillman Avenue, followed by a hitman from the other team, as in "the family." As Jimmy stopped his car in front of 437 Skillman due to a double-parked car blocking his way, the mobster ran up and shot him. He returned fire and the rest of the story is history.

Both shooters survived their wounds and were convicted of all charges and did serious time.

There came a time when I decided to buy the book. I must say it is a well-written exposé on one of the worst criminal gangs I ever heard of. I mean those guys were seriously B.A.D.

After reading the book, I had to agree with Mr. Walker. No doubt God and my patron saint, St. Michael the Archangel, saved me…. AGAIN.

41

GERRY THOMPSON

As I was preparing to leave my home to work a four to midnight tour, I received a phone call from one of my fellow PBA delegates, Johnny Aziz. He told me that Gerry Thompson, a member of his late tour carpool, called him and said that he found out his wife was cheating on him. He also said he wanted to end his life.

John knew Gerry and he knew this was a very serious threat. He convinced him to accept the help our NYPD Health Services Unit would provide.

John was away on vacation, but he contacted Health Services to inform them of the issue. A doctor asked John if he knew someone who would drive to Gerry's home to take possession of his revolvers and stay with him until two representatives from that department arrived. John called me and I called the doctor.

"Doctor Baum, this is PO Fitzgerald calling regarding Officer Gerry Thompson."

"Yes, Officer Fitzgerald, thank you for calling. I understand you spoke to Officer Aziz and you are familiar with this issue?"

"I did and I am."

"Are you able to go to Officer Thompson's home and take possession of his firearms?"

"Yes. I was also told you want me to stay with Gerry until your people arrive."

"Yes, that would be very helpful."

"I can do that, but I need you to call my command and have me assigned to Health Services for today. I'm scheduled to work a four to midnight tour and I will need to have that change of assignment made."

"I'll do that immediately and I would appreciate your leaving ASAP to Officer Thompson's home. How long do you think it will take you?"

"I'm not sure, but it shouldn't take more than forty-five minutes."

"Very good, I'll have our people leave here now. You have my number and please call me when you arrive."

As I drove, I realized the seriousness of what I had let myself in for. I really didn't know Gerry. He worked midnight to eight tours and I did four to midnights. We never worked together nor did we socialize.

My mind raced over this very dangerous, possibly deadly scenario; considering Gerry, by his own admission, was suicidal, I couldn't help but think maybe I was going to be the solution to his problem. Obviously he didn't want to shoot himself because he could have done that already.

I had been in tight spots before so I was not a stranger to adversity, but this was very, very different. I thought about the stories I read about people committing suicide by cop and prayed as I drove that this would not end up as one of those stories. I was not happy with where I was going or what I was being asked to do.

I arrived at Gerry's house and as I drove down his block I could see him standing in front of his home. My heart began to race and I didn't like the look on his face. What have I let myself in for? I drove a good 150 feet past his house to give myself time and distance between us.

I had my off-duty gun in my pocket and as I walked toward

him I had it ready for an easy quick draw. Now try to understand that up to that moment, in my police career, I had been in one very serious gunfight, shot at or threatened with weapons several times, and a few other close calls, but I never had the opportunity to think about the threat/danger I was walking into.

As I approached him I was truly alive and on an adrenaline high. I never took my eyes off his hands and knew exactly what I would do if he made a threatening move which, thank God, he didn't . . . I said, "Hi, Gerry, I guess you know why I'm here."

"Yes, the doctor from Health Services is on the phone and he wants to talk to you."

"I'll talk to him in a few minutes, but first I need to ask you: Where are your guns?"

"My service gun is in my locker and I'll show you where my off-duty is."

He began walking into his bedroom and as he neared a small end table I said, "Gerry, is your gun in that table?"

"Yes, I'll get it for you."

"Gerry, do me a favor, let me get the gun."

He looked at me with a smile on his face; he knew what I was thinking and I guess he didn't want to make my day any more stressful than it already was.

"It's in the top drawer."

"Thanks. Now where is your phone?"

I retrieved the off-duty weapon and got on the phone with the doctor.

"Good afternoon, Doctor."

"Officer Fitzgerald, how are you doing?"

"So far, so good."

"Do you have Officer Thompson's firearms?"

"Yes and no. I have possession of his off-duty revolver. He told me his service gun is in his locker. He owns two firearms. He gave me his locker number and the combination so I can get his service gun from his locker and voucher it for him tomorrow. By the way, Doctor, do you know when I can expect your people?"

"Sergeant White called a few minutes ago and told me they were delayed due to heavy traffic. Would it be possible for you to drive Officer Thompson into our Queens Health Care facility?"

Heavy traffic, what traffic. I listened to the traffic report while driving to Gerry's home and there was no traffic from the Queens line into Suffolk County, where we were.

What a lot of crap. I knew exactly what happened. They didn't have the balls to do what they asked me to do. They knew there was a strong possibility I would be walking into a classic "suicide by cop scenario."

I told the doctor I would bring Gerry to Health Services . . . The hour-and-thirty-minute ride went well and we chatted about the traffic and our command in general. He didn't say a word about what brought us together that day and neither did I.

When we arrived at QHC, I escorted Gerry to the doctor's office. The doctor greeted us as he took Gerry to a small room, then he thanked me and walked me to the elevator. He asked me if I had any personal knowledge of Gerry's marital problems or if we had discussed that issue on the way in. I answered no to both questions. I said good-bye, got on the elevator and drove home.

I felt sorry for Gerry because I knew what he was facing over the next couple of years; that is, if he was retained in the NYPD, which was very doubtful. The Department had a very high suicide rate and rarely allowed a member of the service to return to full duty after it was determined he/she was suicidal.

After months of treatment Gerry was returned to the Nine Four Precinct on restricted duty. No gun, no shield. He was assigned to the third platoon (four to midnight). I also worked that tour, so I got to know him over the next eighteen months. Johnny Aziz was right; Gerry was a very nice guy.

There came a time when he was told he would be retired and given a one third disability pension, which wasn't very much. Johnny and I contacted our Brooklyn North Financial Secretary and asked him to intervene. Jimmy Hogan was the best man for this job because he didn't take crap from anyone.

Jimmy did what he did best. He had Gerry examined by three experts in that field, including a recently retired department psychologist, and they all concluded the cause of his problem was long over. The medical board finally conceded.

Gerry was assigned to a sector on his former late shift. He studied and was eventually promoted to sergeant. The promotion resulted in an automatic reassignment. He completed his twenty years of service, retiring without further incident.

42

BULLET HEAD AND THE FEAST

Every summer Mount Carmel Catholic Church held a two-week-long feast on Havermeyer Street in the Nine Four Precinct. That church and school served our Italian American population in the Williamsburg section. Our precinct sent ten police officers and a sergeant to work the entire fourteen days.

They worked Monday to Friday from two p.m. until closing, which was usually about midnight, maybe one... On weekends they worked from eight a.m. until closing, which was no earlier than two a.m. The bottom line was the same ten PO s got that sweet job every year. They accrued about sixteen days on the lost time sheet and they didn't kill themselves.

I got lucky one Sunday when one of the regulars had to attend his brother's wedding.

Eighteen hours' lost time, a great lunch provided by the people who ran the feast and everyone was there to have a good time. When I returned to work on Tuesday, I asked the roll call man if I could get it again. "Jack, don't even think about it." That's just the way it was.

After I was elected as a PBA Delegate, a friend and member of the Nine Four asked to speak to me about the feast detail.

"Jack, the feast is coming up again and I want to request that assignment. I could use the lost time. My wife and I are expecting next month and I could use the time to help her with the baby."

As a delegate I now had the authority to ask questions about issues related to our police officers. I contacted our Brooklyn North Financial Secretary, Jimmy H., and told him about the conversation I had with Pete.

He did his homework and discovered that many years ago, when Father Angelo was assigned to Mount Carmel, he was put in charge of the feast. That first year he befriended the officers assigned to that detail and he just continued requesting they be assigned year after year. For some unknown reason no one challenged that unfair distribution of overtime . . . Up until now, that is!

With Jimmy's help I was going to "rock the boat." Jimmy reviewed our contract and discovered the Nine Four Precinct commanding officers had violated our contractual agreement with the city with that assignment. He met with me and my two co-delegates and we decided it was time for a change.

This Feast Detail issue should have been an easy fix, but it most certainly was not. For the following reason:

Our commanding officer, Captain Williams, was not easy to get along with. I discovered he was never a street cop. He began his career in a quiet precinct in Queens and took every opportunity to get off the street. He studied while guarding prisoners at the hospital. He studied whenever he could find a job that would allow him time to study on the job. Eventually he studied his way to the rank of captain, but he had very little on-the-job experience. He was what was known as a "Book Boss."

He didn't appreciate the good work the members of the Nine Four were doing and he was also under the misconception that the PBA and its delegates were powerless. In his words: "I am the commanding officer and I'll do what I want to do, the PBA has nothing to say." I can only assume he wasn't paying attention when his instructor in "New Captain School" told the class, "A happy worker is a productive worker." To my knowledge there were very few happy workers in our precinct under his command. Maybe ten!!

To write that he was not very popular is an understatement. Then we have his personal appearance: He was a short, bald, fat, dumpy man with a head shaped exactly like an old round-ball 38 caliber bullet. Ergo the nickname "Bullet Head." I admit not very nice, but his condescending, nasty attitude generated our lack of respect for him.

Jimmy called our CO and requested a meeting to discuss the feast detail. Captain Williams replied there was no reason to meet because there was nothing to discuss. He added that the feast was a nonissue.

Not a smart response, especially with Jimmy H., who then went to see the borough commander, a two-star chief. The chief knew Jimmy was right about the contract and called our CO and ordered him to meet with the PBA and work out this issue before it became an official contractual grievance.

The CO grudgingly agreed to the meeting to "work out" this nonissue, which by now was a serious issue. Two days later I joined Jimmy and my two co-delegates in the captain's office.

The CO began by saying, "I have been told you want to talk about the feast detail. Let's talk."

Jimmy responded, "Captain Williams, I know Chief Manzo has informed you that the methods being used to select the officers assigned to the Mount Carmel Feast detail are in violation of the PBA contract with the city."

"Okay, what changes do you want me to make?"

"We want two changes that will bring that detail closer to our contractual agreement. You are still ahead of the game because we will allow you to compensate the officers with time back in lieu of money. This is what we propose: That feast is fourteen days long, so we want the detail broken down into two one-week assignments. Ten officers week one and ten different officers week two. We want you to make that detail available to everyone in the command with more than ten years' seniority."

The CO was not happy with that idea. By agreeing to it he would be giving up his self-imposed "dictatorial authority" over his command. He would lose some juice. As he considered our proposal we could see his face turning a light shade of pink. Then he asked when we wanted to do this.

My co-delegate Bobby C. said, "Captain we have the list of officers who have submitted their names. I wrote their names on pieces of paper which will be placed in a hat. The names will be drawn at random. We're ready to do this now."

"Okay, let's get this over with. Before we begin I'm telling you now there are three men who I won't even consider. They are not eligible for that assignment."

He gave us the names of the three officers. The reason they were not to be considered was due to minor command disciplines. All three officers were productive members of the command, including my partner Billy C. Billy was one of the most active members in the command, but he was caught getting out of our RMP, on a burglary in progress run, without his hat.

Jimmy responded, "Okay, Captain, I was hoping our three delegates were wrong when they told me you were very difficult to get along with. I can see they were right. May I use your phone?"

"Why do you want to use my phone?"

"No, I won't use your phone I'll make my call from another office."

"Go ahead, make your call."

"Thank you. Hello, Lieutenant Cohen, is Chief Manzo in his office?"

Well folks, short, fat, dumpy Bullet Head bolted out of his chair and actually ended the call by pushing the end-call button on the telephone

"Why are you calling the chief?"

"Because his parting words to me as I was leaving his office were, "If you can't work this out with Captain Williams, I want you to call me. He also said he would then have this meeting in his office where he would take over the negotiations.

"Captain Williams, I interact with six commanding officers in Brooklyn North. Five of them are deputy inspectors. I can't recall having this much difficulty with such a simple issue. Before you so rudely ended my call I heard Lieutenant Cohen tell me the chief was in his office. I'm leaving now. I want to tell him how you are making this so difficult, in person."

With those words Captain Williams went from pink to red. We could also see he was beginning to perspire.

"Get your little pieces of paper and get a hat."

As we left the office Jimmy told the CO we would be back in a few minutes. We weren't expecting the three-officer exclusion part of the deal, so now we needed to improvise. I got my new hat that still had the piece of plastic on the inside center, which created a small pocket.

It was a department-issued hat and they all came with the pocket, so there could be no complaint about that. We had about thirty-five names written on little pieces of paper, including the three who were not to be considered but now were. I took the slips with the names of the blackballed officers and put them into the pocket.

As we walked into the office I could see Williams was almost back to his normal pale color. There was no small talk. He was really pissed off and just wanted to get this over with. Jimmy took the small square slips and tossed them into the hat and asked the captain if he would like to pick the names.

We all knew there was no way he would do any name picking. This just may have been his worst day as a boss. He was a captain and four subordinates, lowly police officers, were dictating policy to him. He would have no part in this travesty, which was almost causing him to have a stroke. Jimmy lifted the hat and asked Bobby C. to pick a name, then he went to Ralph C. and he picked another name, so far so good. Now it's my turn and I picked a name from the pocket. Bill Cahill, one of the men on the shit list and my partner. I could see the captain's face begin to change color. Light pink.

We went around again. This time Bobby C. picked a name from the pocket and as he read it out loud Bullet Head's face went to red, beet red. We were eight names into the twenty names needed to work the fourteen-day feast and it was my turn again.

I went into the pocket and picked the third name on the black-list. As I read that name the captain stood up and said, "The PBA wins. You pick the f***in' names and when you're finished just let me know who's working the feast."

We did as ordered and for the first time in a long time, the selection process was fair. No precinct politics came into play except for the three outcasts who were great cops and deserved a shot at a plum detail.

The priest wasn't happy. He lost his favorites and he didn't know any of the newly assigned officers.. He requested a meeting with Captain Williams who told him the officers assigned to the feast this year was out of his control. He had to abide by the contract. The feast went as expected. The usual minor incidents, due to overindulgence, but no arrests were made.

43

JAMES NAPOLI AKA JIMMY NAP

My father was born and raised in Brooklyn with his four brothers and three sisters. As a young man, before World War II, he worked in the Brooklyn Navy Yard and while there he became close friends with a fellow Navy Yard worker named James Napoli, aka, Jimmy Nap.

During my early teen years I spent a lot of time with my dad. One day as we were driving to my uncle's house, we passed a bar and grill on Metropolitan Avenue in the Greenpoint/Williamsburg section of Brooklyn. He stopped, parked the car, and told me to sit tight as he went into the bar, returning a few minutes later. I asked him why he went there and he said he wanted to see a friend he hadn't seen in a long time, but the man wasn't there.

He went on to tell me that the man's name was Jimmy Nap and they worked together in the Navy Yard a long time ago. That bar, called the Highway Tavern, was his hangout. They used to be close friends, but that ended when my father joined the Police Department and Jimmy went in a different direction. That's how he described their relationship.

Over the years, listening to my dad during conversations about the past, I learned Jimmy Nap was an associate in the Genovese crime family. His forte was gambling.

When I was assigned to the precinct that covered Jimmy's turf, my father told me that if I ever had a problem with any "wise guys" in Williamsburg, just ask to meet with Jimmy Nap and tell Jimmy who I was.

Williamsburg was a well-known mob neighborhood. The movie *Donnie Brasco* was filmed in Williamsburg because that's where the actual incidents took place. The clubs, the bars, the restaurants, and even the apartments where the mob guys lived were in my precinct.

I worked that area for twenty years and during that time I never had reason to contact Jimmy Nap, but I was curious to learn more about my father's old friend. Jimmy was very well known and respected in Williamsburg. One night, while assigned to a Golden Gloves Boxing show at Our Lady of Mount Carmel's church/school, a neighborhood friend gave me an elbow and said, "That's Jimmy Nap," as he walked in with his entourage. Now I knew what he looked like.

About five years later and while assigned to light duty due to a line of duty injury, I asked to work the TS (telephone switchboard). I found that assignment interesting because you had the people from the neighborhood calling requesting assistance with problems that didn't require a call to nine one one. Somebody was playing the radio too loud at five in the afternoon, a car was double-parked blocking someone, et cetera, et cetera, and very often I could handle the problem from my seat at the TS.

At about seven p.m., I received a call from the bartender at a very well-known restaurant in Williamsburg. The word on the street was Creasy's served excellent but expensive Italian food, which is why I didn't have firsthand knowledge.

"Nine Four Precinct, Police Officer Fitzgerald, may I help you?"

"Yes, Officer, I'm the bartender at Creasy's restaurant on Graham Avenue. One of my customers just had his car stolen from in front of our restaurant and he wants to make a report."

"Unfortunately we're very busy and it will probably take at least forty-five minutes before I can have a car respond."

"Forty-five minutes, there's nothing you can do? This guy is one of my best customers and I'm embarrassed he got his car stolen right from in front of our restaurant. Anything you could do would be appreciated."

"What's your name?"

"Jimmy."

"Okay, Jimmy, I'll make you a deal. I go on meal in ten minutes. I'll come to your restaurant and personally take the report if you make two dinners to go for me and my friend."

"Whatever you want, it will be done."

I asked my friend Lieutenant Sullivan, the desk officer, what he would like to have for dinner from Creasy's. Veal cutlet with pasta would be nice. I told Jimmy what we wanted and said I would see him in a few minutes.

It was a simple UF 61 for a stolen car. I did the paperwork and sent the alarm notification, no big deal. While I did that, Jimmy had the chef prepare two delicious veal cutlet parm dinners. As I was leaving with our food, I asked him for his full name and he said James Napoli Jr. I then asked if he was any relation to "the" Jimmy Nap and he said yes, that was his father.

That's when I told him that I was the son of one of his father's old friends from his days working in the Navy Yard. I asked if it would be possible for me to meet his father, as I'd heard so much about him from my father.

He asked me for my father's name and then he told me to call him in about an hour. I returned to the station house, had dinner with Lieutenant Sullivan, and made the call.

Jimmy asked what time I got off and I said ten. He told me to come by the restaurant at that time. By ten fifteen I was walking into the restaurant, where I met Jimmy Jr. He asked if I would like to have a glass of wine and I declined. As we left the restaurant, he told me his father was very ill with a brain tumor.

He took me across the street to a house that looked just like all the other row houses on the block. As I entered the first floor apartment there was the man I recognized as Jimmy Nap from the Golden Glove boxing show. He came over, shook my hand, and said welcome to my home. His home was absolutely beautiful. Expensive hand-carved wood furniture, antique tables, antique lamps; I felt like I was walking into a museum.

He asked if I would like a glass of his homemade wine, which I graciously accepted. As we sat he asked about my father and I told him he passed away several years ago. He began telling me stories about my dad and my uncles. No doubt he knew our family, as he remembered every brother's name and had stories about them all. He said the best of the lot was my father, who saved him on more than one occasion from getting his butt kicked at "the Yard."

I could not believe his memory. I sat listening to him reminisce for about forty-five minutes, enjoying this once-in-a-lifetime meeting with a man who was such a good friend of my father when they worked together decades ago.

Jimmy Nap was not what we think of when we hear the term organized crime. In fact I'm sure very few if any of the people reading this book have ever heard his name. Jimmy was loved and respected in the Williamsburg/Greenpoint neighborhood because he cared about the people in that neighborhood. He was known as a gentlemans gentleman.

At Thanksgiving, he bought a truckload of turkeys and gave them to people who didn't have money for turkeys. When a family was down on their luck, he provided for them until they got back on the feet. Yes, he may have been a member of a crime family, but his forte was gambling.

I looked at my watch and realized it was getting late, so I thanked Jimmy and Jimmy Jr., shook their hands, and told them if there was anything I could do, within my limits as a police officer, to call me. They thanked me and I left, thinking I had finally met my father's friend from many, many years ago. A short time after that meeting I read Jimmy Nap had passed away due to his cancer.

The uniformed patrol force had absolutely nothing to do with organized crime. We had nothing to do with gambling. My interaction with Jimmy Nap that evening was to finally meet a man who was, at one time, close to my father.

Jimmy Breslin, a well-known writer for the *Daily News*, devoted his entire half page article to Jimmy Nap and there wasn't a harsh word written. I still have that article.

P.S. For more detailed information about Jimmy Nap google James Napoli and go to his Wikipedia bio.

44

EVIL IS AS EVIL DOES EVEN AT FOURTEEN YEARS OF AGE

Halloween was one of our busiest nights and the night we came upon two of our well-known young punks was no exception. Bob and I watched as the two fourteen-year-old maggots, each carrying two cartons of eggs, walked past our unmarked car.

There was no doubt they were up to no good. We got out of the car and followed them for a short time and sure enough when they saw a woman with her young daughter coming out of a market on Nassau Avenue, they couldn't resist the targets.

The cretins unleashed a barrage of eggs at the woman and her daughter. They missed, but had no problem hitting every window at the Bumble Bee Market. Splat, splat, splat, all five very large windows were hit with eggs. We were on them like white on rice. We grabbed them, they resisted. We used minimum force to bring them under control, and then we cuffed them.

The woman, a young Polish immigrant, and her four-year-old daughter were frightened but unharmed. She didn't want to make a complaint. The store owner was not so forgiving.

Alex, the owner, knew one of the punks as a frequent shoplifter. He was never able to catch him as he ran out of the store with the goods, but he knew him. Now little Ernie was caught and it was Alex's turn. He didn't know the other kid, but he said he would do whatever we needed him to do. We transported them to the Nine Four SH and after a search, took them into the youth office.

Ernie DeMayo was a true low-life derelict. A young worthless bum. Bob and I arrested him many times for burglary, grand larceny auto, and other crimes. Other officers in the Nine Four arrested him for similar crimes. He was well known in Family Court. His fellow lowlife that evening was also known to us. Johnny Healy was another punk, burglar, car thief, and all-around juvenile delinquent. Two career criminals, but still within the jurisdiction of Family Court . . . Minor leagues.

We knew they were fourteen years old and considering the charge was criminal mischief, a misdemeanor, the most we could do was a youthful offender form, aka a YD card.

We called their parents and told them they needed to respond to the Nine Four SH . . . again, to pick up their boys, but this time they needed to pay the store owner, who wanted his windows washed. Neither had a father living at home, so we spoke to their mothers.

They both asked if we could just send their little boys home and we said absolutely not. Considering their sons' criminal history, I wanted to inconvenience both mothers as much as possible. There were consequences for raising juvenile delinquents and that's why I told the store owner to make sure he hired the most expensive window washer he could find. He responded that he didn't have to look far because the guy he had was very expensive, but he did a great job.

Ernie's mother arrived first with her usual attitude: My little Ernie didn't do anything wrong and you cops are always picking on him. That's why the little bastard was always getting arrested. I made her await the arrival of the other mother, who had to take a cab from the south side, a good fifteen-minute ride. Now we had both mothers in our office and we weren't surprised they knew each other.

We told them about the woman with the child and I could see they were both upset with their children by the way they looked at us, as in: "Is that all they did?" Then I asked how long it would take for them to return with the $200. They both responded in perfect harmony: "Two hundred dollars, what f***en two hundred dollars?"

I must admit I despised the two slugs, but I despised their mothers even more. Their permissive attitude allowed their boys to make life miserable for so many people on a daily basis. Now it was my turn. I had to make their mothers' lives as miserable as possible.

"Oh, Mrs. DeMayo and Mrs. Healy, I guess I forgot to tell you; when your never-do-anything-wrong children were throwing their eggs, they missed the woman and child, but they did hit all the windows at the Bumble Bee Market. The owner wants his windows washed."

Ernie's mother told us she would wash the windows, but I said no, the owner wants the windows washed by his contracted window washer. He will call him tomorrow and the cost for that service is $200.

Mrs. DeMayo said, "Officer Fitzgerald, we will contact the owner and make arrangements to pay him sometime tomorrow."

"Unfortunately that's not an option. You have two choices. Choice number one: You work it out between the two of you, but someone must come up with the two hundred dollars tonight, at which time your boys will be released into your custody.

"Choice number two: My partner and I will be happy to transport little Ernie and little Johnny to Spofford Youth House in the Bronx. I have no doubt you both know where Spofford is. In the morning, you can see them again when they appear in Family Court and at that time you can tell your story about making payment to a judge."

None of that was true, but the mothers didn't know that, so Mrs. DeMayo said she would be back with the money. She returned in about an hour with the cash and both women took their little dirt bag juvenile delinquents home.

My parting remark to both mothers and the young criminals was, "The owner of the market never wants to see either of your boys in his store again. If they walk in the door he will call us and we will make an arrest for criminal trespass. Do you both understand that?" Yes!

Epilogue to the Above Work and The Last Day in the Life of a Young Career Criminal

Over the next four years, Bobby and I arrested Ernie several times.

One cold dark night we were in our unmarked car parked under the trees just inside McCarren Park. That park covers an eight-block area and on a good night it was poorly lit. We were enjoying a container of coffee when we heard what sounded like a gunshot coming from the park house about one hundred yards away.

I drove to the sound and found a body lying face-down in the dirt. We went to aid the person only to discover it was Ernie DeMayo. The now not-so-little Ernie had a bullet hole in his eyebrow and he was dead, dead, dead. As Bobby was calling for an ambulance, the sergeant on patrol, the detectives, et cetera, a young man approached me out of the dark.

"You're Officer Fitzgerald, right?"

"Yes, and you are?"

"My name is Robert DeMayo, I'm Ernie's cousin."

"Were you witness to what happened here tonight?"

"Yeah, I was walking right next to Ernie."

"Okay Robert, can you tell me what happened?"

"Today is Ernie's eighteenth birthday and his mother had a party for him at their house. Everybody was smoking weed, but Ernie told me he wanted to go to the Eagle's Nest Bar across the park to have his first legal beer, so that's where we were going.

"As we walked past the park house, we saw these two Puerto

Rican guys sitting on the ledge by the house smoking. Ernie walked over to this one guy and said, 'Hey spick, give me a cigarette.' The guy stood up and walked over to Ernie. He took a gun out of his jacket pocket and shot Ernie in the face. I ran, the spicks ran and you guys pulled up."

As I was speaking to Robert, the Sergeant arrived, followed by two sectors. I got a vague description of the shooter as well as the other Puerto Rican guy, which Bob transmitted to Central.

Our witness said he wanted to return to the party. He wanted to tell Ernie's mother what happened. No way are you going anywhere. I knew that address and asked a sector to make the notification as I put Robert in the backseat of our vehicle.

The ambulance arrived and pronounced little Ernie DeMayo dead.

The sergeant secured the crime scene and we drove Robert around the neighborhood looking for the shooter. I knew we were wasting our time. We went through the motions, but considering the time lapse and unless the perp had a heart attack and dropped dead crossing the street, we had absolutely no chance of finding him in the dark.

The truth be told: The coldhearted reality of this crime, as far as I was concerned, was the shooter saved the good citizens of Greenpoint as well as all the other yet-to-be victims, a lot of grief. Killing that young, already identified, career criminal was a mercy killing. I know that's not a nice thing to say, but I also remembered that Polish woman and her little daughter. I remembered all the other victims of his never-ending crime spree. Yes, at times God works in mysterious ways and this was just another unsolved homicide in the "Naked City."

45

THE NOT AT ALL INFAMOUS JOHN GOTTI

Christmas morning in our home was a day I looked forward to, especially after our children were old enough to understand and appreciate Santa Claus. If I was scheduled to work an eight to four tour, I would request the day off. With seniority came the strong possibility that request would be granted. It went that way for my entire career, but there was one Christmas Eve when my routine was in jeopardy.

December 24, 1984, I was assigned to the Youth Gang Car with Bobby Mack. The desk officer ordered us to work in uniform so we could answer jobs if and when there was a backlog and we used our unmarked RMP.

December was our busiest month and Christmas Eve was always very busy. There are more homicides, suicides, robberies, and much more street crime in December.

At about eight thirty, sector Adam received a job on Eckford Street: Investigate a possible EDP involved in a motor vehicle accident. EDPs (emotionally disturbed person, aka psycho) were always dangerous, so we informed Central we would respond as a backup.

We arrived as the sector and the sergeant on patrol pulled up. A rather large crowd had gathered and we could see it was a two-car collision with minimal damage. We also saw a man about twenty-one years old yelling into the combination police/fire call box as he was hitting it with a baseball bat. Yes, a very possible psycho.

That call box was a rather expensive piece of equipment found on street corners in every neighborhood. If you needed the police or the fire department, you pushed the designated button and talked to the operator.

On that Christmas Eve our twenty-one-year-old child, John, was having a tantrum; I guess he didn't see the police pull up with our shiny blue and white cars, because he continued to scream into the call box as he did his best to destroy it with his bat.

No one wanted to make an arrest that evening. I definitely didn't want to arrest this guy and it wasn't even our job. I knew the two mopes in sector Adam were useless and as far as this job was concerned, they were spectators. I certainly didn't expect the sergeant to make the arrest. This was a tough one. Someone had to take proper police action for the damaged call box and we had to bring the idiot under control.

Bobby and I weren't used to taking crap from anyone, but on this evening we were going to try to avoid an arrest. I went over and took the bat away from the jerk and told him to calm down; he ignored me like I was invisible. The crowd looked on as this punk made us look bad. Really B. A.D.

He ranted and raved about us friggin' cops taking so long, but he didn't use friggin'. He also complained about the ambulance not responding for his girlfriend and it seems that was what he was screaming about into the call box.

He demanded and I mean really demanded that we take his girlfriend in a radio car to the hospital. I spoke to the girlfriend and she wasn't complaining about an injury. She wasn't even hurt and in fact she was embarrassed for the way her boyfriend was acting.

Folk, this guy was a classic Guido. A wannabe wise guy,

showing off in front of the crowd and his girlfriend. Before we had a chance to tell him what he could do with his demands, the ambulance arrived.

Then I heard someone from the crowd say, in a loud voice, "I wonder just how much shit those cops are going to take from that punk." Yes, a very good question. How much shit are we going to take.

When the EMT approached us, he asked who was in need of medical assistance and that's when the punk told him to put his girlfriend in the ambulance and take her to the hospital, NOW. The EMT asked to see the girlfriend and that's when he went wild.

I don't recall his exact words, but he was nonstop verbal abuse. There came a time when the technician told him to shut up and he responded, "My name is John Gotti and you're going to do exactly what I tell you to do."

Now I get it!!! I understood John's mindset. This jamoke really thought he was the reincarnated infamous Mafia boss, "the" John Gotti

(For those of you not familiar with NYC mob history, the real John Gotti was the boss of the Gambino crime family. He became known as the most powerful and most dangerous boss in the country)

The technician ignored him and questioned the girlfriend about her injury. It was clear her injuries were so minor that she didn't need to be transported to a hospital, but if she wanted to go they would take her. After that brief conversation, she said she didn't want to go to the hospital, but John was on a roll.

The new "Mob boss John Gotti" was having his fifteen minutes of fame and enjoying every minute of it. He could see the crowd watching him carry on and he actually thought they were impressed by his machismo.

As the tech began preparing the required "Refused medical aid" forms, I had the pleasure of informing Johnny boy that his girlfriend changed her mind and wasn't going to the hospital.

I had been down this road many times before with the "wannabe wise guy" members of our Italian neighborhood. I knew exactly where this was going and with the crowd of onlookers watching our every move, I wanted to cover my ass. I went into my "Good Cop" routine and I was an expert at that persona.

The following conversation was loud enough for everyone to hear.

"Mr. Gotti, your friend Angelina has decided she doesn't want to go to the hospital and she will visit her family doctor."

"No F***en way. She's goin' and dat's dat. Get dat in your F***en head now."

"Mr. Gotti, I'm sorry, but it doesn't work that way."

"Don't tell me how it works; just get her to da hospital NOW."

"Mr. Gotti, those officers over there (I put that on sector Adam; it was their job) will prepare the accident report and they will also speak to you about the damage you did to the call box with your bat. The ambulance has other people in need of medical attention and they will be leaving NOW."

His last attempt at immortality came as the technician was returning to the ambulance. I knew exactly what was going to happen and I was ready: Johnny boy Gotti grabbed the tech's arm and said, "I told you to get us to the hospital."

I could no longer stand by and watch this idiot make us look like fools. My pride as a police officer would not permit me to allow this "John Gotti" to continue. NO F***EN WAY!!! As I walked over and grabbed his arm, I said, "You're under arrest."

He tried to punch me, but I blocked it and smacked him across the face with an open hand. ("Bitch slapping" a twenty-one-year-old Guido wannabe wise guy is one of the worst insults you can give.) I knocked him down with the smack, which made it worse. I could tell by the way he looked up at me, he was dazed and shocked.

I could read his little pea brain. He was saying to himself: What the F**k just happened? He had gotten away with so much crap and we, the cops, did nothing and now all of a sudden "KAPOW." He was on the ground looking up with that glassy-eyed look I had seen many times before.

The crowd of people went wild; they clapped and actually cheered my bold move, which felt very good. One man, who I knew from the neighborhood, came over and told me he wanted to buy me dinner. Another woman asked if I was working tomorrow, Christmas Day, and wanted me to come to her home for dinner with her family. It was clear that up until that moment every person in the crowd had lost all respect for the police officers in the Nine Four Precinct for allowing this punk to get away with his wise-guy bullshit attitude.

I went from a feeling of disgust with myself for allowing "John Gotti" to make us look like chumps to a feeling of pride for doing what needed to be done, even though I was probably going to miss Christmas morning with my family.

I was very angry with the two men given the assignment. It was their responsibility to take "proper police action." They should never have let John go as far as he did.

Finally I helped my prisoner up from the street, as he was still dazed. My smack was a true 5 on the Richter scale and could be heard in Chicago. I cuffed him and in a rather loud voice said, "Now, John Gotti, you are under arrest and going to jail on Christmas Eve."

Another round of applause from the crowd. The sergeant thanked me for doing the right thing and said, "Jack, I really didn't want to order anyone to make this arrest, but it had to be done." Then he drove Angelina home. Sector Adam did the accident report.

Bobby and I took John to the Nine Four. I did the printing as Bob did the arrest forms. We made short work of that process before moving on to the BCB. We were pleasantly surprised to find a short line. I was expecting the usual madhouse, but it was still reasonably early and the rush would probably begin later that evening and well into Christmas morning.

Bob knew most of the bosses and cops assigned to BCB. He was temporarily assigned there for several months while recovering from a line of duty injury and that familiarity was going to come into play that evening.

Now that John was handcuffed to the railing, it was clear to him that he was in trouble. This was not the way this scene was supposed to play out. He apologized over and over, telling me he didn't know what got into him. He told us he wasn't a bad guy and then he told us his uncle was Vinny Flynn, a sergeant in our precinct and a great boss.

I called the precinct and got Sergeant Flynn's home phone number. He answered the phone and I asked him if he had a nephew named John Gotti. He said no, but he knew his father for years and the father was a good guy. The kid thought he was a made member of some fictitious crime family because of his name. Vinny went on to tell me that John was a little slow, but deep down not a bad kid. Then he wanted to know why I called.

I gave him a blow-by-blow description of the events that took place that evening. I asked Vinny if he wanted me to cut him some slack and he said if it was possible, but not if it was going to create a problem for me or Bobby.

John Gotti was now a timid, repentant former wannabe wise guy who literally had the error of his ways smacked into him. Bob spoke to the sergeant in charge. He told him about the phone call to our sergeant and asked if we could take John back to the Nine Four and issue him a DAT (Desk Appearance Ticket).

Before the call to Sergeant Flynn, the charges were: Criminal mischief for breaking the call box, obstructing governmental administration, harassment on the technician, failing to comply with a lawful order, and of course resisting arrest to cover my well-deserved smack. All misdemeanors except for the baseball bat assault on the call box. That was felonious criminal mischief due to the cost of the box.

The BCB boss had no problem with our request and made the

necessary changes in their arrest log, which included a few changes to the original charges. This was not a big deal.

We took Johnny back to the Nine Four and explained everything to our desk officer. He too had no problem with the DAT as long as he didn't have an outstanding warrant. We had to redo the arrest forms and the prints with the amended charges.

I changed the felony criminal mischief to a misdemeanor. I had no idea how much the repair to the call box would be, my estimate was based on an uneducated guess, so that change wasn't an issue. He was going to pay for the repair or replacement and that was a guarantee. You damage city property and you WILL pay.

I was doing another member of the service a small favor and I was doing myself a very big favor. The misdemeanor would allow me to be home with my family. I issued him a DAT for criminal mischief as a misdemeanor and resisting arrest.

The end result of that memorable Christmas Eve tour was that the not-so-famous John Gotti, who tried to show off in front of his girlfriend by disrespecting New York's Finest, got bitch-slapped and knocked on his ass in front of the neighborhood he was trying to impress. He had to hire a lawyer to represent him in court, where he pleaded guilty and received a $500 fine plus a bill for the repairs to the call box amounting to $4,500; I was right with my estimate, but it was what it was and he paid the bill.

I received the approval of the neighborhood people who witnessed his tirade. I also received an offer for a free meal, which I never accepted, as well as an offer to have Christmas dinner with another appreciative family, which I also declined. I did get to go home, a little later than expected, but I spent Christmas morning with my family.

Oh, and now for the final insult/disrespect for John: The patrol sergeant who drove Angelina home told me she told him she had never been so embarrassed in her life. She added that her friends told her about my man Johnny, but she didn't believe them. Now she did and she would never talk to or see to him again.

46

THE NOT-SO-HANDY BOMB MAKER

I was on restricted duty that hot Saturday evening and assigned as the "arrest processing officer." I spent my meal hour in the gym, as usual. I worked myself back into great shape and my back injury was no longer an issue. I wanted to return to full duty, but that was up to a department surgeon to give me the go-ahead.

I had already assisted three sector teams and we were down one RMP due to a collision the night before. With three sectors out of service at BCB and one RMP in the shop, we were down to three sectors and a sergeant for the entire precinct. Every precinct in our division was in a backlog with "no units available."

As I was having a cup of coffee with Lieutenant Farrell, we heard a call on the radio.

"Any available Nine Four units to respond to a report of an explosion at One Fifty-Six Green Street? Any available units?" No answer.

"Numerous calls at One Fifty-Six Green Street, any available units? . . . Nine Four sergeant? . . . Any Nine O units available? I now have a report of a large crowd in front of One Fifty-Six Green."

I could feel the adrenaline pumping through my veins. I

wanted to get back in the game. "Put me in coach, I'm ready to play!!!"

I told the desk officer I would volunteer to respond to that location to assist the sector when one became available. That move on my part was a first. Being on restricted duty made me "absolutely positively" ineligible for patrol duty. I could not even leave the station house to go on meal in uniform.

The desk officer knew my dedication to the job, especially when the going got tough. This was one of those times. He took a long hard look at me and I could read his mind: I'm out of my mind for going along with this insane idea.

"Jack, are you sure you're up to this?"

"Yes sir. I'll be there to assist the sector when they arrive and I'm just waiting to see the surgeon to be returned to full duty."

"Change into uniform and take RMP Eleven Forty-Two."

Lieutenant Farrell was a street cop before studying his way up to lieutenant. He knew the job and he knew from time to time, under extreme conditions, you must think outside the box. On that evening our desk officer didn't just think outside the box he thought outside the ball park.

As I returned to the desk I heard sector Charlie acknowledge taking the job. I took the keys for the RMP and told the lieutenant I was leaving. I drove to the job and arrived just as the sector pulled up. When Bill Clementi saw me get out of my car he said, "Jack, what are you doing here? You're still a house mouse. Oh, I get it. The injury to your back wasn't bad enough to get three quarters so you put your uniform on, stole an RMP, and resumed patrol. Good move, it might even work. No doubt Psych services will find you absolutely out of your friggin' mind and give you the disability for being crazy. Why didn't I think of that?"

"Very funny, Billy, let's get to work."

There was a very large crowd gathered in front of 156 Green. The sidewalk, the street halfway up and halfway down Green, was wall-to-wall people. There were only three of us, so we didn't even consider trying to move the crowd. They were just standing around, so no big problem.

I knew many of the residents in that part of the precinct, so when I saw Jimmy Sydlanski, I asked him if he knew what happened.

"Jimmy, did you see what happened here?"

"I didn't see anything, but I heard an explosion. Joe Ortiz knows more about what happened."

"Yo, Joe, you got a minute?"

" Yeah Jack, what can I do for you?"

"You saw what happened here?"

"Yeah. Me and Lenny was hangin' out on his stoop when all of a sudden kaboom. The windows on the third floor of that house got blown out and the glass fell all over the sidewalk. Good thing nobody was hangin' out over there."

"Jimmy, Joe, don't go too far in case I need to ask you a few more questions."

I entered the building and found Bill and his partner on the third floor in apartment Three L. I had never seen the aftermath of an explosion before, so this was going to be a first. We found the results of the blast in the front/living room. The middle room showed signs of damage, but the kitchen was clean. The two front windows, gone. Blown out. You get the picture.

We found most of a dead body as well as a few body parts in that front room. We also found a few parts in the middle room. That guy was literally blown to pieces and the blood splatter was everywhere.

I found what appeared to be two pipe bombs on the floor, in a box, in the middle room. I used my Sherlock Holmes powers of deduction and came to the conclusion the damage was caused by a bomb.

I was the senior man on the scene, so I took charge. I found a phone and called Lieutenant Farrell.

"Lieutenant, Officer Fitzgerald reporting: I'm on the scene with sector Charlie."

"Thanks for calling. Jack, Your timing is right on. The Borough just called and the chief was notified about the explosion. I need as much info as you can give me at this time. You know the drill: who, what, when, where, and why."

"Lou, at this time I can give a partial answer to your question. What—an explosion that I believe was caused by a pipe bomb. When—Central received the first call at exactly nine fourteen. Where—One Fifty-Six Green Street, apartment three left on the third floor.

"Now for my report: There was an explosion resulting in one 'very possible' dead body, damage to the apartment and we found what looks like two pipe bombs. I have safeguarded the bombs without moving them.

"There's a large crowd in front of the building, but they're just standing around. We need the sergeant on patrol when he's available. The bomb squad ASAP, the Duty Captain, any available sectors for crowd control, and an ambulance when one becomes available. No need to put a rush on the bus, this guy isn't going anywhere.

"Sector Charlie began a building evacuation minutes after we arrived and Bill Clementi just told me everyone from this building is on the street. They are now evacuating the two adjacent buildings. At this time we have done all we can do. "

"Good. Keep me informed."

While the sector safeguarded the scene, I went outside to find someone who lived in the building.

A man approached and said he lived on the second floor.

"What is your name, sir?"

"Mike and you are Officer Fitzgerald, right?"

"Yes Mike, I can definitely use your help."

"Officer, can I ask what happened on the third floor?"

"Yes, but can I ask you if you know the guy who lives in that apartment?"

"I really don't know him. He moved in about two months ago

and keeps to himself. He's Puerto Rican and doesn't speak much English."

"Thanks Mike. I'm sure you figured out there was an explosion in that apartment. We're trying to figure out what caused that explosion and now we need everyone to move away from the front of this building."

As I was about to return to the apartment, the Duty Captain arrived. It was none other than my former sergeant and now captain, Tim Snyder. Of all the DCs that could have shown up, he was the best. Nothing rattles Captain Snyder. The members of our command who knew him gave him a nickname, to wit, Sergeant Cool or Sergeant Fonz., but now he was Captain Cool and Captain Fonz. Those nicknames were used with utmost respect for his ability to remain calm under pressure. Timmy had class and I never saw him sweat.

I took him to the crime scene on the third floor, where we joined Bill Clementi and his partner Bob Connolly. He took one look around and asked, "Have you searched the apartment for additional bombs or bomb-making material?"

"Yes and no. We did find two more bombs under this table and we did our best to safeguard them without touching them. We haven't had time to search further."

"Good work. Bill, you take the kitchen. Bobby you take the middle room and Jack take the front room. I want you all to do a superficial search of every part of your designated area without touching or moving anything. Do you all understand what I just said?"

"Yes, Captain."

"Where's the house phone, I need to call the Borough."

As we were searching our designated areas the sergeant arrived, followed by another sector. The first thing Sergeant Jefferson said was, "Jack, are you lost? What are you doing here?"

"No, Sarge. Due to this dire circumstance and the lack of manpower, I am doing what needs to be done. If this scenario goes down the way Lieutenant Farrell and Captain Snyder hope it does, I am not here. I am at the Nine Four doing my arrest processing job."

"I get the picture. Jack, sector Charlie and sector Frank are outside moving the crowd, do me a favor get the names and contact info for everyone who has knowledge of what happened here tonight. I told him I has accomplished that mission soon after arrival.

As the sergeant waited for Captain Snyder to end his call, I brought him up to speed. There was no mystery with regard to what happened and the why question would be answered by a different agency in the NYPD after an investigation.

Finally two detectives from the bomb squad arrived and I showed them where the two pipe bombs were. Detective Adams took one look at the metal pipes and asked if the building had been evacuated . . . Yes. I then heard him call his office requesting the bomb disposal truck be dispatched to our location.

The captain called Lieutenant Farrell to let him know he was on the scene and had called the Borough Office. Then he said, "Lou, have you made any entries in the log regarding Jack Fitzgerald responding to this job?"

"No and unless there came a time when I needed to, I wasn't going to"

"Don't. I'll take care of that if it becomes an issue, which I don't think it will. You did what needed to be done and you did the right thing. The bomb squad just arrived and they're waiting for their bomb disposal truck before they move the two bombs. I'll keep you informed.

The captain gave me the keys to his unmarked RMP and told me he needed his attaché case. As I walked to his car I could see the entire block had been evacuated. The only police presence was an Emergency Service truck about one hundred feet away. On the way to the car I walked past the ESU sergeant as he was talking to two of his officers.

He stopped me and asked if I knew I was walking through a restricted area. Then he ordered me to leave the area and join the two sectors doing crowd control on the corner two hundred feet away. It wasn't so much his words as his condescending attitude and the wise guy smirk on his face.

The way I heard the question was: Hey stupid, are you some kind of idiot? Don't you know they have bombs in that building?

He was a young sergeant and clearly new to the role of supervisor. I also believe he was trying to impress the other ESU officers. I was not young and I had a lot more street experience than he did, so I took the high road. I walked just out of hearing range of the other two officers and said, "Sergeant, can I speak to you over here for a moment."

"Yes, what do you want?"

"Sergeant I am aware of the bombs in that building. I was one of the first officers on the scene. I found the two bombs. I helped the sector evacuate the building and I've spent the past forty- five minutes in the apartment not ten feet away from where the bombs are located.

"Captain Snyder, the Duty Captain, has made me his aide. I am going to his vehicle to retrieve his attaché case as ordered. If you have a problem with that, I suggest you speak to Captain Snyder. You can find him at the scene of the explosion on the third floor of One Fifty-Six Green."

He had no response. He turned and walked back to his truck as I went to the car. I found the attaché case and returned to the crime scene. (Note: I had nothing but respect for everyone assigned to Emergency Service Unit. They have a very difficult and very dangerous job. I did not want to disrespect that sergeant in front of his men, but I did need to let him know I would not accept his disrespectful condescending attitude.)

The captain asked me to draw a sketch of the apartment identifying where the dead body as well as the body parts were found. I also noted where I found the two pipe bombs. No need to use a tape measure, just approximate, the crime scene photos would tell more than my sketch. As I worked on that sketch, the ambulance arrived and pronounced the dead guy officially DOA.

The Crime Scene Unit was on the way to take photos of the apartment and the medical examiner would arrive whenever he got there.

Detective Adams spoke to Captain Snyder.

"Captain, the bomb truck is on the way with a thirty-minute ETA. If the two adjacent buildings haven't been evacuated, now is the time to get that done. As you know, the bombs are unstable, so when the time comes for me to take them to the truck, I need all members of the service to be out of the building."

I overheard Detective Adams during his conversation with the captain and told him both buildings had been evacuated by the sector.

It was a little after twelve thirty . . . Captain Snyder ordered the sector to remain on the scene until they were relieved by the late tour. We returned to the station house and he spent a good half hour making entries in the Log and bringing the desk officer up to speed. Then he called the Borough and did the same with the officer on night duty.

I helped prepare the numerous reports needed for this incident. I had all the names, addresses and phone numbers of witnesses that could possibly be called upon down the road if needed.

By three fifteen, we were pretty much finished with the massive amount of paperwork required for this job. Captain Snyder said, "Jack it's been a long stressful night, how about breakfast?"

"Sounds good, where are we going? There's no decent place open at this time around here."

"Here's the keys, you drive."

"Where are we going?"

"Do you know how to get to Junior's?"

"Of course."

"Drive."

I enjoyed spending some time with a good friend over breakfast. He paid the bill and as he did that I ordered three large containers of coffee and a cheesecake for the desk officer, the telephone switchboard operator, and the PAA (Police administrative aide) in the 124 room (clerical office) . . . I paid that bill.

We returned to the Nine Four just as the late tour sector arrived from the crime scene. The bomb squad had safely removed the two bombs and the medical examiner did what he needed to do and the body was removed to the Kings County Hospital Morgue.

It was five a.m., the end of another long, eventful tour. A good tour. No, make that a very good tour.

Epilogue

The dead bomb maker was a member of the FALN, also known as the armed forces of the Puerto Rican National Liberation organization.

That radical group came on the scene at 1:29 p.m. on Friday, January 24, 1975. They planted a large bomb in Fraunces Tavern on Pearl Street in lower Manhattan. Fraunces Tavern is a landmark restaurant in the Wall Street area. (Ralph Washington gave his farewell speech to his officers there in 1783.) The tremendous explosion rocked the building and caused the death of four executives from Wall Street as they were having lunch. Many others suffered severe injuries.

The FALN claimed responsibility. Their message was that they were dedicated to using violence to free their island from the grips of the United States.

Their weapon of choice was the pipe bomb. They continued planting bombs in Manhattan, Chicago, Washington, DC, Newark and Miami, killing and injuring more than 130 innocent victims.

With regard to Lieutenant Farrell: My only concern with him allowing my response to that job was within our command. The only person who would make an issue of it was our commanding officer. I asked Captain Snyder, as a favor to me, to speak to our CO and explain that my presence at that scene was essential to the successful conclusion to a dangerous/deadly situation. He went further: He wrote a letter of commendation for the lieutenant.

When all was said and done, Police Officer Fitzgerald completed his tour as the arrest processing officer without interruption.

The final/end result of this very long tour was: One—I was happy that I was given the opportunity to perform as a police officer again. Two—Lieutenant Farrell was pleased with his letter. No one ever said a word about my involvement. As far as the NYPD was concerned there was no change of assignment for me. I was the arrest processing officer and as far as my name on the reports: As we say in Brooklyn, "Who knew?"

During my twenty-six years "on the job" I met and worked under many very good supervisors. Lieutenant Farrell was one of the best.

Lieutenant Farrell passed away shortly after his forced retirement due to the sixty-two-year age limit. "Tom" loved "The Job." He was a special person. I remember one four to twelve tour when I went a little over the line and he needed to read me the riot act. I was wrong and deserved the verbal reprimand. Two hours later, he asked me if I was stopping, for a pint, after work. Every member of our command respected him to the max and he lived for what he did. I have no doubt Lieutenant Farrell died from a broken heart.

God bless you, Lou, you are a legend to everyone who knew you. Captain Snyder was a one-of-a-kind boss. I don't recall a time when he needed to give an order to a member of the command. He was so well liked and respected, all he needed to do was suggest police action was required and it was done. He led from the front. Timmy was and still is my friend and I have nothing but the utmost respect for him.

Timmy: You are truly the BEST.

47

THE BRAND NEW WHITE SATIN JACKET

During my last year as a police officer and due to permanent injuries sustained during two separate RMP accidents, I was placed on restricted duty.

As a senior member of the command and the senior PBA delegate (union representative,) I was given a choice of assignments. The timing was perfect; the designated "arrest processing officer" retired, so that position was available. I'll take it.

That job was relatively simple: When a police officer arrived with a prisoner(s), that officer would do all that needed to be done in front of the desk officer, to wit, a prisoner search. He would give the name(s) and charges to the DO. He would take his prisoner(s) into the arrest processing room adjacent to the desk and that's when I would be called.

While the arresting officer prepared his/her required forms, I took control of the prisoner(s). Before they went into the cell I would always do another prisoner search just in case the AO missed something. On occasion it did happen. Then I took their fingerprints. If they wanted to make a phone call, I would make that happen. When that was done I would help with the paperwork. That assignment was usually methodical . . . until it wasn't.

One evening, two of our very young, relatively inexperienced police officers arrested two nineteen-year-old men from our Williamsburg (Italian American) neighborhood. They were charged with disorderly conduct, sexual harassment, and resisting arrest.

According to the arresting officers, Anthony and Carmine were at the corner of Graham Avenue and Conselyea Street harassing and annoying pedestrians as they walked by, giving special attention to the young ladies. They were trying to grab certain body parts as they passed. Someone called 911, our officers responded to investigate and were met by Mr. Anthony Wannabe Wise Guy and his sidekick Carmine Bagadoughnuts.

The two Guidos had been drinking and smoking weed, so they were combative from the get-go. When our officers began to question them their response was a ration of crap, resulting in their arrest. They felt they had done nothing wrong so they resisted and a minimum amount of force was used to handcuff them.

When they arrived at the SH I could see both officers were close to the breaking point and just about ready to smack one or both upside the head. I've been there many times and know the feeling. It's like, I didn't come to work today looking to have my balls busted by a couple of stupid drunks.

I told the officers I would do the required search in front of the desk officer while they took a few minutes to relax and get a cup of coffee. There was no need to rush this process and they could use a break.

To say the two punks had a bad attitude would be an extreme understatement, especially Anthony. Anthony was a Super Macho Guido wearing a beautiful, ultra-shiny/almost glowing, white satin jacket. It was nice and Anthony was feeling important as he strutted around wearing it. He was somebody and he thought who the f*** he was. He was definitely the lead singer in that duet.

Now it was time to move on to the arrest processing room and into the cell. That room is about 25' x 15' including the cell. The room also contained a desk used by the arresting officers and a cabinet containing all the items needed to fingerprint prisoners, to wit, a secured glass ink plate, fingerprint ink, and fingerprint cards.

Now I must tell you about fingerprint ink. It is a gooey, very dense, paste-like substance. Pitch black and it comes in a tooth-paste-like tube. It is so hard to wash off your hands, we used rubber gloves when fingerprinting.

Back to the two jerks. Once Anthony got comfortable with his new surroundings he picked up where he left off, verbally harassing and abusing both arresting officers. He told them that he paid their salary. They were just public servants yada, yada, yada.

This went on for several minutes and I could see both officers straining to keep their cool while they tried to concentrate on the arrest forms. Every time he was asked a question he had a nasty vulgar response.

"Anthony, what is your full name?"

"Anthony Mister Anthony. Just call me Mister Anthony."

"Anthony, what is your address?"

"Ask your mother, she knows where I live."

"Anthony, what is your date of birth?"

"Youse are so smart, youse can figure it out."

"Anthony, where were you born?"

"Up your mother's ***."

I couldn't allow this verbal assault to continue. My job was to assist the arresting officers and that is exactly what I was going to do. I asked both officers to join me outside the APR.

"Mike, Pete, don't let this idiot get to you. I know exactly what you're thinking, but it's not worth it. Been there, done that. He wants to get to you. He wants you to go into that cell and throw him a beatin' so he can give you a civilian complaint and then he'll lawyer up and sue you and the city. You're pissin' him off by remaining calm. You're not responding and that is a good thing. Listen to me: Relax. Stay cool, let me do what needs to be done."

"Thanks, Jack, you are reading our minds."

"The last thing I want to say is: No matter what I say in that room, do not show emotion. Do not get upset, do you both understand?"

"Yes."

"Yes."

We returned to the room and I got ready for fingerprinting. Three cards each, ink, and the roller. I'm good to go. I took Carmine out first. He was beginning to sober up and the fun had come to an end. He complied with my instructions, fingerprinting went well. I took him to the restroom to wash his hands and all the while his out-of-control idiot goomba never missed a beat with his verbal assault on the arresting officers. This jamoke had a black belt in mouth karate.

Now it's Anthony's turn.

"Anthony, listen to me, I'm tryin to help you out over here. I heard the answers you gave your arresting officer. If you try that with me you're not getting out of here today. You do understand that, right?"

"What do you mean?"

"Come on, Anthony, do you know where you are and why you're here?"

"Yeah, but we didn't do nuttin' to those girls. We didn't do nuttin' at all and those two cops just want to bust our balls for no reason."

"Anthony, you look like a smart guy. You do want to go home sometime today, right?"

"Yeah."

"Okay. Right now that officer has you down as a John Doe. You know what that means, right?"

"No."

"It means you won't get a desk appearance ticket and you won't be going home today. Let me talk to him and see if he'll redo everything. But you must tell him you're sorry for acting like a jerk."

Anthony had trouble with my idea, but he wanted to go home.

He did apologize to the arresting officer and the forms were completed.

Now we're back to fingerprinting.

"Anthony, it might be a good idea if you took your jacket off before I begin fingerprinting you. This ink is impossible to get out of clothing and that is a nice jacket."

"Yo, let me worry about my jacket, just do what you gotta do so we can get outta here."

As I began rolling his fingers, he went back to abusing the arresting officers. He had apologized and provided the info required for the arrest forms, but he was relentless. I knew where I needed to go with this.

I began agreeing with him. I asked him if the officers abused him in any way, which I knew they didn't and he said no. I asked him if they had advised him of his rights and I knew they did as I heard that part. Yes they did.

I then told the officers I had no idea why they were picking on him as he seemed to be a nice guy. I told him to let me know if the officers did anything they shouldn't do. He came to the conclusion that I was his friend and on his side. Finally he had someone who would "be wit' him."

This conversation went on the entire time it took to print him and when I was finished I asked one of the officers to take him to the bathroom so he could wash his hands.

They left the room and I took the tube of ink and layered it on the glass plate. I put so much ink on that plate faggadaboudit. Then I took my right hand with the rubber glove on it and mushed it into the ink. When I was finished, that glove was absolutely coated with the black gooey, black, blacker than black glue-like ink.

I went to the restroom and took control of my new best friend, Anthony. We chatted for a few minutes as he worked hard to clean his hands. Finally he was ready to return to the cell. I unlocked the cell door with my left hand as I guided him into the cell by placed my right hand on the back of his beautiful white satin jacket.

"OH NO! Anthony, I'm so sorry, I forgot about the ink. Look what I did to your jacket. I'm so sorry."

Carmine took one look at the jacket and said, "Holy shit, Anthony, look at your jacket." My man Anthony took the jacket off and just looked at the picture perfect imprint of a "Black Hand" in the middle of the back of his jacket.

When he finished throwing and kicking the garment all over the cell he stopped and gave me a long hard look: At that moment he knew what I did and he also knew why I did it. I could read his mind. "I f**ked wit your boys and now you got even. You f**ked wit' me!!!" I gave him a slight nod. He knew that I knew that he knew.

Anthony may not have been the valedictorian of his high-school class but he was street smart. He knew the rules and on that afternoon he discovered I knew and went by those same rules.

The desk officer, who was a good friend and knew me better than most people, came to see what was happening. As he entered the room I was telling Anthony how sorry I was and reminding him of the warning I gave fifteen minutes ago about the damage the ink could do. I also told him he could sue the city for a new jacket and I would admit my mistake.

Anthony didn't say another word. About a half hour later both prisoners were removed from the cell by the arresting officers. They both received their desk appearance tickets and were released. My man Anthony left his jacket in the cell.

The arresting officers were very happy as they knew regardless of what took place in court, justice was done, and they thanked me later.

The desk officer, who will remain nameless, had one thing to say: "Jack, only you could have pulled that off."

48

THE STORM TROOPER

For a short time while assigned to the Nine Four Precinct I worked with a fine police officer named Jimmy Machine. Jimmy was a proactive professional who enjoyed being a cop. Jimmy was also one of the toughest cops on the job and one of my boxing coaches.

It was ten minutes to four in the a.m. and our meal hour was coming to an end. As we were leaving the station house, the vestibule door opened and a woman carrying a young boy walked in.

It was about ten degrees out and all she had on was a housecoat and slippers, the child wore pajamas and no shoes. It was obvious they were very cold, but there was more to this scene than the temperature. The woman approached the desk officer and in broken English began telling him that her husband was drunk and had beaten her because she complained about him and his drunken friends who had a party at their house that night.

We told the DO we would take the woman and child home and handle the assignment. Jimmy notified Central we had a pickup, Ten Fifty-Two family dispute, at the station house and we were off to 876 Manhattan Avenue with two complainants.

There was no doubt the woman was deathly afraid of her

husband, because as we pulled up in front of their house she began to shake and it wasn't from the cold. We exited the RMP and made our way to her third-floor apartment. She didn't have a key so we told her to knock on the door and ask her husband to let her in. Then I told her to return to the second floor with the child.

When the door opened we were met by a guy about six foot three weighing in at about two hundred and eighty pounds. He was clearly drunk, a nasty state of drunk, and in a mean mood. Speaking in a heavy German accent he demanded to know why we were there. We had no right to enter his apartment and we were fascist pigs' yada, yada, yada. I got the impression he didn't like Jimmy because I knew he couldn't be talking about me. We moved him into the kitchen where we had more light. We could see the remains of a party. Several plates containing stale cold cuts, salads, bread and two empty quart bottles of vodka.

Jimmy, who is also a good size man, but in great shape, told him he had to leave the apartment for the night or get arrested for assaulting his wife,. We could see that thought wasn't getting through to his vodka-soaked brain.

"Vot you mean leave? I not goingk anywhere. My wife go."

I said, "What is your name?"

"Vy you vant my name?"

I could see this wasn't going well, but I knew I now had his attention.

"I need your name so when we take you to the hospital and the doctor asks us for your name we will know what to tell him."

"Vot hospital, you crazy man. I no need no hospital. "

"If you don't leave now, we will arrest you. If you resist arrest, you WILL DEFINITELY go to the hospital."

"You no arrest me, I arrest you."

And with that response he picked up a large carving knife from under a napkin on the kitchen table and stabbed Jimmy in the stomach. The good news was Jimmy was wearing his heavy leather, horsehide, uniform jacket.

He caught him in the one area where the leather was double thick, at the waist. The thrust sent Jim back, but the knife still penetrated the leather and punctured his skin. Thank God the wound wasn't very deep.

Now it was my turn. He came at me with the knife, but I saw it coming and hit him with my super-duper heavy-duty ebony nightstick. The Louisville Slugger of all nightsticks and without a doubt the best baton to have when you want to stop a crazed man coming at you with a knife and you don't have time to get your revolver out. He was lucky; I absolutely, positively would have shot him.

I caught him a good shot and he crumbled to the floor. He was semiconscious and bleeding with a wide three-inch gash on his forehead. Jimmy took his jacket off and we could see the wound wasn't very deep, but he was bleeding. He used his handkerchief to stop the bleeding.

Jimmy went to the second floor and told the woman it was safe to return to the apartment. He walked her directly into the bedroom away from the kitchen. I called for an ambulance for our prisoner, who was about to fulfill my prophecy: He was going to the hospital.

Jimmy handcuffed the prisoner and applied a hand towel to his head, attempting to stop the bleeding. By the time the ambulance arrived we went through two towels and were on the third. Head wounds usually cause massive bleeding and this guy had a good size gash.

Go ebony nightstick.

The ambulance took Jimmy's prisoner to Greenpoint Hospital with an assigned foot man, where he received seventeen stitches to close the wound. There was no more fight in that German puppy.

I took Jimmy to St. John's Hospital in Queens, where he received three stitches and a tetanus shot. We returned to the Nine Four SH. While Jimmy prepared the forms required for his line of duty injury, I returned to the wife at her apartment.

I told her she would be needed in Brooklyn Criminal Court the next day to speak to an ADA and to assist in the prosecution of her husband for assault on her and her son. I wrote those instructions for her and told her if they needed transportation to court we would provide that for them. She thanked me and said she would need transportation.

It was at that time, standing in her living room, that I noticed a photo hanging on the wall. That photo was of a very young soldier. I took a closer look and discovered it was a picture of a Nazi SS Storm Trooper.

I asked her who that was and she told me it was her husband from WW II. He joined the army when he was sixteen. He was a highly decorated soldier who killed many Americans during the war. He was still a Nazi fanatic and hated the NYC Police, which obviously prompted his assault on Jim.

The disposition for this incident: I arrested the storm trooper and charged him with attempted murder, assault second degree, possession of a dangerous instrument, and resisting arrest.

Jim went on sick report due to his wound. He recovered and returned to work shortly after the stitches were removed.

The wife was afraid to proceed with her complaint, which was SOP, but the storm trooper still had to answer for the assault on Jim

He had no prior arrest record and was allowed to plead to assault second degree and possession of a dangerous instrument. The Nazi spent nine months as a guest of the NYC Department of Corrections.

49

THE SOUTH SIDE BIKERS GANG

Over my many years assigned to the Nine Four Precinct I was the captain's "go to" man. Commanding officers changed and my title changed, but my assignment pretty much stayed the same. I went from the Youth Car to the Youth Gang Car to the Quality of Life Car to the Conditions Car. When the CO received a complaint from the community, my partner and I would be called into his office and given the assignment.

There came a time in the late seventies when street gangs were on the rise and Brooklyn was infested with them. We had our share in Nine Four. We had two black gangs from the Cooper Projects and three Puerto Rican gangs from the north side, which was a multiethnic neighborhood. Prior to the gangs, the Puerto Rican people lived in harmony with the Polish and some Irish. Then those same peace-loving people became victims.

Our neighboring precinct, the Nine O, had a far greater gang problem. Their worst gang was known as the South Side Bikers. They were violent criminals.

I know something about gangs. In the late fifties and early sixties, my teenage years growing up in Bushwick/Ridgewood Brooklyn, our local gang was the Halsey Bops. They hung out in Halsey Park, three blocks from my home, but that entire area was their turf. Back then gangs were into turf wars and control of their neighborhood.

If, let's say "The Saints," our closest gang from Queens, ventured into Halsey Bop territory, they would have a "gang fight," They used fists, car antennas, maybe a couple of knives, and possibly a "zip" gun. (A zip gun was a homemade weapon made from a piece of car antenna and fired .22 caliber bullets.) A zip gun was accurate from about an inch and a half, but a .22 caliber round could kill you as sure as any other bullet if it hit you in a vital area.

There would be injuries, but it was rare to have a kid seriously hurt or killed. Those gangs and that style of gangsterism ebbed in the early sixties.

Gangs came alive again in the Bronx in the early seventies and spread into Harlem and eventually into Brooklyn. That new breed was more concerned with moneymaking criminal activity and the only time turf came into the picture was when someone tried to make a move on a drug location owned by another gang. The end result of that maneuver was usually serious injury or death to the interloper. And the days of the zip guns were long gone.

The new improved "Gangstas" packed .38s, 9 millimeter handguns and shotguns. The multi-shot assault weapons currently in use were not available at that time.

My partner in the Gang Car was Bobby Mack. Bobby was the bravest man I ever worked with. A proud member of the First Cavalry in Viet Nam. A helicopter gunner. A two-time recipient of the Purple Heart as well as many medals for bravery. He had no fear. Together we had near total control of the gangs in our precinct. We walked a thin line when it came to their constitutional rights.

Example: If we caught a gang member wearing "colors," they were ours. (Colors were denim jackets with the name of the gang on the back. Much like the type the motorcycle gangs wear.) We took the mutt into the station house and issued a universal summons for GP (General Principle). We confiscated the jacket, hung the trophy on our wall in our Youth office, and sent him on his way with a warning: Next time you won't be so lucky.

The walls of our Youth Office were covered with colors identifying five different local gangs. Those jackets were meant to bring fear to the community and that wasn't going to happen in the Nine Four. Bobby and I would be bringing the fear and eventually the "Gangstas" got the message.

The citywide gang problem was so serious the officers assigned to monitor and deal with that criminal activity were given more latitude when enforcing those laws. The gangsters were not in the habit of making civilian complaints, not that anyone in CCRB would have given it much consideration, so we were able to use our imagination. Ergo, we stopped and searched everyone who even resembled a gang member. We made many arrests and we took a lot of weapons and drugs off the street.

Our gang condition never became what would be considered "out of control" for two reasons. One: Our gang population wasn't nearly as high as some other precincts'. Two: We never allowed them room to grow. The Nine O had two men assigned to their Gang Car (Bobby Island and Lenny Christopher). They had a larger Puerto Rican population resulting in a far greater Puerto Rican gang problem. Both officers were dedicated to solving their gang problems and they did a great job, but on occasion they would request a sit-down over coffee to discuss our mutual interest, to wit, gang activity.

"Jack, can you and Bobby meet with me and Lenny in about one hour?"

"Yes, what's up?"

"I'll tell you when we meet."

We met for coffee at the Kellogg diner just inside their precinct boundaries.

"Jack, Bobby, how you guys doin'?"

"We're okay and you?"

"Busy as usual. One of our gangs is moving into your precinct and we want to bring you up to speed. The Bikers are making a

338 | JACK FITZGERALD

move into the Nine Four. That social club on Franklin and Clay is owned by Roberto Ramos. Hector Ramos, the president of the Bikers, is his cousin and they're setting up shop in that club."

"We're talking dope and guns, right?"

"Yeah. Me and Lenny have been turning up the heat on them for a couple of months already and the word we got was they feel it's time to move somewhere where they're not well known. Hector worked out a deal with Roberto and we just found out they're already in that club."

"We don't spend much time in that corner of the precinct. Not much happening there, but now we will. Thanks for the heads-up. No doubt we'll be calling upon you guys soon. Do they know about our 'no colors' rule?"

"We don't think so, but even if they do you know they're going to test you. They don't know you and they'll see how much they can get away with."

"This is going to be interesting. We thanked Bobby and Lenny, then drove to the station house. Our CO wanted to be informed about any issues that could possibly affect our precinct. There wasn't a question about "if" we could handle this new development, but how long it was going to take.

The boss pulled out his social club file and found two "Kites" (Intelligence reports) on that club. Most of the social clubs had complaints from neighborhood people for one reason or another, so two was nothing to be alarmed about.

I told the CO we would keep him informed. Bobby and I decided it was time to call in a marker from one of our gang informants. Carlos was a member of one of our gangs who fed us intel. We in turn cut him some slack. We did what we needed to do to get the job done, but we never went over the line . . . In all honesty and keeping my promise to be as truthful as my memory will allow I must modify that statement: We did what we needed to do to get the job done and there were a few times when we needed to go a tad over the line, but only when absolutely necessary and when required under dire circumstances.

It took us a while, but eventually we found Carlos. Our routine with him was simple: If we needed to speak to him we would just pull up, get out of our car, and toss him as though we were going to arrest him. We would let him know we needed to talk . . . now or in a little while. If he said now, which was usually the case; we would cuff him to the first notch on the handcuff and put him in our car. We would drive to a secluded area, he would take the cuffs off, and we would talk business.

"Carlos, how you been doin'?"

"Doin' good, how 'bout youse?"

"Good, listen, what's up with the club on Clay and Franklin?"

"You know that clique from the south side, the Bikers, right, well they be hangin' out in that club and sellin' shit. I hear they be sellin' shooters, too."

"How long has that been going on?"

"'Bout three weeks."

"Carlos, I thought we could count on you. What took you so long?"

"Sorry 'bout that."

"We need to know what's going on in that club."

"What you need to know?"

"We need to know how much shit they're selling and what kind. We need to know when they bring guns to the club. We need to know who's buying the guns. We need to know all that and we need to know about it yesterday. Do you ever hang in that club?"

"Nah, but Jose goes there once in a while to cop, but you can't talk to him. I'll find out and call the precinct tomorrow. What time should I call?"

"Three would be good, but if we're not in just leave a message and we'll catch you on the street."

At three we were in the muster room waiting for roll call. Sergeant Kelly came in and told me I had a call. I knew it was Carlos.

"Nine Four Precinct, Police Officer Fitzgerald, how may I help you?"

"Yeah, it's me Carlos."

"Good to hear from you. You got something for me?"

"Yeah."

"We'll see you at the lumberyard at six. I'll tell the guard to let you in like always."

"See you at six."

We had a secure, fenced-in, out-of-the-way lumberyard in a corner of our precinct, just off the East River. We made that our rendezvous spot when meeting with informants. The security guard knew us and if we told him to let someone in that person was given a pass.

We were waiting when Carlos arrived.

"Carlos, how you doin'?"

"Good."

"What do you have for us?"

"I saw Jose and he said that clique is deep in that club. They be sellin' crack and weed every day and if you want a shooter they will make that happen."

"Carlos, if you really want to help us we need more information."

"What do you need to know?"

"How much crack and weed do they keep in the club? How many guns do they have? We want to shut them down and put them in jail, so we need to know more about what's going on. Do you understand?"

"Yeah, I know what you talkin' about. Let me see what I can do. I'll get back to you."

We returned to the SH and prepared an intelligence report. That document went to the CO and then on to the "proper authority," in this case Narcotics for the dope and ATF (Alcohol, Tobacco and Firearms) for the guns. This criminal activity needed to be reviewed by them before we made a move.

The gang members came and went in a van, so we never

needed to address our ban on colors issue. They drove to the club, parked in a legal spot, and when it was time to leave they just drove off. The chances were no one had a driver's license, but we weren't about to interfere with an ongoing department investigation due to a traffic infraction.

There came a time, about two weeks later, when I received a call from Lenny Christopher. We met with him and he gave us color photos of Hector. I called Narcotics and ATF to see where they were with our intelligent report . . .

Nowhere. I knew this issue was small potatoes for them, but we needed to follow department guidelines / procedures.

Bobby and I went to see our CO and brought him up to speed.

"Captain, I just got off the phone with Narcotics and ATF regarding the Biker Social Club issue. They both told me our report was at the bottom of their list of things to do. They added that if we wanted to make a move they wouldn't have a problem with that and if we needed their help there were no guarantees of a speedy response."

"Okay. Make your observations and let me know before you do anything."

We knew a couple who were very active with the Franklin Avenue block association and they lived across the street from the club. We met with them and asked if we could set up a movie camera in their apartment overlooking the club . . . Yes.

It didn't take long before we had several hours of good video clearly identifying the players in this game. We met with our CO and gave him what we had.

"Jack, Bobby, how did you make out?"

"I spoke to Vinny and Ann Palumbo from the Franklin Street Block Association. You know who they are, right?"

"Yes, they're very active in that area."

"They live directly across from that club and we asked if they would mind if we made observations from their apartment. I told them we would be in civilian clothes and discreet when coming and going. They both said they would do whatever was necessary to close that club. Captain, I've been down this road before. If you will allow Sergeant Kelly and his Anti-Crime team to work with us, I know we can resolve this problem and make a few gun and drug collars as well."

Bobby and I met with the captain, Sergeant Kelly, and his Anti-Crime officers.

"Okay, Jack, Bobby, how can we help with that Biker condition?"

"It's pretty simple; Bobby and I will be watching the club from the apartment across the street. We already have video and there is a lot of coming and going in the club from about five to midnight. The plan is when we see someone enter and leave within a few minutes; we will call you on channel two with a description. All you need do is wait until the target gets far enough away and do a stop and frisk. Chances are you'll come up with dope and maybe a gun."

Over the following two weeks Sergeant Kelly and his Anti-Crime team made many arrests for possession of narcotics as well as seven gun collars. One afternoon the sergeant requested we meet with the captain to see how far we would take this:

Sergeant Kelly began, "Captain, my team has worked with Jack and Bobby for two weeks and during that time we've made twenty-seven arrests for possession of narcotics. Some grass, but mostly coke and crack. We've taken seven guns off the street, but we haven't had much time to do our anti-crime work. How much longer do you want us to work on this assignment?"

The captain said, "Jack, Sergeant Kelly is right, it's time to bring this assignment to a close.

"Captain, Bobby and I were talking about that earlier today. We're beginning to lose control of our conditions and that's not good. We don't see an end in sight. The customers get arrested, they're back on the street in a couple of days and they're back for more. I wish I had someone on the inside who could give us more intel, but that clique is from the south side and they don't get along with our crews.

"It would be nice if we could get help from Narco and ATF, but they won't touch this small potatoes kite. As I see it, the good news is we're making good arrests and we're getting guns off the street. The bad news is our other conditions are getting sloppy and the longer we're away, the longer it will take to bring them back. Sergeant Kelly wants to get back to his street crime enforcement, so it's your call, boss, but Bobby and I agree with Sergeant Kelly. It's time to bring this to a close."

"Okay. Sergeant, you, Jack, and Bob come up with a plan to bring this assignment to a successful conclusion."

The result of that meeting was: I was going to try to get Carlos to get more info about how much dope and how many guns they had in the club. Bobby and I went on the prowl looking for our man Carlos.

Lo and behold we found him with his homies hanging out on Huron and Manhattan. We pulled up and Bobby gave them the regular "Break it up, no hanging out," Carlos looked at me and I gave him the slight nod. He knew we wanted to talk.

We drove to the lumberyard and waited about ten minutes. "Carlos, what's happenin'?"

"What's happenin', you know what's happenin', your boys be bustin' the entire neighborhood. Julio had a warrant so he be in. Louis, little Jose and Jesus all got grabbed wit' dope or guns. These are my people, when this be ova?"

"I'm glad you asked. We want to close this down. We want to close the club and lock up as many Bikers as possible. We want to get as much dope and as many gun as we can get.

"We need you to get as much information as you can about when they have the guns, the dope, and when they have more of their people there. The sooner you find out, the sooner you get the street back to normal."

Bobby and I met with Sergeant Kelly and the CO the next after-noon. We told them about the meeting we had with our informant and we decided it might be a good idea to lay off the club until our guy got back to us.

It took Carlos three days and then we got a message to meet him at the lumberyard.

"Carlos, what's up?"

"Okay, listen, Jose went in the club and said they always have plenty of dope and shooters in there. The best time to bring it down is Saturday night after eight. It's Roberto's birthday and they be havin' a party. They be a lot a Bikers there and plenty a dope and guns. Oh, Jack, you know Hector Ramos killed his boy Carlito, right?"

"Yeah."

"You and Bobby better be careful; that dude be crazy."

We had our final meeting with Captain Mazon and Sergeant Kelly.

The CO said, "If possible I want to handle this within the command. Jack, how many people do you think will be in the club?"

"It's a birthday party, so maybe a high of about twenty, possibly a few more, but not less than fifteen. We can expect most of them will be armed and high on crack. As you know, Bob and I are solo qualified, so I strongly suggest we bring shotguns to this party. Nothing brings a chill to a hot party like a twelve-gauge."(At that time the department was experimenting with one man patrol units.pproved volunteers spent three days at the outdoor range learning everything there was to know about the twelve gauge shotgun. We fired about one hundred rounds of the high powered ammo every day and it was intensive training with that weapon.)

"Good idea, bring the guns. Sergeant, you have six men, Jack and Bob make nine. I want you to have three sectors standing by. I'll assign every available PO to a sector or a special. Do you think you can do this with fifteen men, including yourself?"

"Yes."

That Saturday evening I arranged to have Jose go into the club to make sure the party was on. He went in as we waited. He came out and took his hat off. The show is about to begin.

Bobby and I joined Sergeant Kelly and his six men as we all walked up to the door. It was unlocked. We rushed in and yelled, "Everyone on the floor." There were exactly fourteen men and nine women in the club, including Hector. The six uniforms came in and we cuffed our prisoners. We searched every inch of the club and came up with a half a kilo of cocaine, six ounces of crack cocaine, a kilo of marijuana, ten handguns, and a sawed-off twelve-gauge shotgun.

The end result of this South Side Biker issue was:

Twelve gangsters were arrested for possession of drugs and/or weapons. Roberto Ramos got arrested on his birthday for possession of drugs and guns. I collared Hector Ramos for homicide, possession of drugs, and a weapon. He had a loaded .38 caliber revolver in his jacket pocket. We cut the women loose because there was no way to connect them with the criminal activity. Twelve Bikers pleaded guilty to possession of drugs and/or weapons. They all had prior arrests so they went upstate . . . Roberto, the club owner, took the weight for the five guns found in the back room. He also pled guilty to possession with intent to sell the drugs. He had two prior convictions for drugs, so he did hard time upstate where he celebrated five more birthdays. My man Hector pled not guilty to the homicide.

My involvement with the homicide charge was zero. My testimony at the grand jury was narrowly related to the arrest at the social club and the possession of the gun which, by the way, was the gun he used to shoot his homeboy and VP, Carlito.

I was notified to appear in Brooklyn Supreme Court. I met with the DA, was prepped and ready to go. The docket was called and Hector decided to take a plea. Seven years minimum, inside.

The South Side Bikers ceased to exist. Carlos was happy, as was Jose, because they got their streets back. Bobby and I told them we owed them one, so they knew if the time came they got caught with a nickel bag of weed we would allow them to toss it down a sewer. That was a small price to pay for all the help we received from them.

Our CO was happy because by closing that social club, every club in that area got the message: You conduct criminal activity in your club . . . you go to jail.

Sergeant Kelly and his Anti-Crime team were happy because they got their numbers for several months by getting the drugs and especially the guns off the street.

Vinny and Ann Palumbo were very happy. With the club closed they were able to get a good night's sleep. No more loud music. No more street fighting and there were no more occasional shots fired from across the street.

Bobby Mack and I bought Lenny and Bobby dinner at Little Europe, a nice restaurant in our precinct, with some of the overtime money we made on this very good arrest. Bob and I also received department recognition, to wit, Meritorious Police Duty and a letter of commendation from the Brooklyn North Commanding Officer.

50

THE GUNFIGHT AT 195 MCDONOUGH STREET

The following is a blow-by-blow description of what took place one cold December morning with a full explanation for my dedication to St. Michael the Archangel.

In December of 1973 I was assigned to the Eight One Police Precinct in the Bedford-Stuyvesant section in Brooklyn, New York. The Eight One was a very busy and dangerous place to work. Every precinct in Bed-Sty was busy and dangerous.

They were dangerous areas for the police officers assigned to work those precincts, but much more dangerous for the citizens living there, due to the high crime and mortality rate suffered by and committed by the residents.

That morning I worked a midnight to eight a.m. shift with my partner Robert Thomas; remember that name. We had a very early meal. From two to three we were in the station house and off the radio. At three we notified Central we were resuming patrol and were immediately given an assignment, to wit, investigate two men with guns holding a hostage at 195 McDonough Street, third-floor apartment.

When we arrived, another sector was there to back us up. Bob

348 | JACK FITZGERALD

rang the first-floor bell and an elderly woman came to open the door

I said, "Good morning, ma'am, sorry to bother you, but we have a report of criminal activity on the third floor. Do you know of anything happening on that floor?"

"No."

"Have you heard any noise or know of anything unusual happening anywhere in the building?"

"No."

"The caller stated there were two men with guns holding a hostage on the third floor. Would you know anything about that?"

"No."

"We need to check it out."

With those last words the woman returned to her first-floor apartment. Bob and I, accompanied by Lenny Palmari and Kevin Shore, climbed the two flights of stairs to the third floor. We found two apartments on that floor. I was the senior man on the scene, which made me the person in charge until a sergeant arrived. I went to the front apartment door with Palmari, the junior man. I could see light coming from under the door and I asked my partner and Kevin to go to the rear door. We knocked on the doors, announced our police presence; no response.

I could hear someone moving around and whispers in the front apartment. There was definitely someone in there and unless he was whispering to himself there were at least two people in that apartment. I returned to the first floor and had another conversation with the elderly woman.

Knock, knock, knock.

"What do you want?"

"Police Officer Fitzgerald again, I need to talk to you."

She opened her door and I got the message she was not in a talkative mood.

"Why you bothering me? I told you they ain't nothin happenin in my building. Just go away."

"We can't do that. I know there are at least two people in the front apartment and they won't open the door. This is a very serious assignment and we can't leave without checking it out, so unfortunately if they won't open the door, I will kick it in."

"WHAT! You ain't kickin' my door down. Are you crazy? Where you goin'? Get back here. Get outa my house, now."

As she continued to yell her objections, I returned to the third floor. I told Bob that when he saw me ready to kick the front door he should do the same to the rear door.

There wasn't much room between my door and the handrail at the stair line, due to a fire escape ladder going to the roof. I put my back to the ladder and kicked the center of the door.

As I kicked the door, the inner plywood frame, a thirty-by-thirty-inch piece, broke in two and one large piece fell into the room. I immediately heard numerous gunshots and a bullet cracked the remaining piece of plywood about three inches from my head. I could see a man to my left. Most of his body was hidden behind a bedroom wall in a crouched position, but I could see him peeking from behind the wall, gun in hand, shooting at me. I instinctively retreated until my back hit that ladder, about two feet away.

I saw Palmari retreating down a few steps and without thinking I moved forward toward the door. The initial shock was wearing off and with that large piece of wood gone I could see into about half of the room. I could see a man with a large Afro haircut, sitting in a green lounge chair with its back against the door. I also saw the gunman behind the wall still shooting at me. I returned fire, one shot. He dropped his gun and fell to the floor.

The hostage, that was forced to sit in the chair by his nephews, lunged out onto the floor near the gunman and just lay there. I forced the door open by pushing the chair into the room and I was totally focused on the guy I shot and his gun lying about one foot from where he fell. My partner Bob Thomas, Kevin Shore, and Palmari followed me into the apartment. As I was retrieving the weapon from the floor, Kevin Shore called my name and I turned in his direction.

He was taking a gun out of the hand of another armed gunman who, in ultra-slow motion, was trying to raise it, no doubt, to shoot me. As he did that he was doing his death gurgle.

I checked the criminal I shot and he was unconscious, so I went over to the other shooter and he was dead. I checked on the man who had been sitting in the chair and found he had been shot on his right side, but he was alive and conscious.

We called for an ambulance, as well as the sergeant on patrol who was the same boss who responded a short while earlier and did not do his job. Bob called the station house with the house phone and explained what took place to the desk officer. The DO notified the Duty Captain, detectives, Crime Scene Unit, medical examiner, et cetera.

Now for the most important part of my story: Two weeks prior to that morning, Father Blyleven, a priest from Spanish Harlem, came to our command and asked the desk officer if he could address the troops after roll call.

He received permission from Police Headquarters and had been giving his talks to police officers working the high crime areas for many years.

Father Blyleven told us that when Pope Pius XII came to New York City in 1965, he was invited to the mass the Pope said in Yankee Stadium. He brought two shoe boxes filled with small aluminum St. Michael the Archangel medals with him. When the Pope blessed the people and religious medals/articles, he held his boxes high.

He then told us that St. Michael was the patron saint of police officers. So who knew? I certainly didn't.

As we left the muster room, the priest handed every man a medal that was about the size of a dime. I took that medal and added it to the chain I wore around my neck next to the gold Miraculous Medal my wife gave me when we got married.

Now for the bottom line: As the two would-be assassins were shooting at me, everything went into slow motion. I'd heard about that phenomenon, but never experienced it before that morning. Immediately after I fired my gun and while I was in that trancelike state, the smoke from my gun rose toward me and the smell of the gunpowder brought me back to reality. At that exact moment I grabbed for my St. Michael medal on my chain around my neck under my uniform.

Those few minutes in my twenty-six-year career will remain burned into my memory forever. I have total recall of that experience and the most outstanding memory is that moment when I grabbed my medal. I have no doubt St. Michael saved me that morning because I never saw the gunman, Raymond Thomas, to my right, as he was hidden behind a coffee table and out of my sight, but he could see me in the doorway.

The Crime Scene investigation revealed that he fired five shots in my direction and those bullets passed through the door frame or were lodged in the plaster wall just next to where I was standing. One round struck his uncle sitting in the chair, hitting him in the side. Then he fired one round into his own chest and he had one round left in his .380 semiautomatic, which I found when I cleared his weapon.

His brother Robert fired several shots in my direction and they all went over my head or around me, missing me by inches. I know St. Michael saved my life that morning by causing that low-life would-be assassin to shoot himself with what he probably thought was his last bullet.

I have reviewed that moment over and over in my mind and I still do to this day, but maybe not as much as before. The reason I am so sure, besides me grabbing my medal immediately after I came back to reality, is—that if the unseen gunman hadn't killed himself, he would have had me totally exposed when I entered the room. He was hiding about four feet away and with two shots left he couldn't have missed me.

The brother I shot died three days later. Uncle Raymond Thomas spent over one month in Kings County Hospital due to extensive internal injuries.

Now for the official report that was prepared by the investigating detectives after interviewing the uncle, his friend who made the calls, and the owner of the house.

The two brothers, Raymond Thomas and Robert Thomas, were wanted fugitives. They were wanted in both Phoenix and Tucson, Arizona, for numerous robberies, attempted murder, felonious assaults, possession of weapons, and sale of drugs. A total of fourteen separate grand jury indictments. They came to New York because they knew their uncle, Raymond Thomas, was a bartender at the Big "T" bar, which, at that time, was a known hangout for the Black Liberation Army. (In fact, about three months after my incident, there was a widely publicized shootout at that bar between the BLA and our NYPD and several criminals were killed.)

The brothers went to the uncle's apartment and told him they wanted to sell the drugs they brought with them out of his bar. He said no. They told him he would not be allowed to leave the apartment until he agreed to their demands

On the morning of December 15, his friend, who lived across the street, came to check up on him. The friend hadn't seen Raymond for a few days and wanted to make sure he was all right. He knocked on the door at about two fifteen and the brothers let their uncle answer, but would not allow the friend into the rooms.

Raymond told his friend he was okay, but whispered that he was being held hostage by his nephews and they had guns. The friend left and called 911. The 911 operator dispatched a sector that was backed up by the sergeant on patrol. They arrived at the house, rang the bell, and the same woman I met opened the door. They asked her, as I did, if she knew of any problems in her building and she said no, so they left and gave the job back as unfounded.

My partner and I were on meal and never heard the job. Our backup was on another job at that time and didn't hear the job either. When the friend saw the responding units leave without even going into the house, he called again and that was the call we responded to at three a.m.

A search of the apartment yielded two kilos of heroin and four kilos of marijuana, as well as a scale to weigh the drugs, and small nickel bags for the grass and glassine envelopes for the dope. The two automatics were from a collection stolen in Arizona and valued at $2,500 each. When I took the guns to our ballistics lab for analysis, the detective knew they were collector's pieces and ran their serial numbers. That's how he discovered they were stolen and the value listed on the report of theft.

I never received a report regarding the results of the ballistics tests on the guns because both brothers were dead.

After being interviewed by the detectives and the Duty Captain at the scene, we were ordered to take all the recovered property to the station house to be vouchered. When I arrived at the house, the desk officer told me our commanding officer wanted to see me in his office.

I went into the office and was surprised that he had responded at that early hour. He congratulated me for a job well done and asked me to sit and tell him what happened. A short while later the Borough Commander, a two-star chief, entered the room, walked over, shook my hand, and said, "On behalf of myself and the Police Commissioner, we congratulate you for the action you took this morning." Then I had to start telling my story all over again.

As I was giving my CO and the chief the blow by blow, the desk officer entered the room and told the captain the news media was on the phone and wanted the facts for their reports to be aired on the radio. The CO asked me if I would mind giving them a firsthand report and I agreed, but only after I called my wife, my mom, and my dad.

I explained exactly what happened several times to different radio stations and I gave them the facts and the names of all involved. Every station called back to confirm the names of the perps, the uncle, and my partner.

Most of what needed to be done, regarding my involvement with that incident, ended about twelve hours after it began.

I worked into the day tour vouchering evidence, to wit, the guns, drugs and the drug paraphernalia. At about two thirty I was ready to call it a day when my former boss in the Taxi Truck Surveillance Unit arrived. Captain McQuen was now Inspector McQuen and assigned to Brooklyn North. I hadn't seen him in quite a while, but he was one of the best supervisors I ever worked for and he appreciated my work ethic.

He found me in the arrest processing room.

"Jack, I heard you had an eventful late tour."

"Yes sir, truer words were never spoken."

"How are you feeling? Would you like to visit KCH to be checked out?"

"No, I'm good, but I would like to get home."

"You're scheduled for another late tour tonight, but I can't allow you to return to patrol duty yet. You need a few nights away from the street. I am assigning you to the Borough Office for your late tour tonight, in civilian clothes. Stop at the Eight One and take an unmarked RMP to the Academy with your service revolver, their guns as well as all the drugs you recovered this morning. I'll call the CO of ballistics and have the guns test-fired while you wait. While there you can also deliver the narcotics to the lab for analysis." (Our ballistics unit and narco laboratory were located in the NYPD Academy.)

At eleven p.m. I was standing in front of the same desk officer who worked the previous late tour. He asked how I was and said, "Jack, good work last night. Inspector McQuen doesn't want you in uniform. You're assigned to the Borough Office tonight as well as the next three nights. Use unmarked RMP nine thirty-six." He told me what I already knew, but he added that as soon as I returned with the RMP I was excused for the rest of this tour as well as the next three late tours.

My commanding officer submitted my name as well as the names of my partner and our backup for department recognition.

They all received department recognition, to wit, Exceptional Merit. I received Honorable Mention. My Honorable Mention then went to the Honor Board for further review.

In June of 1974, I was ordered to report for the Medal Day ceremony held at One Police Plaza. One day, every year, our mayor presents medals to members of the service for action taken the previous year. I received the Michael Delehanty Medal for Valor from Mayor Beame for my gunfight at 195 McDonough Street.

On that day my wife and children were present to watch as the mayor placed my medal around my neck. Also present was my father, retired Patrolman James Raymond Fitzgerald. (In June of 1959, I was present at City Hall to watch Mayor Robert Wagner pin the Michael Delehanty Medal for Valor on my father's summer blouse.)

After the ceremony, a reporter from one of our local newspapers asked to speak to us. He was writing about Medal Day and when he discovered my father had received a medal years before, he wanted to know more about "our" stories. During that interview my father noticed the reporter was wearing a Marine Corps pin on his lapel.

He mentioned that his father, my grandfather, Marine Corps Gunnery Sergeant Major John Fitzgerald, was awarded the Congressional Medal of Honor for action taken in Cuba during the Spanish–American War. The end result of that interview: This was the first and only time a father and son received the same medal. And we were both descendants of a Medal of Honor recipient.

That reporter wrote a very complimentary article.

In conclusion: One day, a couple of years later, I was waterskiing off my cousin's high-speed boat near Jones Beach, Long Island. He was going fast and I was up on one ski (slalom). I lost my balance when I hit a wave created by another boat and took a bad spill, causing injury to my knee. The worst part: I hit the water with such force that I lost both medals I had around my neck. The St. Michael medal and my Miraculous Medal were gone forever. I was crushed, but my wife came to my rescue. We went into the Jewelry Exchange in Manhattan where she bought me the gold St. Michael the Archangel medal I now wear.

Epilogue

The only remaining issue I needed to address before I was, in my mind, whole again, was the fact that my new medal wasn't blessed by the Pope. A major part of the medal I lost.

I decided that rather than have it blessed by a priest, which wouldn't have been a bad move, I would wait until I had a chance to visit Rome. That Pope blessing was just that important to me.

Then in October of 1979, I heard Pope John Paul II was coming to New York to say Mass at Yankee Stadium. I knew there was no way I wasn't going to that Mass. I also knew there would be a great police presence. I hoped I would go "on duty," but if that wasn't possible I would take the night off and find a way to get in. Now, we all know there are only so many seats in any ballpark and every Catholic Church in the NYC area received a given number of tickets to disperse to their congregation.

Our church had a raffle and as much as my wife, daughter and son wanted to attend and see the Pope, I didn't enter. I just don't trust raffles and considering they only had about fifteen tickets, I knew who the lucky winners were going to be. Every priest was going to win a ticket and a few special friends would take the remaining seats. Ergo, I took my best option and went to my CO.

I explained my reason for wanting to work that detail and he said, "No problem." He was sending five men from the Nine Four and my partner, Bob Mack, and I would be the first two on the list. Then he told me he was sending five men to Shea Stadium the next morning. The Pope was saying Mass there as well. He asked if we wanted to be assigned and I said yes.

So we worked that night when the Pope said Mass at Yankee Stadium and when he blessed everyone I took my new medal off my neck and raised it to be blessed. The next morning we were early arrivals at Shea Stadium. I parked our car and found the section we were assigned to.

The night before, we were assigned to the second tier, which was reasonably close to the altar, but at Shea Stadium we were one level off the field. Knowing my wife and kids really wanted to see the Pope, I found the usher in charge of our area. I asked him if it would be possible to bring my wife and children to see the Pope. He said, "Have them come in and I'll find seats for them."

I called my wife and it was still very early, so my son and daughter hadn't left for school yet. She called the school had them excused for the day, drove in to Shea, and when they arrived I was waiting for them in the parking lot. I took them to our section and the usher found them great seats as promised. That morning I had my medal blessed by Pope John Paul II for the second time.

Then in December of 1989, our NYPD PBA Boxing Team, which I was a member of, went to Rome to compete in the Rome police, seven-country tournament. Of course while in Rome we went to St. Peter's and the Vatican on Sunday, where Pope John Paul addressed the crowd gathered in St. Peter's Square from his window.

When he blessed the crowd, I again had my medal in my hand and for the third time had it blessed by our Pope John Paul II.

So now you know the whole story. I have never taken the time to sit down to write what took place that morning, but now I have and I will keep what I have written for my grandchildren. I still have great difficulty talking about what took place and it was much easier writing about it. I hope you enjoyed reading my story and every word is true.

— Jack Fitzgerald

Made in United States
North Haven, CT
14 June 2022

20227129R00217